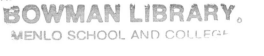

THE
POLITICS
OF
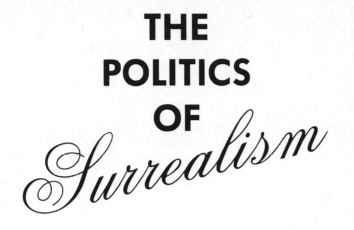

THE
POLITICS
OF
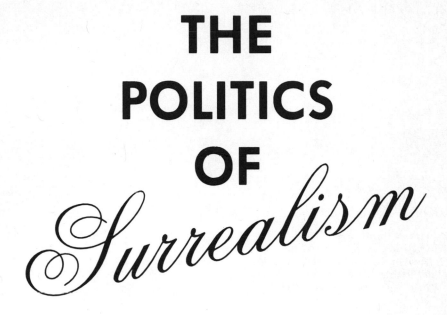

Helena Lewis

PARAGON HOUSE PUBLISHERS

NEW YORK

First edition
Published in the United States by
Paragon House Publishers
90 Fifth Avenue
New York, New York 10011

All photographs in insert by Man Ray. Courtesy
Juliet Man Ray and Artists Rights Society.

Library of Congress Cataloging-in-Publication Data

Lewis, Helena.
   The politics of surrealism / Helena
Lewis.—1st ed.
     p.   cm.
   Bibliography: p.
   Includes index.
   ISBN 0-913729-44-2.   ISBN 0-913729-91-4 (pbk.)
   1. Surrealism—France. 2. Arts, French. 3. Arts, Modern—20th
century—France. 4. Arts—Political aspects—France. 5. Artists—
France—Political activity. I. Title.
NX549.A1L48   1988
700'.944—dc19   87-16986

To the memory of my husband,
Leonard Seelig

Contents

Preface

Surrealism has had an incalculable impact on contemporary culture but, underlying its aesthetics is a fundamental ideology vital to its development, and only through a thorough knowledge of its history and politics can the movement be fully understood. In the past, it was not uncommon for individual artists to become activists but with World War I, a new phenomenon appeared. *Avant-garde* movements committed themselves *en bloc* to political parties as enthusiastically as they espoused particular theories of art and, at least in this century, art and politics have been inseparable. In the 1920s and 1930s, it was taken for granted that art has a social content and that artists ought to work for social change. The German Expressionists took part in the street fighting in Germany after the war, demanding a proletarian revolution and, like the German Dadaists, were forced into exile when the Nazis came to power. The Futurists in the Soviet Union and Italy were also, in very different ways, politically committed. Vladimir Mayakovsky and his circle in the USSR were dedicated to the Bolshevik Revolution, while the Italian Futurists, led by Filippo Marinetti, published manifestoes glorifying war and nationalism and some became ardent supporters of Mussolini. But, of all these groups, the Surrealists developed the most sustained and coherent political beliefs.

The Dadaists, forerunners of the Surrealists, exemplified the pessimism of the World War I generation by their nihilistic rejection of traditional values. Their destructiveness and violence expressed their anger at the moral bankruptcy of Western culture. But the Surrealists gave Dadaist "anti-art" a positive meaning. For them, the abolition of logic meant the creation of a new art form based on chance, dream, fantasy and the irrational. They were able to transcend the negativism of Dada because of their reaction to the most significant historical event of the era: the Russian Revolution. It gave them faith in the possibility of the radical transformation of society.

Surrealism is an extremely eclectic movement that has borrowed from such disparate sources as Hegel, Marx, Lenin, Trotsky, the Romantics, Eastern mysticism, psychoanalysis, Cubism, Futurism and anarchism. It was also influenced by the late nineteenth-century poets Rimbaud and Lautréamont, eccentric author of *Les Chants de Maldoror,* and the Surrealists' love of fantasy led them to claim kinship with an astonishing variety of artists from Hieronymus Bosch to Lewis Carroll. Even the new findings in physics influenced their philosophy which emphasizes the importance of chance, of coincidence, and of relativity; and André Breton, founder and leader of the group, has claimed both Einstein and Heraclitus as Surrealist "heroes." But the movement owes as much, if not more, to Freud and Marx. Freud was almost unknown in France until the Surrealists "discovered" him and became fascinated with his theory of dreams, and they were the first to translate some of his works into French.

The Surrealists also became Marxists and it is in their political commitment that they differ most from the Dadaists. They joined protest demonstrations, wrote manifestoes against war, nationalism, militarism, racism, colonialism, and Christianity; and fought against all forms of oppression. They were horrified at the spread of fascism and supported the Popular Front in the Spanish Civil War. They also advocated general strikes and favored the idea of a Surrealist "revolutionary myth" of direct action. They joined the French Communist Party and worked in its organizations from 1927 to 1935, despite increasing strains. The inevitable break occurred after socialist realism became official policy because they feared that any attempt to force art into a rigid mold was bound to destroy it. Some of their most prominent members broke with the group at this point to become Communist militants and the others were faced with the task they set themselves of trying to build a "third force" out of the non-Communist Left. They allied with Trotsky in 1938 when Breton visited him in Mexico and the two issued a joint manifesto calling for a new organization of revolutionary artists free from the dictates of Party directives and based on complete liberty of expression. After World War II, the Surrealists found themselves isolated from the mainstream of left-wing politics because they adamantly adhered to their own libertarian socialist position. But the movement continued its astonishing levels of creativity, its influence has grown immeasurably, and it has never abandoned its unique synthesis of Marx, Freud and Rimbaud.

1

Introduction: Dada and the Great War

Our generation was formed through the absurdity of war.

—André Malraux,
Les Conquérants

Dada Anti-Art

That art is a reflection of society may be difficult to document, but it is undeniable that the Surrealist movement grew out of the ruins of a world shattered by war. Dada, its violent and nihilistic forerunner, manifested the despair and disillusionment felt by so many young artists and intellectuals in the face of the Great War, and it was an international phenomenon that erupted almost simultaneously in Zurich, New York, Berlin, and Paris. These groups shared a moral revulsion against the whole tradition of European civilization that seemed bent solely on its own destruction. The young Dadaists, many of whom later took part in founding Surrealism, had a profoundly negative outlook toward the future and though Dada was apolitical at the beginning, it was born of the politics of war, and this paradox was revealed by the general character of the movement. Dada, in essence, was revolt against war. None of these artists could bring themselves to work for the rebuilding of a society that had proven itself so morally bankrupt and they rebelled against the accepted values because these had all succumbed to rabid militarism. Ilya Ehrenburg, a Soviet novelist living in Paris, rightly insisted that "Dadaism has more to do with the battle of the Somme, with uprisings and putsches . . . than with what we usually consider art."[1]

1

The artists channeled their total rejection of society into pure acts of defiance and, with all their energy, they threw themselves into protests against their whole cultural heritage. Jean Arp, the painter, felt that the refusal to compromise, which they carried to the point of complete nihilism, actually constituted an inverted idealism, and he maintained that "Dada was more than a kettle-drum, a big noise, and a joke. Dada protested against the stupidity and vanity of mankind. Among the Dadaists, there were martyrs and believers who sacrificed their lives in the search for life and beauty."[2] The movement began in Switzerland in 1916 with a few expatriate artists who had escaped the war by fleeing to Zurich. They gathered at the Cabaret Voltaire, a little artists' café run by Hugo Ball, a pacifist who had left Germany one step ahead of the police. As Ball explained, "it is necessary to define the activity of this cabaret; its aim is to remind the world that there are independent men, men—beyond war and nationalism—who live for other ideals."[3] Others in the group included Tristan Tzara, its first leader, and Marcel Janco, both Rumanian poets; Hans Richter, German painter and film maker; and Richard Huelsenbeck, a German writer who became a psychoanalyst in New York. Arp, from Alsace, was also part of the original group as was the painter, Sophie Taüber, who later became his wife.

In various memoirs, they all stressed the direct relationship between the war and the origins of the movement. As Huelsenbeck said, "none of us had much appreciation for the kind of courage it takes to get shot for the idea of a nation which is at best a cartel of merchants and profiteers, at worst a cultural association of psychopaths who . . . marched off with a volume of Goethe in their knapsacks, to skewer Frenchmen and Russians on their bayonets."[4] Arp, too, stated that "in Zurich in 1915, losing interest in the slaughterhouses of the World War, we turned to the Fine Arts. While the thunder of the batteries rumbled in the distance, we pasted, we recited, we versified, we sang with all our souls. We searched for an elementary art that would, we thought, save mankind from the furious folly of those times."[5] And Tzara declared bitterly

> this war was not our war; to us, it was a war of false emotions and feeble justifications. . . . Dada was born of a moral need, of an implacable will to achieve a moral absolute. . . . Honor, Country, Morality, Family, Art, Religion, Liberty, Fraternity,

etc. [*sic*]—all these notions had once answered to human needs, now nothing remained of them but a skeleton of conventions.[6]

This hatred of war was inherited by the Surrealists who were always profoundly anti–militarist, anti–nationalist, and anti–imperialist.

The Cabaret Voltaire artists were from the beginning in revolt against "establishment" art. Only the most daring of their contemporaries were exhibited, among whom were Picasso, Braque, Kandinsky, Archipenko, and the Futurists Marinetti, Prampolini, and Boccioni. Showings consisted of a *mélange* of all the arts and a communal art or *Gesamtkunstwerk* seems to have been the goal.[7] The "young ladies" of a local dance school joined them in performing "Cubist dances," there were readings of the poetry of Max Jacob, André Salmon and Alfred Jarry, and recitations of the Dadaists themselves. The music of Milhaud and Satie was performed, as well as the "bruitist" music of the Futurists, notably Marinetti's symphony, a "chorus of typewriters, kettles, rattles and pot covers, which had created such a stir in Milan."[8] Other *anti-art* experiments included the *sound poem,* an invention of Hugo Ball, which consisted entirely of meaningless syllables strung together, and the *simultaneous poem,* Tzara's contribution, in which different voices recited the various parts all at once usually in different languages.[9] The graphic artists experimented with *collage,* the pasting of photographs, bits of paper, or even garbage as Kurt Schwitters did, more or less at random on the canvas. As Max Ernst, who was first a Dadaist, then a Surrealist painter, "explained" it,

> A ready-made reality (a canoe), finding itself in the presence of another and hardly less absurd reality (a vacuum cleaner), in a place where both of them must feel displaced (a forest), will, by this very fact, escape into a new absolute value, true and poetic: canoe and vacuum cleaner will make love. The mechanism of collage, it seems to me, is revealed by this very simple example.[10]

Later, the *simultaneous poem* evolved into the collective writing of the Surrealists and the *sound poem* into their famous experiments in automatic writing. *Collage,* which originally was *anti-art* in character, evolved into a positive art form utilizing the principle of chance as a creative force. But for the Dadaists, who were against all principles, such antics had a purely destructive shock value.

The first Dada event was an evening of dance, music, theory, manifestoes, poems, pictures, costumes, and masks, all going on simultaneously.[11] Naturally, it ended in a riot. Hugo Ball recited a phonetic poem of meaningless syllables while attired in a cylindrical cardboard costume which, unhappily, hampered his escape from the wrath of the audience. There was "Negro music," that is, loud banging of drums, a manifesto by Tzara, "we demand the right to piss in different colors!" and a "Cubist dance," a boxing match, and "more outcries, the big drum, piano, and impotent cannon, cardboard costumes torn off by the audience . . . simultaneous poem for four voices and simultaneous work for 300 hopeless idiots."[12] Clearly, Dada was out to shock.

> To outrage public opinion was a basic principle of Dada. . . .
> The devising and raising of public hell was an essential function of any Dada movement, whether its goal was pro-art, non-art, or anti-art. And when the public, like insects or bacteria, had developed immunity to one kind of poison, we had to think of another.[13]

No event was considered a success unless it ended in a free-for-all.

If they had any credo, it was implicit in their communal and anonymous art expressed with complete spontaneity, coupled with the desire to show society how much they despised it. They soon turned against Futurism and Cubism because these schools had specific aesthetic principles while Dada "not only had no program, it was against all programs."[14] The Futurists became particularly abhorrent to them when the Dadaists learned of their intense nationalism and militarism[15] and they broke with the Futurists because, as Huelsenbeck said, "Marinetti and his group love war as the highest expression of the conflict of things."[16] Although Dada was anti-war, its nihilism had its own strong implications of violence. The destructive character of the movement became more pronounced when Tzara replaced Ball as editor of *Dada* after the first issue and in this manifesto of 1918 his extreme negativism is striking.

Dadaist Disgust
Every product of disgust capable of becoming a negation of the family is *Dada;* Protest by fists with all one's might in

taking destructive action is *Dada;* . . . abolition of logic . . . is *Dada;* . . . abolition of memory is *Dada;* abolition of history is *Dada;* abolition of property is *Dada;* abolition of the future is *Dada;* absolute and indisputable god-like faith in every product of immediate spontaneity is *Dada*.

In all of his early manifestoes, the reader is assured that "Dada means nothing."

Only spontaneity or the substitution of chance for deliberate artistic creation was permitted. All else was to be destroyed for, as Tzara declared, "there is a great task of destruction and negation to accomplish. We must sweep and clean!"[17] Chance played a vitally important role in the visual arts and it was also the idea behind Tzara's famous "recipe" for poetry which, judging by his work, he followed faithfully. His intention was to produce a poem totally devoid of meaning by completely eliminating the conscious role of the artist.

Take a newspaper. Take a pair of scissors. Choose an article from this newspaper which is the same length that you want your poem to be. Cut the article out. Then carefully cut out each of the words of the article and put them in a bag. Shake softly. Take out each word one after the other. Copy them down conscientiously in the same order that they came out of the bag. The poem will resemble you. And there you are, a writer of infinite originality and charming sensibility.[18]

It is clear from this "recipe" that chance was used in a negative sense, with the intent of destroying aesthetic values. There may have been, at least in the minds of some, the hope of creating a new art form, and even a new social order, but this was never really made explicit. For the present, all action had to be purely destructive.

Naturally, they hated capitalism, as they hated all bourgeois institutions, but the Dadaists were certainly not consciously political. They rejected all ideologies, as this manifesto by the French Dadaist poet, Louis Aragon, shows:

No more painters, no more writers, no more musicians, no more sculptors, no more religions, no more republicans, no more royalists, no more imperialists, no more anarchists, no more socialists, no more Bolsheviks, no more aristocrats, no more armaments, no more police, no more countries, enough of all these imbecilities, no more, no more, no more, no more, no more.[19]

Even though Lenin was in Zurich, living on the same street as the Cabaret Voltaire, the group had virtually no contact with him. Obviously, the Russian revolutionaries at that time were as uninterested in art as the Dadaists in politics and, although both groups had in common a desire to destroy the system, the Bolsheviks, unlike the Dadaists, had a definite and positive goal and a whole system of theory and tactics for achieving it. Richter made only one reference to Lenin in his memoir when he said that "Radek, Lenin and Zinoviev were allowed complete liberty in Zurich. I saw Lenin in the library several times and once heard him speak at a meeting in Berne. . . . It seemed to me that the Swiss authorities were much more suspicious of the Dadaists, who were after all capable of perpetrating some new enormity at any moment, than of these quiet, studious Russians."[20]

An exception to the apolitical character of Dada was Ball who, by the end of 1916, was deeply involved in politics. But by then he had disassociated himself from the movement, and become editor of a radical pacifist weekly in Berne. Richter, too, began writing for a newspaper that attacked the war and the social irresponsibility of contemporary artists.[21] But Ball and Richter were German and the movement in Germany was the only one that had a political dimension. There was no collective political activity of any kind involving the groups in Zurich, Paris, or New York, because most Dadaists rejected the idea of progress. "Naturally, we cannot believe in any possibility of ameliorating social conditions," declared André Breton, a surprising statement from the future founder of Surrealism.[22] Nevertheless, they were regarded as dangerous by the authorities because of their categorical denial of nationalism. Georges Hugnet, a French writer who became a Surrealist, stated that "in those war days, Dada's internationalism was an element in its subversiveness and in France it was believed to be a German movement in which French writers compromised themselves."[23] There was, at least implicitly, a threat to established society in Dada's nihilism, and its heirs, the Surrealists, made this threat explicit by becoming overtly political.

Dada in Germany

German Dada, from the beginning, was linked with radical politics because of the extreme political instability of the country at the end of the war. The German artists were radicals of various kinds who viewed the defeat with equanimity and, indeed, hoped and expected that this defeat would bring about socialism. They were immediately aware of the profound significance of the Russian Revolution because it seemed obvious to them that Germany would be next. They lived, for a while, in an intensely revolutionary situation with an uprising in Berlin and a short-lived "Soviet" in Bavaria, unlike their counterparts in Paris, New York, and Zurich. Yet their approach to revolution was typically Dada, preserving a strong element of humor, and a refusal to be completely serious even when they were in the middle of the fighting in the streets.

Dada began in Berlin, even before the war ended, when Huelsenbeck returned there in 1917. Among the group were Johannes Baader, Wieland Herzfelde and his brother, John Heartfield, who had anglicized the name, Raoul Hausmann, the painter, George Grosz, famous for his savage caricatures, and Hanna Höch, known for her photo montages. Ernst, originally of the Zurich group, and the artist, Johannes Baargeld, founded Dada in Cologne and collaborated on a Marxist-oriented review, *Der Ventilator.* The German circle was political from the start and, for some of its members, art became completely subordinated to politics. Communists and Dadaists collaborated on such periodicals as *Die Aktion,* and there seemed to be no incompatibility at this time between revolutionary politics and *avant garde* art. This period of easygoing collaboration contrasts sharply with the decade of the 1930s; however, in Germany just after the war, there was such a continual series of revolts, both Left and Right, that nobody was very doctrinaire. As Hugnet explained,

> They believed that the poetic and political attitudes were not incompatible . . . and that a politically revolutionary action corresponds in essence to such a social attitude. They wanted to hasten through their writings the decomposition of bourgeois art and thought . . . [and] they did not hesitate to express their political options publicly. I do not believe that at that time anyone thought of imposing this or that poetical formula, or of creating a proletarian literature. The problem

and the alternative did not bother anyone very much; there were other fish to fry.[24]

It seemed that the German Communists at that time welcomed them as allies.

During the street fighting of 1918–1919, the Dadaists naturally sided with the workers. As an expression of solidarity, it was decided to distribute their review, *Jedermann sein eigner Fussball* (Every Man His Own Football), in the streets. At the height of the Spartacist revolt of January 1919 in Berlin, the Dadaists, singing anti-military songs, went marching into the working-class districts hawking the review, and obviously providing much-needed comic relief. As Walter Mehring, one of the German group recalled, it sold very well and "Jedermann sein eigner Fussball" became a popular expression of contempt for authority. "Our Dadaist procession was greeted with delight as spontaneous as the *on y danse* of the Paris mob in front of the Bastille." But they were arrested and charged with "seeking to bring the armed forces into contempt and distributing indecent publications."[25] Mehring stated that they were actually sentenced to eight months in jail but managed to win the case on appeal. Herzfelde did, in fact, go to jail for disrespect toward the army, and the police closed down their first Dada exhibit because its *pièce de résistance* was an army officer hanging in effigy from the ceiling with a placard around its neck that read, "killed by the revolution."

The German group issued extremely provocative manifestoes and one by Huelsenbeck and Hausmann is particularly memorable for its intriguing mixture of Dada nonsense and Marxist doctrine.

I. Dadaism demands:

1. The international revolutionary union of all creative and intellectual men and women on the basis of radical Communism.

2. The introduction of progressive unemployment through comprehensive mechanization of every field of activity. Only by unemployment does it become possible for the individual to achieve certainty as to the truth of life and finally become accustomed to experience.

3. The immediate expropriation of property (socialization) and the communal feeding of all; further, the erection of cities of light and gardens which will belong to society as a whole and prepare man for a state of freedom.

II. The Central Council demands:

a) Daily meals at public expense for all creative and intellectual men and women on the *Potsdamer Platz*.

b) Compulsory adherence of all clergymen and teachers to the Dadaist articles of faith.

c) The most brutal struggle against all . . . so-called "workers of the spirit" . . . against their concealed *bourgeoisism*.

d) The immediate erection of a state art center, . . . The concept of property is entirely excluded from the super-individual movement of Dadaism which liberates all mankind.

e) Introduction of the *simultaneist* poem as a Communist state prayer:

f) Requisition of churches for the performance of *bruitism, simultaneist,* and Dadaist poems.

g) Establishment of a Dadaist advisory council for the remodeling of life in every city of over 50,000 inhabitants.

h) Immediate organization of a large-scale Dadaist propaganda campaign with 150 circuses for the enlightenment of the proletariat.

i) Submission of all laws and decrees to the Dadaist central council for approval.

j) Immediate regulation of all sexual relations according to the views of international Dadaism through establishment of a Dadaist sexual center.

This remarkable manifesto was signed by the "Dadaist Central Revolutionary Council" and, despite its deliberately humorous content, the signers were clearly committed to playing a revolutionary role. They were serious about their activism and, as Huelsenbeck stated, "while Tzara was still writing 'Dada means nothing' in Germany, Dada lost its uncommitted character with its very first move."[26]

Another manifesto, *Dadaisten gegen Weimar* (Dadaists Against Weimar), declared "The OBERDADA will be proclaimed as PRESIDENT OF THE GLOBE. . . . We shall blow Weimar sky-high. . . . Nobody and nothing will be spared. Turn out in masses! (signed) The Dadaist Central Council of World Revolution."[27] Baader actually went to the State theater during the ceremony inaugurating the Weimar Republic with flyers of this bizarre manifesto which he threw to the audience from the balconies. He avoided jail only by pleading mental instability, but Dada had succeeded in insulting the highest government officials in Germany and in winning for itself the reputation of being a dangerous, subversive group.

The peak of the movement came in 1920 in Cologne with an exhibition which one had to enter through a public urinal. Its main attraction was a young girl, dressed in white as though for her first communion, reading pornographic poems. It, too, was closed down by the police, this time on grounds of obscenity. That same year Huelsenbeck and Hausmann undertook a lecture tour through Germany to Prague for which Huelsenbeck gave himself the title of "Commissar of the Arts." The lectures were strongly in favor of the Russian Revolution, and audiences were extremely hostile. In Prague, they were doubly hostile to the two who, besides being socialists, were also Germans, and the government forbade any more Dada demonstrations in Czechoslovak territory.[28]

By 1922, some of the most active members—Grosz, Heartfield, and Herzfelde—had become militant Communists, Ernst had gone to Paris and Huelsenbeck had resumed his medical studies, so German Dada died out as a collective movement. Hugnet remarked of the German group that it "came to politics through poetic revolt, and politics absorbed Dada."[29] However, Richter thought that they were never really Communists, or anything so definite in terms of politics.

> At one moment, they were all for the *Spartakus* movement; then it was Communism, Bolshevism, Anarchism and whatever else was going. But there was always a side door left open for a quick getaway, if this should be necessary to preserve what Dada valued most—personal freedom and independence. . . . The flirtation with Communism was solely the product of this *anti-everything* mentality, not of any devotion to the doctrines of Karl Marx, [for] Dada in its pure state was pure revolt, ANTI-EVERYTHING!

Richter added that their political naïveté was so extreme that when Gabriele D'Annunzio captured Fiume in September 1919, they were delighted by what they considered a perfect Dada gesture. They sent him a telegram saying "If Allies protest telephone Club Dada Berlin. Capture of Fiume Dadaist masterstroke. Will make every effort to secure recognition [signed] Hausmann, Huelsenbeck, Grosz, Club Dada."[30] They simply failed to see the strong implications of fascism and militarism in D'Annunzio's act.

Huelsenbeck, however, does not agree that the German Dadaists had an "anti-everything" ideology. He stated that "our work in the Cabaret Voltaire had, from the very beginning, an anti-militaristic, revolutionary tendency,"[31] and that "Dada is German Bolshevism."[32] He also pointed out that "Adolf Hitler's rage against the Dadaists proves that they were on the right path."[33] Indeed, Hitler considered them sufficiently important to mention them in *Mein Kampf,* where he described Dada as "spiritual madness" and "art Bolshevism."[34] In fact, after his rise to power in Germany, a exhibition of "Dadaistic Works of Shame and Filth" was organized to educate the German people as to the dangers of decadent and subversive art.[35]

Although the German artists were politically naive and far too undisciplined to be entirely serious about their politics, they were internationalist in spirit and possessed an intuitive, though crude and uninformed, radicalism that found expression in their alliance with the Spartacists and other revolutionary groups. The "true" Dadaists cherished spontaneity too much to make a permanent political commitment, as Richter pointed out, but their instinctive anti-war and anti-capitalist sentiments were shaped and refined by the Surrealists as they developed political consciousness.

The Grande Finale: Dada in Paris

After the war, artists from various countries converged on France, which now became the center of the movement. German Dadaists, such as Ernst, came to Paris, as did some of the New York group. Many New York Dadaists were Europeans who, like their counterparts in Zurich, had fled to the United States to escape being drafted. The most famous was the Frenchman, Marcel Duchamp, whose painting, "Nude Descending the Staircase" had been a *succès de scandale* of the 1913 Armory show. The painter, Francis Picabia, half French, half Cuban, was part of the circle, as was the American, Man Ray, later known for his Surrealist photography. During the war, these three had produced the same kinds of *anti-art* as the Dadaists in Zurich. Duchamp introduced a new aesthetic concept, the *ready-made,* forerunner of the Surrealist *objet-trouvé,* which was simply a mass-produced, manufactured object. His famous "Bottlerack," arbitrarily exhibited as sculpture, became notorious but most shocking of all was a urinal, entitled "Fountain," signed "R. Mutt," that had been indignantly rejected by the New York Independents Exhibition in 1917. Man Ray anticipated the Destructionists of the 1960s with his "Object to be Destroyed," a metronome with the photograph of an eye glued to it.[36] Picabia also ridiculed establishment art in true Dada fashion with his ironic "Portrait de Cézanne," a stuffed monkey glued to a board. Duchamp became a great "anti-hero to the movement for his superbly Dadaist gesture of abandoning art for chess, thus giving perfect expression to the Dadaists' conviction that life is absurd. A curious figure, an American named Arthur Cravan, also became a favorite "anti-hero." He was an amateur boxer who once fought Jack Johnson, the heavyweight champion, and survived to edit a Dada-type review called *Maintenant*. He provoked a great scandal when, instead of giving a lecture at the Independents Exhibition as he was scheduled to do, he proceeded to strip off his clothes and ended by getting arrested. To escape from the draft, he fled to Mexico where, in 1918, he killed himself by drowning.[37] He was much admired for his Dada life and especially his death because the idea of suicide was tremendously fascinating to both Dadaists and Surrealists and it was an important theme in their work.

In 1919, Man Ray and Picabia came to Paris and New York Dada died out. Paris Dada began "officially" with the eagerly awaited arrival of Tzara from Switzerland. The French artists had long been in touch with the Zurich group and had contributed to their journal and the Paris review, *Littérature,* had in turn published Tzara, who served as a kind of catalyst for launching Dada in France. In addition to Breton and Aragon, the group included the poets Paul Eluard, Benjamin Péret, Jacques Rigaut, Philippe Soupault and the future journalist, Georges Ribemont-Dessaignes. To celebrate Tzara's arrival, *Littérature* organized a matinée on the "new art." The public appeared, unaware of the intended farce, to find Picabia ostensibly lecturing on art, but really erasing lines on a blackboard as fast as he drew them. Tzara, after announcing a manifesto, read from the telephone book, while the others rang cowbells and drowned him out. Ribemont-Dessaignes addressed the audience in such an insulting fashion that he caused a riot, and the first Paris Dada event was judged a huge success.[38] Their provocations became extremely intense as their pessimism proved amply justified by the cynicism of the post-war era. They envied their German counterparts the sheer excitement of their times because in France it was simply "business as usual."

The French Dadaists also angrily denounced war and the evils of patriotism. They jeered at the idea of heroism, for what more meaningless death could there be than to die for one's country on a battlefield? They were even convinced that only the mediocre had survived and Ribemont-Dessaignes reflected this cynicism in his "Time of Heroes."

> It is the hour of the heroes. And what heroes! All those who had courage are dead, also some others who didn't have it but who, having to choose between revolt and death, took a chance on the latter, because it was easier. More intellectuals were killed than returned from the war because intellectuals are physically weaker. Therefore, among those who returned safe and sound, the majority are imbeciles.[39]

Life is absurd and the Dadaists strove to express this conviction in all their activities. Matthew Josephson, as a young American writer in Paris, was bewildered to discover a whole group of obviously talented young men writing nothing but manifestoes, organizing demonstrations, and sworn to give up their literary careers. He was sure that "in secret they were writing," but, while he may have been right, the feelings of disgust expressed in their collective protests were clearly genuine.[40] André Gide was one of the few prominent writers they admired because he, too, symbolized revolt with his famous cry, "Families, I hate You!"[41] Especially appealing was his idea of the *acte gratuit,* personified by Lafcadio, the delightful and amoral hero of *Les Caves du Vatican* (translated as *Lafcadio's Adventures*). The Dadaists took this idea from Gide's comic novel quite seriously: to save a life one day, and commit a completely unmotivated murder the next, fitted perfectly with their doctrine of the absurd. In one humorous incident the group, gathered in a cafe, found a wallet left by a waiter and, of course, revolt against morality demanded that they take it. Much discussion followed as to what to do with it. If they returned it, as some of them wanted to do, because the waiter was a poor working man, they would be guilty of having acted according to bourgeois morality. In their dilemma, they gave the wallet to Eluard for safekeeping until they made their decision, but he took it upon himself to return it and thus bore the brunt of their reproaches.[42] As so often happens with Dada, there are different versions of the same events, and Eluard said that the wallet had been stolen from a priest and given to a waiter, thereby satisfying both their revolt against morality, and their vehement anti-clericalism.[43] But both versions reveal the fact that, while the Dadaists professed to be against all values, they had definite empathy with the poor, behaving toward the working class at least with a "bourgeois" sense of honor.

The *acte gratuit,* however, had its serious side for, taken to its logical conclusion, the act of ultimate absurdity was suicide and its philosophical justification became a significant element in the movement. A young soldier, Jacques Vaché, became a most important "anti-hero" as the perfect embodiment of Dada and, although he was never a member, he was a seminal figure. In the opinion of one critic "the Dadaists—and the Surrealists as well, as a matter of fact—may trace their descent from the picturesque Jacques Vaché."[44] Breton met him in 1916 while serving in a military mental hospital where Vaché was a patient. Breton, who at that time was writing imitative Symbolist poetry, was electrified by Vaché's contemptuous remark that "art is a stupidity."[45] He was in complete revolt against society and, like the Dadaists, was disgusted with the war. He liked dressing up as a German officer to show his complete rejection of patriotism and said, "I object to being killed in time of war. . . . I only hope They don't blow my head off while They have me in their power."[46] His philosophy was summed up in his concept of "umour," [*sic*] which he defined as "a theatrical uselessness (without joy) of everything," and it expressed his conviction that existence is absurd.[47]

Vaché's death was the grimmest practical joke of all. He committed suicide in 1918 by taking an overdose of opium and, in a horrifying *acte gratuit,* he apparently also administered a deliberately fatal overdose to an unsuspecting companion. But Breton's admiration only increased. "It is to Jacques Vaché that I owe the most. The time I spent with him in Nantes seemed almost enchanted."[48] The manner of his death was especially "admirable in that it appeared to be accidental," and the death of Vaché's friend was merely a "final amusing escapade."[49] Thus, largely through Vaché's example, the doctrine of suicide became increasingly important for the Dadaists and the Surrealists as well, several of whom actually did kill themselves. There seemed to be only two alternatives, given their negativism: one, to follow nihilism to its extreme of death; the other, to engage in incessant, meaningless activity as an expression of futility.

1920 was the climax of the Paris movement and their various

offenses were given a great deal of adverse publicity, which naturally delighted them. The high point of the year was a soirée in the dignified *Salle Gaveau* where, among many other outrages, Philippe Soupault appeared and, as he called out the names of the Pope, Clemenceau, and Foch, balloon caricatures came out of a large box and floated up to the ceiling. Tzara announced to his great satisfaction that, "for the first time in the history of the world, people threw at us not only eggs, salads and pennies, but beefsteaks as well. It was a great success."[50] But by this time, a terrible thing began to happen: the public began to enjoy these events and people came in such numbers that they had to be turned away at the door. Even worse, from the Dadaists' point of view, they tried to understand and sympathize with their moral and intellectual rebellion. As Malcolm Cowley said, people seemed to agree that "now it was time for a literary movement that would outdo the politicians in lunacy."[51]

Public sympathy and understanding were clearly intolerable, so another tack had to be taken and Breton had a new idea: the Dadaists would hold a mock trial of Maurice Barrès. In his youth he had written iconoclastic works and had admired Stendhal and Nietzsche for their rebellion against bourgeois morality. But he had become a rabid nationalist, a *revanchist,* an anti-Dreyfusard, and a leader of the reactionary and ultra-patriotic *Ligue de la patrie française.* All of this naturally made him a perfect target for the wrath of the group, however, Breton's idea did not meet with unanimous approval. Tzara opposed it on the grounds that it would be demonstrating humanitarian principles when the essence of Dada was to have no principles and Picabia was opposed because it sounded "too serious," and Dada was a joke. But Breton managed to have his way, and the "criminal" Barrès was put on trial for "Crimes against the Security of the Human Spirit."[52] Barrès publicly scoffed at the mock trial; nevertheless he found it convenient to be out of the city when it took place. Breton was the judge, Ribemont-Dessaignes was the prosecutor, and Aragon and Soupault were the counsel for the defense. Tzara and the others were witnesses, and Péret was very moving in the role of the unknown German soldier. Tzara tried to make it the usual Dada farce but Breton was determined to make the trial a severe indictment of the man who symbolized everything they despised, even though being serious was a cardinal sin.

Breton was already beginning to assert the leadership which

he was to exercise over the Surrealist movement and Tzara's role was being usurped. Even as a very young man, he was extremely dominating and had already surrounded himself with a group of artists and poets who regarded him as their leader. It was clear that, aside from his sincere desire to give a new substance to Dada, there was also a personal conflict between him and Tzara, who had been its original founder. Tzara, Picabia and some of the others resented Breton's attempts to give Dada a new direction and a purpose, which seemed to them completely contrary to its essence. The schism widened when, in 1922, Breton proposed to hold an international congress of artists "For the Determination of the Directions and the Defense of the Modern Spirit," but Tzara, Picabia, Eluard, and Soupault flatly refused to participate. An angry manifesto, *Coeur à barbe* (The Bearded Heart), appeared attacking Breton and the idea of the Congress as contrary to the true meaning of Dada, and Breton was forced to drop the project.[53] Its spirit was no longer a unifying force and by 1923, the movement as such no longer existed. "Dada is dead!" exclaimed Péret.[54] "Let go of everything. Let go of Dada. Let go of your wife. Let go of your mistress. . . . Let go of a need for a life of ease. . . . Take to the road!" was Breton's nonchalant farewell.[55] Breton and his friends had reached an impasse and it was time to move on.

The constant, directionless activity was, in the end, destructive of Dada itself because, as the critic, George Lemaître said, it was inevitable that its absolute negativism would bring about its own dissolution. He pointed out that the Dadaists were not psychologically cut out to be nihilists. They had too much exuberance and vitality and eventually their energy was bound to lead them toward genuine commitment.[56] Also, the movement possessed a moral fervor which, although negatively expressed, had to produce its opposite, a positive program with definite goals and ideals. It did, in fact, have a function which was to disrupt the complacency of society and especially to destroy established cultural values. As Tzara had said, it had a great task to perform of clearing away the old order. If this was so, then there had to be the idea of building anew, so it was not surprising that the Surrealists, who evolved out of Dada, would be deeply politically committed.

2 The Negation of Negation: Surrealist Revolt, 1920–1925

> I demand that he who still refuses, for instance, to see a horse galloping on a tomato should be looked upon as a cretin. A tomato is also a child's balloon—Surrealism, I repeat, having suppressed the word "like."
> —André Breton, *What is Surrealism?*

Dreams and Trances: The First Manifesto

The Surrealist movement is often said to have begun in 1924 with the publication of the *First Manifesto of Surrealism,* but there was a transition period between 1920 and 1924 during which Aragon, Breton and Soupault, three of the founders of the movement, edited the journal, *Littérature.* One of its most important texts had been the *Lettres de guerre* (Letters from the War) of Jacques Vaché, so much admired for his double crime of murder and suicide. It also published Jacques Rigaut's essay on suicide in which he sentenced himself to death ten years hence and actually carried out his intention, killing himself in 1929.[1] His act of self-destruction was hailed by the Surrealists and they elevated him, along with Vaché, to the ranks of Surrealist "saints." René Crevel's suicide in 1935 also met with a similar response and it is clear that Surrealism, although it tended to deny its heritage, retained a strong element of Dadaist nihilism and love of violence. However, while retaining the anti-social character of Dada in many respects, Surrealism did so in the name of a new principle, that of revolution, which at first meant the liberation of mind and spirit, but later came to include political and social revolution.

At the end of 1919, *Littérature* published a significant work, *Les Champs magnétiques* (Magnetic Fields), which has been described as "the first authentic Surrealist text."[2] A collaboration of Breton and Soupault, it was the first experiment in automatic writing and it was based, in part, on the principles of Freud. Breton had been fascinated by Freudian theory ever since 1916 when, as a medical student, he had worked with shell-shocked soldiers. In 1921 he had even made a "pilgrimage" to Vienna to meet Freud, but it had been an utterly fruitless encounter. Breton complained that "I could only get generalities out of him such as 'your letter was the most touching I have ever received,' or, 'happily, we can count on youth,' and the statement that he didn't much like France, 'the only country to remain indifferent to my work.' "[3] Freud professed complete bewilderment at the things the Surrealists were trying to do and he was frankly puzzled when Breton asked him to contribute accounts of his patients' dreams to a collection the Surrealists planned to publish.

> The superficial aspect of dreams, what I call the "manifest dream," holds no interest for me. I have been concerned with "latent content," which can be derived from the "manifest dream" by psychoanalytical interpretation. A collection of dreams without associations and knowledge of the context in which it was dreamed, does not tell me anything, and it is hard for me to imagine what it can mean to anyone else.[4]

In his opinion, dreams had significance only in a psychoanalytic setting when patients using the method of free association, uncovered their unconscious meaning.

But the Surrealists were not interested in employing Freud's methods as therapy; they had developed what they considered to be a revolutionary application of Freudian theory. They were interested in dreams and free association purely as a method of liberating man's creativity, not as a cure for neurosis and they believed that true poetry comes only from the unconscious, the irrational part of man's nature. Man has been too long stifled and inhibited by logic and rational thought, and it was their task, as they saw it, to liberate his mind. They wanted to teach man to rediscover his own unconscious and show him how to grasp the imaginative fantasies that lay hidden, even from himself. The method utilized in *Les Champs magnétiques* was of central importance to Surrealist ideology and, to Breton, it had the force of a revelation. One evening, just before falling asleep, he experienced an intensely vivid visual image of a man cut in half by a window, which had enormous significance for him. "Occupied at that time as I was by Freud, and familiar with his methods of examination which I had had occasion to practice on patients during the war, I resolved to obtain from myself what I had tried to obtain from them: a monologue spoken as rapidly as possible without any intervention of the critical faculties . . . which would be as close as possible to *spoken thought.*"[5]

Automatic writing, or "psychic automatism"—a better term since it was applied to painting as well as to writing—became the most important Surrealist method. While it was true that the Dadaists dabbled in it, they did not do so systematically in a spirit of scientific inquiry, nor with the goals the Surrealists had. The Surrealists now considered themselves scientists because they were serious explorers of a new world: the unconscious, the dream, the fantastic, or the "marvelous," a favorite word in their vocabulary. They stressed the systematic, experimental, and *scientific* character of their new method, in contrast to the destructiveness and anarchy of Dada.[6] Of course, they had their own special definition of science which had nothing to do with logic, quite the contrary. They were conducting "research" in the field of language, in its irrational, unconscious origins, rather than writing poetry in the usual way. Soon all the Surrealists were enthusiastically trying their hand at automatic writing. "It was a time when, meeting in the evening like hunters after a day in the field, we made the day's accounting, the list of beasts we had invented, of fantastic plants, or images bagged."[7] Naturally, it was against the "rules" to change a word of what was written, and the results were uneven, to say the least. Some very striking images were produced, but much of it is quite unreadable and, as Aragon said, "even if you write wretched idiocies by a Surrealist method, they will still be wretched idiocies, with no excuses."[8] Apparently, many of the poets and painters were never entirely satisfied with this method because, like Aragon, they confessed years later that they did not always abide by the rules, but deliberately altered their compositions. Nevertheless, for a long time, psychic automatism was hailed as the gateway to the "marvelous," the key to the liberation of man's imagination.

Another method of finding true poetic inspiration was by séances. These were conducted according to prescribed ritual in darkness and in silence, with everyone holding hands around the table. But, as Breton insisted, "It goes without saying that . . . at no time did we adopt a belief in spiritualism. As for myself, I formally refuse to accept the notion that there could be any kind of communication between the living and the dead."[9] The ritual was only used to create a trance state which appeared to be even a more direct route to the unconscious than automatic writing. "An epidemic of trances broke out among the Surrealists. . . . There were some . . . who now lived only for those moments of oblivion when, with the lights out, they spoke without consciousness."[10] But the poet, Robert Desnos, who had appeared able to fall into a trance at will, said he had really faked these hypnotic states.[11] As for Crevel, "he very soon withdrew in bitterness from the sessions of hypnotic sleep, and later . . . accused Breton of having prolonged the evenings mercilessly in order to bring his subjects beyond sanity, just to prove that this was not a game, nor simply minds playing with words."[12] These experiments were, in fact, very upsetting. Crevel and several others once tried to hang themselves and, on another occasion, Desnos chased after Eluard brandishing a knife, so Breton had to put an end to them.[13]

The third and most important method of research into the unconscious was the dream. Accounts of dreams appeared regularly in *La Révolution surréaliste* along with automatic poems. To further knowledge of the world of dreams, a "Bureau of Surrealist Research" was opened and an advertisement for it proclaimed "we are on the verge of a revolution! You can take part in it!"[14] The revolutionary goal of Surrealism, as Breton explained it, was the merging of two opposites into one continuum. "I believe in the future resolution of these two states of dream and reality, seemingly so contradictory, into a kind of absolute reality, a surreality."[15] The Surrealists demanded the subordination of logic to the irrational. Their conviction that there was no true dichotomy between dream and reality was a vital part of their philosophy for, as they insisted when they joined the Communist Party, there is no inherent conflict between Surrealism and Marxist theory, since Surrealism was also materialist, with its belief in *one* reality. In this, they were influenced by the French psychologist, Pierre Janet, who, in his theoretical work, opposed Cartesian dualism and stressed the material nature of the products of the mind. He denied that thought existed independently of image or word and, like him, the Surrealists insisted they were not idealists and that they

believed that thought is inseparable from its physical manifestations.[16]

Another important aspect of their "research" was a series of
word games they invented. The best known of these was "le
cadavre exquis," so-called from the first sentence obtained when
they played it, "the exquisite corpse will drink the new wine." It
consisted of writing a noun on paper, folding it so the word
couldn't be seen, passing it to one's neighbor who would write a
verb, and so on, until complete, perfectly grammatical but non-
sensical sentences were produced. They stressed the fact that the
aesthetic results were unimportant and it was only the process of
experimentation that interested them and Breton explained that
this art was to be "an instrument of self-discovery, not an end to be
savored."[17] One important effect of these experiments was that, as
with Dada, the artist submerged his own individuality into that of
the group. This "poetic anonymity" was further developed in
Ralentir travaux (Slack off work), a collection of poems written by
Breton, Eluard, and René Char, in which it is impossible to tell
which lines were written by which poet.[18] This was precisely the
intention of the three who were trying to follow the Comte de
Lautréamont's dictum that poetry should be made by all, not by
one.

Breton clarified these ideas in 1924 in the *First Manifesto of
Surrealism* which is fundamental to an understanding of Surrealist
thought. He praised Freud for being the first to comprehend the
value of dreams, and professed his desire to see "the dream applied
to the solution of the fundamental problems of life."[19] He condemned logic and realism, because "the realistic attitude of
thought, inspired by positivism, from Saint Thomas to Anatole
France, seems to me to be clearly hostile to all intellectual and
moral advances. I have a horror of it because it consists of medi-
ocrity, hate, and dull conceit." He also praised madness saying "I
could spend my life trying to discover the secrets of the insane,"
and he demanded total freedom for the imagination, declaring that
"liberty is the only word that has the power to exalt me. . . . To
reduce the imagination to slavery would be to betray whatever
sense one has of absolute justice."[20] The *First Manifesto* also contained his famous definition of Surrealism:

> SURREALISM, noun, masc., pure psychic automatism
> by which it is intended to express, either verbally or in

writing, the real function of thought, in the absence of any control exercised by the reason and outside of all aesthetic and moral preoccupations.

Encycl. Philos.—Surrealism is based on the belief in the superior reality of certain forms of associations neglected until now, in the omnipotence of the dream, and in the disinterested play of thought. It leads to the destruction of all other psychic mechanisms and substitutes itself for them in solving the principal problems of life. The following have sworn to ABSOLUTE SURREALISM: MM. Aragon, Baron, Boiffard, Breton, Carrive, Crevel, Delteil, Noll, Péret, Picon, Soupault, Vitrac.[21]

Breton then elaborated on this mock dictionary and encyclopedia definition by adding that Surrealism was the "magic art" whose secrets he proposed to reveal. In a passage that recalled Tzara's "recipe" for a poem, he said,

Write quickly, with no preconceived subject in mind, quickly enough so that you cannot recall what you have written and so that you will not be tempted to re-read it. . . . Continue as long as you please. . . . After a word whose origin seems suspect to you, put any letter whatsoever, the letter *1* for example, and retrieve the arbitrary character of the writing by making this letter the first one of the following word.[22]

The "Surrealist voice" was within the compass of everyone's unconscious for the artists declared that they had no talent, they were merely "modest copying machines." In another passage reminiscent of Tzara, Breton stated that "it is even permissible to entitle POEM the results obtained from the most random possible gathering of headlines and scraps of headlines from the newspapers."[23] He explained that the movement was not at all concerned with aesthetics, but only with the search for the "marvelous." Surrealism was fighting a "war of independence," it attempted a whole new way of seeing the world and it must be credited with establishing the primacy of the unconscious, of dreams and of fantasy in art. This new approach that deliberately exalted the unconscious above the rational, even to the point of forbidding the artist to change a word in his own work, was the original meaning of the Surrealist revolution. But the Surrealists had no desire to remain a small, esoteric group pursuing their "researches." On the contrary, they were eager to publicize the fruits of their experiments and urged anyone who would listen to try them too.[24] They were proselytizers spreading Surrealism among the masses. They handed out leaflets in the streets before every new project and assured everybody that they, too, could be artists if they would only release the hidden creativity in their own unconscious minds. They insisted that talent is irrelevant and that, using the methods of psychic automatism, anyone is capable of creation. Everyone has an unconscious; therefore, everyone is a potential poet. This was the exciting new discovery they tried to communicate.

First Public Protests

The Surrealists spent their time in cafés playing their "games," practicing their automatic writing, relating their dreams to one another, and often gathering in the evenings at the home of Breton, who had recently married the first of his three wives, Simone Kahn. He set the tone of this collective life and was the man who dominated and shaped the group. Almost everyone who met him has agreed that he possessed an amazingly magnetic personality and, remarkably, he was able to forge a number of highly individualistic artists into a coherent movement. They willingly abided by the "rules" he laid down, one of which was that all literary and artistic productions had to be approved by the group before they could be published or exhibited. Another was that regular work, especially anything that could lead to a successful career, was forbidden. Breton, Aragon, Jacques-André Boiffard, and Francis Gérard all abandoned their medical studies and others deliberately left the university without getting a degree.[25] Many of them lived under real hardships; in fact, Breton said that he often went without food in those days and he attributed his vivid fantasies to hunger. But, in compensation one could enjoy the fanatically intense friendship and loyalty of the group which was a continual source of inspiration to its members.

Their major goal was to place the dream and the unconscious at the highest level of art but, like the Dadaists, they were determined to destroy traditional culture by ridicule and even by violence. Their first public "scandal" was caused by an insulting pamphlet they wrote called *Un Cadavre* on the death of Anatole France. He was very much a national hero, but to them he symbolized the hated literary establishment, the epitome of bourgeois pretension and, in short, he was everything they despised. Just as he had earlier organized the Barrès trial, Breton was the impetus behind this attack in which all the Surrealists gleefully participated. The spectacle of a country in mourning for a national hero was too great an opportunity to be missed. France's brain was even dissected for the benefit of science and a Dr. Guillaume seriously reported that it was "the finest brain that can be imagined, in the extent, number, and delicacy of circumvolutions, the curliness, as we say. . . . Not to preserve such a brain would be a crime against science. . . . France's brain corresponds in every point to his genius at the same time that it explains it."[26] This passage was simply reprinted by the Surrealists without comment—none being needed. But they also collected the greatest insults they could concoct to show their utter contempt:

THE MISTAKE
I think it's a remarkable idea to waste any time addressing farewells to a corpse from which the brain has been removed! . . .

Philippe Soupault

AN OLD MAN LIKE THE REST
The face of glory, the face of death—the face of Anatole France living or dead. Your kind, corpse, we don't like. . . .

Paul Eluard

REFUSAL TO INTER
Loti, Barrès, France, any year deserves a gold star that lay these sinister gentlemen to rest; the idiot, the traitor, and the policeman. And I should have no objection to wasting a special word of scorn on the third. With France, a bit of human servility leaves the world. Let the day be a holiday when we bury cunning, traditionalism, patriotism, opportunism, skepticism, realism, and lack of heart. . . .

André Breton

HAVE YOU EVER SLAPPED A DEAD MAN?
One does not imagine Baudelaire, for example, or anyone else who stood at that extremity of spirit which alone defies death, celebrated by the press and his contemporaries like a vulgar Anatole France. . . . He wrote quite badly, I assure you. . . . I consider any admirer of Anatole France a degraded being. It delights me that the *littérateur* hailed simultaneously today by the imbecile Maurras and doddering Moscow should have

written the most dishonoring of prefaces to a tale of Sade's, who spent his life in prison. . . . There are days I dream of an eraser to rub out human filth.

Louis Aragon[27]

This protest amounted to a compendium of the grievances they had against society and it provoked an extremely hostile reaction from the press, which pleased them greatly. The right wing *Action Française* threatened that "efforts will be made to reduce them to silence," and other newspapers proposed to punish them by not giving them any publicity and by refusing to review their books and exhibitions.

Shortly afterwards, the Surrealists demonstrated at a banquet held in honor of the poet, Saint-Pol-Roux, whom they admired. They were invited guests, and at first had no thought of being disruptive, but some of the speakers proved too reactionary for them to be able to sit by in silence. The actress, Mme. Rachilde, in the course of her talk, declared passionately that "a Frenchwoman could never marry a German," and at that point, the Surrealists could no longer contain themselves. Breton cried out that she was insulting his friend, Max Ernst, and all of them began shouting "Long live Germany! Down with France! Long live China! Long live the Riff!" The speakers were prevented from continuing and the evening turned into an actual brawl. It ended with many Surrealists being arrested and one, Michel Leiris, being badly beaten by the police. To their delight, Mme. Rachilde insisted publicly that she had been the victim of German agents. The *Association des écrivains combattants* (Association of Literary War Veterans) condemned the Surrealists' action as an "insult to French thought" and an "outrage to all who fought and died for France."[28] This, of course, was exactly the kind of reaction they desired, since they were determined to shock the whole bourgeois world.

At this time, a serious colonial rebellion of the Riff in Morocco had begun and France was obliged to send a large army to put down the revolt. In the increasingly ultra-patriotic climate of opinion, the Surrealists were actually regarded as traitors to their country, just as the Dadaists had been during World War I. Feeling against them was aggravated even more when they issued an *Open Letter to Paul Claudel, French Ambassador to Japan* in response to an attack by Claudel, who had said

> As for the present movements, not one can lead to a genuine renewal or creation. Neither Dadaism nor Surrealism which have only one meaning: pederasty. . . . Many are surprised that I am [not only] a good Catholic, but a writer, a diplomat, French ambassador, and a poet. But I find nothing strange about this. During the war, I went to South America to buy wheat, tinned meat, and lard for the army, and managed to save my country some two hundred million francs.

They could let neither these insults nor these amazingly fatuous comments pass. They fired back a violently angry retort which was also an important statement of their early ideas.

> Sir, the only pederastic thing about our activity is the confusion it introduces into the minds of those who do not take part in it. . . . We fervently hope that wars and colonial insurrections will annihilate this Western civilization. . . . One cannot be both French ambassador and a poet. We take this opportunity to disassociate ourselves publicly from all that is French, in words and in actions. We assert that we find treason and all that can harm the security of the state . . . much more reconcilable with poetry than the sale of "great quantities of lard." . . . Write, pray, and slobber on; we demand the dishonor of having treated you once and for all as a pedant and a swine.[29]

Two major tendencies of Surrealist thought can be seen here: hatred of the Western world and especially of war, characteristics stemming from Dada, and also a new belief in the East as a superior culture that will annihilate the West.

La Révolution surréaliste

In 1924, the Surrealists began publishing their own periodical, *La Révolution surréaliste,* which appeared irregularly until 1929, and successive issues show startling changes in their thought. At first, they were essentially apolitical and they were surprised when Aragon's remark, quoted above, equating the reactionary writer Maurras with "doddering Moscow," provoked a hostile reaction from the Left. A polemical correspondence with *Clarté,* a small Marxist journal close to the Communist Party, followed, that was published both in *Clarté* and in *La Révolution surréaliste.* Jean Bernier, one of *Clarté's* editors, berated Aragon for "the stupidity more comical than odious," of which he was guilty, but Aragon replied that he had "little taste for the Bolshevik government or for Communism in general. I have always placed the spirit of revolt far above politics. I simply shrug my shoulders at the thought of the Russian Revolution . . . it is nothing more than a vague ministerial crisis." Bernier retorted by accusing Aragon of erecting "mysticism in the place of politics," and another editor, Marcel Fourrier, added, "Aragon, that pure anarchist, . . . feels the same horror at the Russian Revolution as all other Frenchmen of his class," and he's no better than the right-wing Barrès. Having the last word in *La Révolution surréaliste,* Aragon replied, "I want none of your half-measures. Your Millerands equal theirs. They have the minds of bankers and you, their apologists, are making a simple legal crisis out of the inimitable cause of revolution."[30]

These polemics reveal that the two groups had as yet no common ground. The Surrealists were idealistic, even mystical, in spite of their claims to the contrary, and they were certainly anarchistic. Aragon often wrote for *Le Libertaire,* an anarchist organ, and in the first issue of *La Révolution surréaliste,* there was a picture of Germaine Berton, surrounded by all the Surrealists, posed as though they were gazing admiringly at her. She was an anarchist terrorist who had recently assassinated an *Action française* leader, Marius Plateau, and Aragon declared fervently that "this woman symbolizes the greatest defiance of slavery that I know."[31] In other articles, the Surrealists demanded total liberty, with no restrictions for anyone. They wanted freedom for prisoners, freedom from military service, freedom for mental patients, sexual freedom, and freedom from all the traditional taboos of Western culture. Surrealism, at least in its early period, was clearly in the anarchist tradition.[32] They could not admire the Russian Revolution because it seemed too orderly, too directed and, as Aragon had indicated, too incomplete. A different government was not the revolution of men's minds that they wanted and it seemed to them that the changes wrought by the Bolsheviks were merely superficial. Their idea of revolt was much more grandiose: it was spiritual rebellion they advocated, not a change in social and economic structure. Yet, the Surrealists did have, as heirs of Dada, a contempt for bourgeois society that was expressed in virtually everything they did and the angry exchange of letters was forgotten a year later when there was a rapprochement with *Clarté.*

La Révolution surréaliste imitated a scientific journal in format. Throughout its pages were reports from the newspapers of strange cases of suicide that, in their continuing fascination with the subject, they undertook to collect. Along with these were dreams, automatic texts, accounts of occult phenomena, and of all sorts of irrational behavior. "We must arrive at a new declaration of the rights of man," declared the editors, Pierre Naville and Benjamin Péret, while a flyer with the first issue set forth their purpose: "The unconscious activity of the mind seems not to have been explored until now . . . LA RÉVOLUTION SURRÉALISTE proposes to liberate this activity. . . . If you are in any way the enemy of positivism, . . . and if you are ready to enter the unexplored field of the Dream, read LA RÉVOLUTION SURRÉALISTE."[33] The issue of January 1925 contained a manifesto, *Ouvrez les prisons, licenciez l'armée,* demanding freedom for common criminals and the abolition of the army: "Social coercion has had its day. Nothing, neither acknowledgment of crimes committed, nor contribution to national defense can force a man to give up his freedom. The idea of barracks are commonplace today. These monstrosities no longer astonish you. . . . Set the soldiers and convicts free!"[34]

The Surrealists were beginning to grope toward some kind of action, although the word "revolution" still signified a revolution of ideas, as in this leaflet, signed by the whole group and handed out in the streets.

DECLARATION OF JANUARY 27, 1925

With regard to a false interpretation of our enterprise, stupidly circulated among the public, . . . we declare as follows: . . .

1. We have nothing to do with literature. . . .

2. Surrealism is not a new means of expression, . . . nor even a metaphysic of poetry. It is a means of total liberation of the mind. . . .

3. We are determined to make a revolution.

4. We have joined the word *surrealism* to the word *revolution* solely to show the disinterested, detached and even entirely desperate character of this revolution. . . .

8. We are specialists in Revolt. There is no means of action which we are not capable of employing.

9. We say in particular to the Western world: *Surrealism*

exists . . . and it is determined to break apart its fetters, even if it must be by material hammers!

Bureau of Surrealist Research[35]

Another tract of this time also illustrated the optimistic belief that the movement had the power to change consciousness. "The immediate reality of the Surrealist revolution is not . . . to change anything in the physical . . . order . . . as to create a movement in men's minds. . . . Everyone faithful to the Surrealist revolution is obliged to believe that the Surrealist movement . . . is really capable of changing something in the minds of men."[36]

A new mysticism was briefly interjected into the journal in the third issue of *La Révolution surréaliste.* Its theme was a comparison of the contemplative philosophies of Asia with the falseness of Western religious values. There were several manifestoes on this subject, written by Antonin Artaud and one, *Letter to the Rectors of European universities,* denounced Western education. "You know nothing of the mind. You ignore its most vital and most secret ramifications. In the name of your own logic, Messieurs, life stinks."[37] Another hurled insults at the Pope and at Christianity. "We declare war on you, Pope, dog! . . . From start to finish, your Roman mascarade shows a hatred of the immediate truths of the spirit,"[38] Jean Koppen insisted that it is always necessary to spit at "a servant of the bearded whore of Nazareth" whenever you meet one on the street.[39] Anticlericalism was an important element of Surrealism and the group always professed a vehement atheism. This was actually one of its less original characteristics since *manger du prêtre* (priest-eating) is a favorite pastime of French intellectuals. But the Surrealists carried their hatred of religion to violent extremes: they even decorated their toilets with sacred objects stolen from churches. Nevertheless, there was also a laudatory manifesto, *Address to the Dalaï-Lama,* which revealed a singular lack of knowledge concerning Eastern religion. "We are your very faithful servants, O Great Lama. Give us . . . your wisdom in words that our contaminated European souls can understand. . . . Teach us material levitation of the body . . . because you know freedom of the Spirit, . . . O Pope of the True Spirit."[40] In the same vein was a *Letter to Buddhists* that praised the spirit of the East in contrast to the contemptible materialistic society of the West. It was clear that ignorance of the Eastern world in no way prevented the Surrealists from using the

East as a symbol for true freedom when they wished to condemn their own culture.

In the name of complete liberty for all, they published *Lettre aux médecins-chefs des asiles de fous* (Letter to the Heads of Insane Asylums). "The insane are the individual victims *par excellence* of social dictation. In the name of that individuality which is essential to man, we insist on the liberation of these convicts of sensibility. . . . Kindly remember, tomorrow morning, when you make your rounds, that . . . your only advantage over these men is that of force."[41] The Surrealists were always fascinated by mental illness, not as a state of disease, but of pure creativity, because mental patients had the great advantage of having escaped from the prison of logic. *La Révolution surréaliste* printed extracts from some remarkable writings and drawings of mental patients and the fiftieth anniversary of Jean-Martin Charcot's great discoveries in hysteria was celebrated in its pages. An interesting literary experiment, *L'Immaculée conception,* published in 1930, was undertaken by Breton and Eluard in which they deliberately simulated states of insanity in order to heighten their creative sensibilities and facilitate the production of automatic writing.

An article by Eluard against colonialist exploitation appeared in which he said that the West was doomed, repeating Artaud's theme, but on a more realistic plane.

> The peoples struggling for their independence will soon perceive that they are capable of overthrowing their masters, whether native or foreign. . . . The taste for liberty will develop in fighting for it. How is it possible that the most stoic of these slaves would put up with the imbecilic cruelties of white decadence forever? . . . The white man is only a corpse stinking in the nose of the yellow man.

He concluded that one day soon, men of all colors will be free of missionaries and soldiers, the "jackals and vultures of the West" who oppress them.[42] Anti-colonialism was also an enduring Surrealist theme and generalized violence was advocated by Desnos, who protested the "westernization" of the whole world. He attacked the League of Nations for passing resolutions against narcotics and pornography saying "it seems to me that your society has as its main goal the struggle against liberty," and he declared that the only solution was "revolution, that is to say the Terror . . . only the guillotine could, by dark strokes, enlighten that mob of adversaries. . . . Ah! Let that sympathetic machine of deliverance be erected on a public square."[43] The Surrealists' consistent and furious opposition to nationalism in any form was expressed, also by Desnos, who was a Jew, in "Pamphlet contre Jérusalem." "Allow me to express, in a writing that is not anti-Semitic, all the horror I feel at this rising nationalism. . . . Here is a sentimental movement, born of the League of Nations, pushing for the reconstruction of Zion and the foundation of a Jewish state as ridiculous and artificial as Poland."[44]

The entire third issue was thus dedicated to the proposition that the West, with its vicious nationalism, its colonialist exploitation, and its coercion of peaceful citizens, was doomed. The agents of its destruction were to be Asian hordes pouring out of the East, while a spiritual rebirth was to come about when Eastern mysticism overcame Western materialism. But as they began to move from a revolution of the mind to some kind of commitment to action, certain inconsistencies began to appear, and ideological differences began to show up, as seen in this memorandum:

> The undersigned, members of *La Révolution surréaliste,* meeting on April 2, 1925 in order to determine which of the two principles, Surrealism or revolution, ought best to guide their activity, having failed to resolve this question, are agreed, however, on the following points:
> 1. Before any Surrealist or revolutionary preoccupation, that which dominates their minds is a certain state of fury.
> 2. They think that on the path of that fury, they are most likely to attain what could be called Surrealist illumination.
> 3. One of the first goals is to elucidate a few points which this fury should most particularly attack.
> 4. For the moment, they see only one positive point to which all the members of *La Révolution surréaliste* must give their support: knowledge that the Spirit is an essentially irreducible principle which cannot be fixed either in life or beyond.[45]

Their dilemma was clear: whether to join with a revolutionary movement or to remain isolated and follow their own path, "the life of pure Surrealism," as Naville later called it. They could not as yet agree on a course of action, and this was shown by the fact that Breton took over the editorship of *La Révolution surréaliste* from Naville, Péret and Artaud with the fourth issue on as a result of an internal power struggle. Here again, Breton asserted his own leadership of the movement in order to guide it along the paths he envisioned. Naville and Péret were still too immersed in the farcical anti-art aspects of Dada, while Artaud's mystical paeans to the East were really irrelevant to the Surrealist revolution, in Breton's opinion. The Surrealists, however, were still open to the charge that they were armchair revolutionaries and indeed, their concept of revolution had a purely metaphysical value. Perpetual revolt, along with threats of violence, were treated as an end in themselves; even the calls for bloodshed, destruction, and the guillotine, were merely metaphorical.

A New Political Consciousness

With the fifth number of *La Révolution surréaliste,* the Surrealists made a decisive commitment to revolution in the political sense. A new vocabulary was evident in their journal as they began to express themselves in Marxist terminology. In this issue, Breton reviewed Trotsky's biography of Lenin and said that while he himself was not totally committed to the Russian Revolution, "their enemies are our enemies," and that, in his opinion, the major achievement of the Russian Revolution had been to destroy the old order: "I think . . . that Communism, by its existence as an organized system, has alone brought about the greatest social upheaval, . . . defensible or not in itself from the moral point of view, . . . it was thanks to this instrument that the walls of the old order have crumbled."[46] He ended by enthusiastically crying "Hurrah for Lenin!" and "I bow to Leon Trotsky!" There was also a "Lettre d'André Masson," that was unusual because the visual artists rarely wrote for the journal; at most, they signed the manifestoes, in which Masson also declared his adherence to the cause of revolution. "I believe that . . . every man who wants revolution . . . is necessarily led to consider that the only socially valuable upheaval in our times is the Dictatorship of the Proletariat as Marx conceived it and as Lenin actualized it. Once and for all, I have broken with 'revolutionary bohemianism.' "[47]

Once again, it was Breton who determined the new course of Surrealism and who, simply by his extraordinary ability to command, was able to persuade most of the group to make a political commitment along with him. There was nothing in Breton's personal history to account for his attraction to either poetry or to revolution. His relatively poor, lower middle-class family was apparently quite conventional, although Breton was always very reticent about his background. It was his parents who chose a medical career for him, and when he abandoned his studies, they withdrew their support and broke off relations with him completely. In his determination to be a poet, he was encouraged and influenced by Guillaume Apollinaire and he had begun publishing poetry very early in his life.

Other than this generalized rebellion, the only remotely political sentiment Breton revealed was his detestation of war. This was an intense and immediate reaction to the terrible conditions encountered at the hospital in Nantes, and it was reinforced by the Dadaists, whom he later joined. It was understandable that, given their anti-militarism, he and his friends would be horrified at the outbreak of a new war, the colonial conflict with the Riff in Morocco and they had to find a more serious means of protest than simply perpetrating another of their many "scandals."

The quarrel between Aragon and the *Clartéistes* had been resolved, the two groups had become friendly, and the young Marxists of *Clarté* had begun to exert a political influence over the Surrealists. Breton realized that Surrealism was beginning to run the risk of sterility, in spite of its many manifestoes and demonstrations, just as had happened to Dada, and it had become clear that the vitality of the movement was at stake. It was now obvious that, while verbal and symbolic violence might cause a momentary shock, the bourgeois world was not at all threatened. If the "revolution in men's minds" was ever to become a reality, it would have to be through other means and gradually, the definition of the Surrealist revolution expanded to include revolution in the political sense. David Gascoyne, an English Surrealist poet, pointed out that "political problems had to force themselves to the consciousness of anyone demanding absolute freedom," and that "Marxist principles gave Surrealism unity and purpose. Without this philosophy, it could never have survived."[48] Brenton understood that surrealism needed Marxism for its own creativity.

The immediate occasion for their first truly political protest was provided by the Moroccan war, which they vehemently denounced. The war against the Riff was intensifying in 1925. Abd-el-Krim, the leader of this struggle for national independence, was finally defeated in 1926, but it took a combined force of French and Spanish troops numbering more than 150,000 to do it. The intellectual establishment in France had published a manifesto in support of the colonial policies of the government called *Les Intellectuels aux côtés de la patrie* (Intellectuals in Support of the Nation). The Surrealists responded by signing a counter-manifesto circulated by the French Communist Party and published in *L'Humanité,* entitled *Les Intellectuels contre la guerre du Maroc* (Intellectuals Against the War in Morocco). But most significant was the manifesto, *La Révolution d'abord et toujours* (Revolution First and Forever), written jointly by the Surrealists and the editors of *Clarté,* and published in both journals. This protest was also signed by the *Philosophies* group, among whom were Henri Lefebvre, Georges Politzer, Norman Guterman, Georges Friedmann, and Paul Nizan, and by the writers of *Correspondance,* a Belgian Surrealist review edited by Camille Goemans and Paul Nougé.

After a lengthy preamble in which the signers declared their opposition to the whole body of European thought and civilization, and announced themselves in favor of the liberation of all the peoples of the world, they called for the following revolutionary program:

> 1. The magnificent example of an immediate disarmament [was] . . . given to the world in 1917 by LENIN at Brest-Litovsk, a disarmament of infinite revolutionary valor. We do not believe that *your* France would ever be capable of following suit.
> 2. Most of us being eligible for the draft, and destined to wear the miserable sky-blue uniform, we energetically reject . . . such a subjugation, since for us, it is a simple fact that France does not exist.
> 3. We fully approve and countersign the manifesto issued by the *Comité d'action contre la guerre du Maroc,* all the more so since at present, its authors are being threatened with legal proceedings.
> 4. Priests, doctors, professors, *littérateurs,* poets, philosophers, journalists, judges, lawyers, policemen, academicians of every sort, all you signatories of that imbecilic paper, *Les Intellectuels aux côtés de la patrie* (Intellectuals in Support of the Country), we denounce you. . . . Dogs on hind legs, chewing on the bone of the only thought you have, that of profiting from *la patrie.*
> 5. We are the revolt of the Spirit. We think of bloody revolution as the inexorable vengeance of the mind humiliated by your works. We are not Utopian; we can only con-

ceive of this Revolution in its social form. . . . The idea of Revolution is the best and most effective safeguard of the individual.[49]

This manifesto represented a new orientation for the Surrealists. It was certainly not true before this that they conceived of revolution only in its social form; in fact, this is precisely what was new. The idea of collaborating with other groups was also new, but they had a compelling motive. As Fourrier of *Clarté* explained, "the events of the war with the Riff literally hurled us into each other's arms."[50] Breton concurred, saying that

> No coherent political or social attitude made its appearance until 1925, that is to say (and it is important to stress this), until the outbreak of the Moroccan war which, re-arousing in us our particular hostility to . . . armed conflicts . . . abruptly placed before us the necessity of making a public protest, *La Révolution d'abord et toujours,* October, 1925. Surrealism . . . suddenly perceived the necessity of . . . dialectical materialism, insisting on the *supremacy of matter over mind.*[51]

With *La Révolution d'abord et toujours,* Surrealism entered what Breton called its "reasoning phase," becoming politically conscious. The Riff war was important enough to give their movement an entirely new ideological direction and field of action because they were profoundly disgusted with the resurgence of imperialistic exploitation. Therefore, in 1925, with France in the throes of another war, the Surrealists, with some claim to consistency, could begin to consider themselves Marxist revolutionaries. Many critics have claimed that they simply dabbled in politics, but in reality, politics played a central role, as was demonstrated by the fact that it was the war in Morocco, with all its imperialist and militaristic implications, that thrust the movement into a new, overtly political phase.

The Riff war produced this change in Surrealist thought largely because of the developing political consciousness of Breton. It was his leadership that transformed Surrealism from a small group of anarchistic artists into an organized movement with revolutionary political as well as aesthetic goals. The process of gradually turning to Marxism and to the Communist Party, which the historian Annie Kriegel describes as the "dynamics of conversion," was, of course, not peculiar to Surrealism. It was fairly common for young intellectuals to become Communists after passing through an ideological phase of anarchism. But, according to her, this kind of "conversion" was apt to produce tremendous tensions between these intellectuals and the Party because they tended to cling to their intellectual independence even after their adherence and this was to be the fundamental cause of conflict between the Surrealists and the Communists.[52]

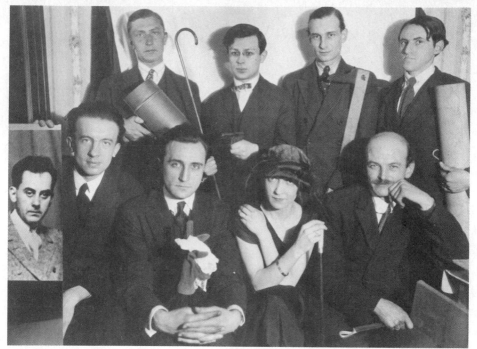

Top, from left to right: Paul Chadourne, Tristan Tzara, Philippe Soupault, Serge Charchoune. *Bottom:* Man Ray, Paul Eluard, Jacques Rigaut, Mick Soupault, Georges Ribemont-Dessaignes, circa 1922.

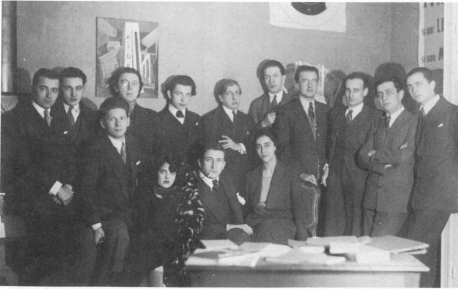

Top, from left to right: Jacques Baron, Raymond Queneau, André Breton, Jacques Boiffard, Giorgio De Chirico, Roger Vitrac, Paul Eluard, Philippe Soupault, Robert Desnos, Louis Aragon. *Bottom, from left to right:* Pierre Naville, Simone Collinet-Breton, Max Morise, Marie-Louise Soupault, 1924.

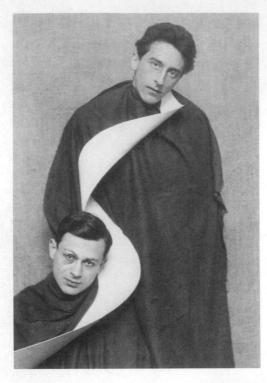

Jean Cocteau, *(top)*
Tristan Tzara,
circa 1922.

Antonin Artaud, 1926.

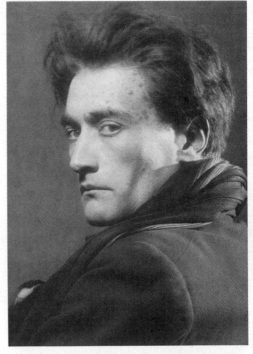

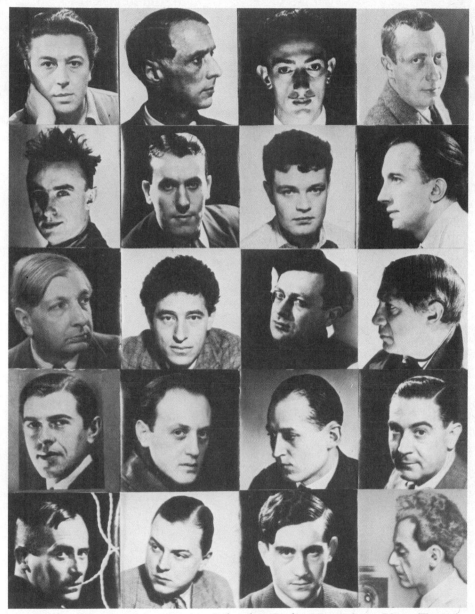

André Breton, Max Ernst, Salvador Dali, Hans Arp, Yves Tanguy, René Char, René Crevel, Paul Eluard, Giorgio De Chirico, Alberto Giacometti, Tristan Tzara, Pablo Picasso, René Magritte, Victor Brauner, Benjamin Péret, Gui Rosey, Joan Miró, E. L. T. Mesens, Georges Hugnet, Man Ray, 1934.

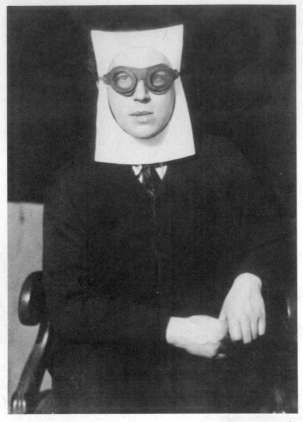

André Breton, circa 1930.

Paul Eluard, André Breton,
1930.

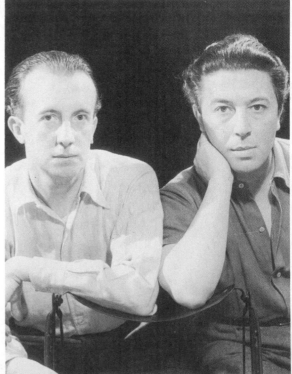

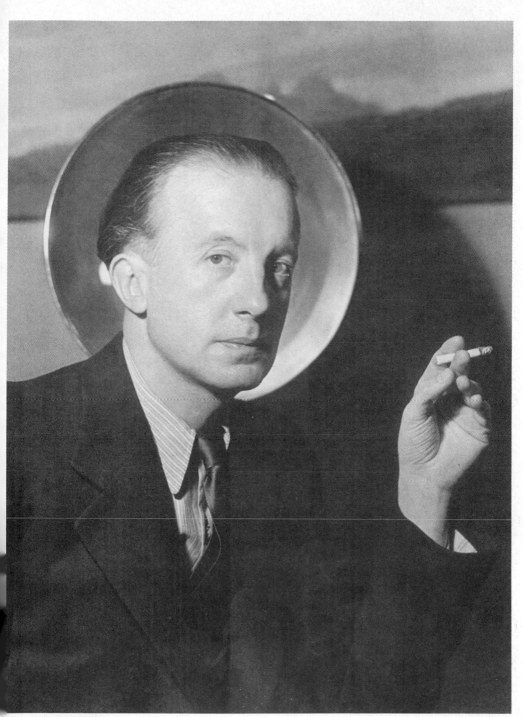

Paul Eluard.

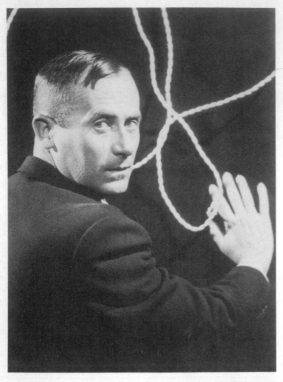

Joan Miró, circa 1930.

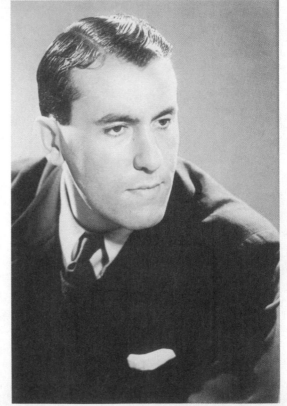

René Char.

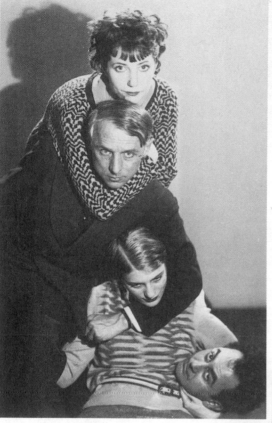

Marie–Berthe Aurenche,
Max Ernst, Lee Miller,
Man Ray.

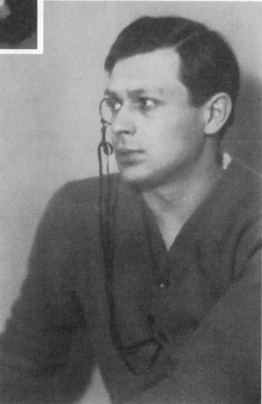

Tristan Tzara.

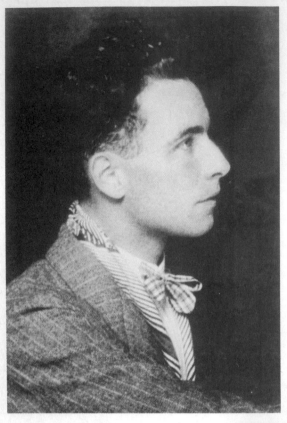

Louis Aragon.

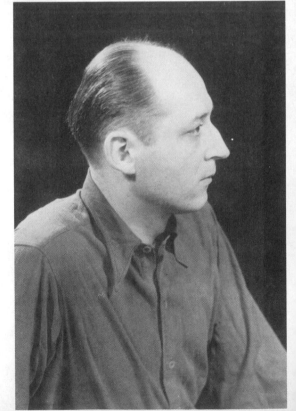

Benjamin Péret.

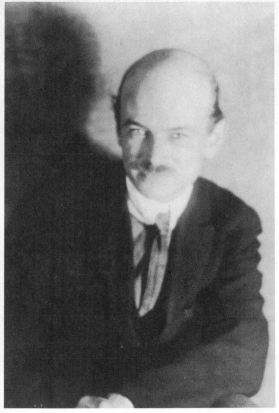

Georges Ribemont–Dessaignes.

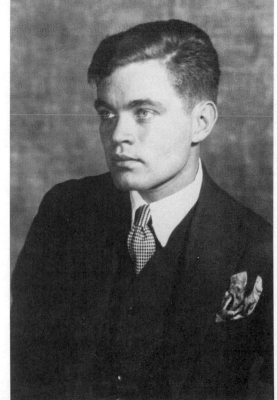

René Crevel.

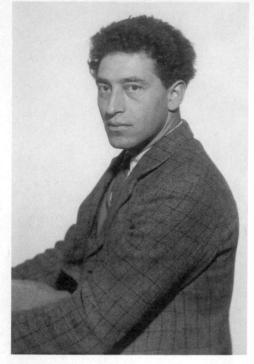

Alberto Giacometti, circa 1934.

Luis Buñuel, 1929.

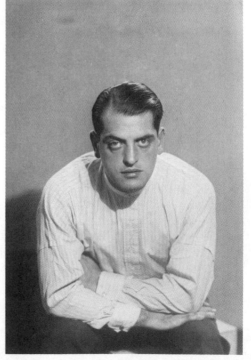

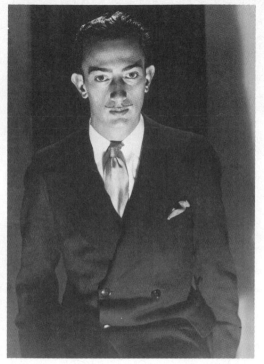

Salvador Dali, 1929–31.

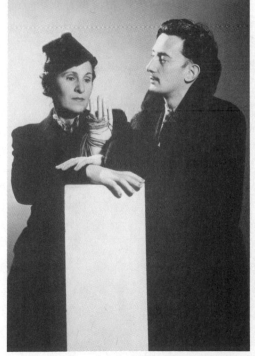

Salvador Dali, with his wife, Gala, 1936.

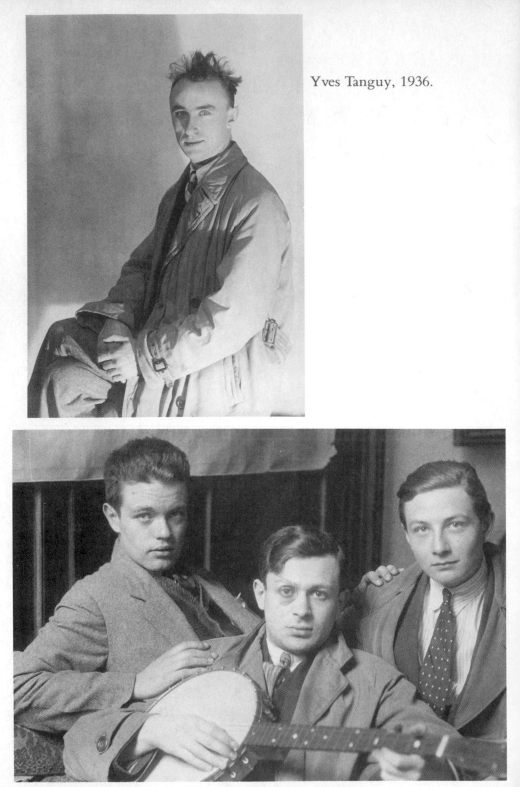

Yves Tanguy, 1936.

René Crevel, Tristan Tzara, Jacques Baron, 1928.

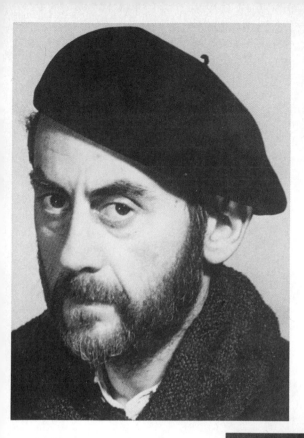

Man Ray. Self-portraits.

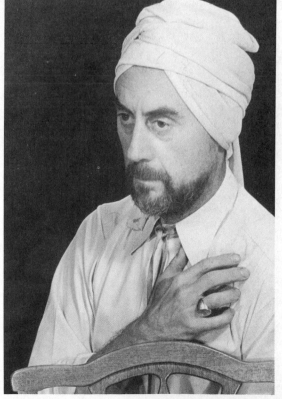

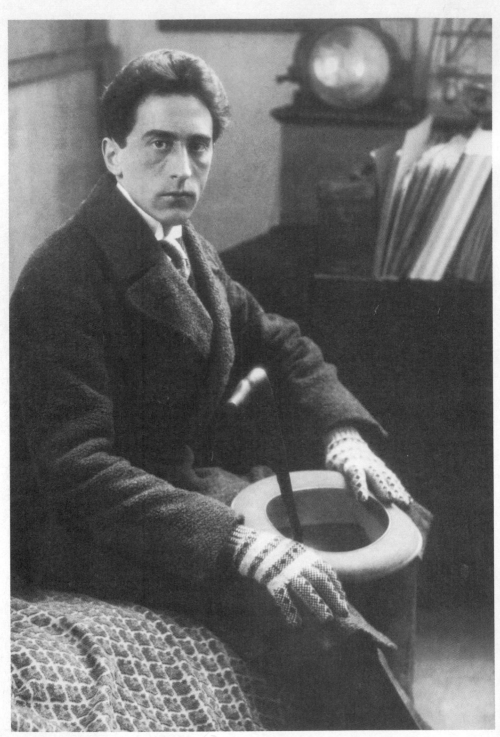

Jean Cocteau, circa 1924.

3

Surrealists and the Clarté Movement

> Surrealist activity had to cease being content
> with the results (automatic texts, the recital of
> dreams, improvised speeches, spontaneous
> poems, drawings and actions) which it had
> originally planned.
> —André Breton, *What Is Surrealism?*

Political Evolution of *Clarté*

The relationship with *Clarté* marked the beginning of a period
of intense political involvement for the Surrealists, and the difficulties they experienced in attempting to collaborate prefigured
those they were to have for years with the French Communist
Party. The *Clarté* movement, from which the journal took its
name, was founded just after World War I by Henri Barbusse and
several other pacifist liberal intellectuals. In France it was headed
by the writers Barbusse, Jules Romains, Romain Rolland, and Paul
Vaillant-Couturier, one of the founders of the French Communist
Party, with the support of Anatole France, who was not actually a
member. The original idea behind the formation of *Clarté* was
frankly elitist. An "international of the mind" was to be organized
by intellectuals in each country who were to be bound together by
vaguely socialistic, humanitarian, and pacifist ideals and they were
to use their influence to prevent further military aggression. Such
groups actually did come into existence in Sweden, where the
organization published its own journal; in England; and in several
cities in France. In addition, Barbusse was able to persuade a

number of famous intellectuals outside of France to sign a declaration in support of the new movement. Among them were Benedetto Croce, Albert Einstein, Maxim Gorky, Selma Lagerlöf, Upton Sinclair, Bertrand Russell, Heinrich Mann, Magdeleine Marx, and Stefan Zweig. Most of these, however, played no active role.

Because of the great prestige of Barbusse, author of *Le Feu* (translated as *Under Fire*), an anti-war novel he published in 1916 at the risk of a military court-martial, many young radicals joined. *Clarté* condemned the Versailles Treaty, especially its "war guilt" clause which put the blame for causing the war solely on Germany. It opposed the Allied intervention in Russia in 1919 and questioned the efficacy of the League of Nations which it believed was designed principally to enforce the provisions of Versailles, and editorially, it was a strange mixture of pacifism, liberalism, and Marxism. By 1920, it was going through a decline dating from the failure of the general strikes that May, and it had no consistent policy toward the schism at the Congress of Tours that resulted in the founding of the French Communist Party. Its editors disagreed on what attitude to take toward the Third International, and *Clarté* suffered from much confusion as to what its role should be. Gradually, some young Communists acquired a decisive influence on the board, and the journal began to support the Third International and became an organ dedicated to violent attacks on bourgeois intellectual life. It even attacked its own literary founders, especially Rolland and France, and it wrested control entirely from Barbusse, who was no longer associated with the review after 1923. Barbusse professed to support the Third International, but he disavowed *Clarté* on the grounds that it had become too narrowly political. He complained that "it was not dignified enough, did not take a high enough stand or handle ideas on a broad basis, but was content to be just a small Communist review."[1]

By 1924 the editors, who had taken over from the original members, were Jean Bernier, Marcel Fourrier, and Victor Crastre, along with Camille Fégy, Georges Altmann and Paul Guitard, who were also on the staff of *L'Humanité*. Although *Clarté* never became an official Communist periodical, for several years it had a close relationship with the French Party and the International, both of which, between 1923 and 1925, were going through a period of great change. This was the era of the "bolshevization" of the Party, of "going to the masses," and of "purifying" the ranks of Party members in various countries. The new hard line coincided with the failure of the last attempts at revolutionary uprisings in the West, with the rise of Mussolini, and the suppression of the Italian Communist Party. The *Clartéistes,* seeing the success of the relatively conservative *Bloc des gauches,* a coalition of political parties, the obvious strength of the bourgeoisie, and the weakness of the French proletariat, concluded sadly that these were not revolutionary times in France.[2] Indeed, the French Party failed to attract the workers in any significant numbers, so *Clarté,* putting aside for the time being the possibility of direct revolutionary action, opted for the task of undermining bourgeois culture.[3]

From the very beginning, the Surrealists had regarded as theirs the task of destroying Western cultural traditions, so it seemed that the goals of both groups were similar, in spite of their very different origins. With this in mind, the desire of the editors of *Clarté* to collaborate with the Surrealists became readily understandable, notwithstanding the recent quarrel that had taken place over Aragon's anti-Soviet statement in *Un Cadavre.* The Surrealists had also independently taken the same position as *Clarté* on the war with the Riff. They had been the only ones outside on the Communist Party to oppose it, and this had led them to their first common protest, the manifesto against the Moroccan war. Personal factors also contributed to their desire for collaboration because Crastre was a great admirer of Breton, and Bernier was acquainted with Breton and Aragon. *Clarté* had even published some of Eluard's poetry so there was already much common ground.

The *Un Cadavre* polemics did not prevent their eventual rapprochement because, as Fourrier pointed out, they had really been on the same side on the question of Anatole France.

> *Un Cadavre* was the only protest raised by French revolutionary intellectuals against the Master, false great man, idolized at the same time by the editors of *Action française* and those of *L'Humanité.* This was the first time that the writers of *Clarté* and those of *Un Cadavre . . .* found themselves so totally in accord concerning such a precise objective.[4]

In addition, *Clarté* itself had published a special number, *Clarté contre Anatole France* in November 1924 which condemned him as a traitor, a chauvinist and a social democrat. This issue had also praised the Surrealists' *Un Cadavre* except, of course, for denouncing Aragon's gratuitous insult to Moscow. Bernier had described it as "a brief and virulent pamphlet, full of excellent things." He had called Eluard "a true poet," and Breton "the most fanatically honest mind of his generation." As for Aragon's remark, Bernier was willing to concede that perhaps Moscow was a bit too impressed with the prestige of Anatole France but "that was simply a question of politics and that, my dear Aragon, does not concern you."[5] *Clarté* and *La Révolution surréaliste* were the only two periodicals to denounce France while not only the conservative newspapers but the Socialist and Communist press had joined in praise of him.

Bernier, who wanted the rapprochement, deeply regretted the quarrel, but Fourrier demanded to know "how can we ally ourselves with men who drag the Russian Revolution in the mud and who completely misunderstand the revolutionary value of Marxism?"[6] He did not at first want to collaborate with the Surrealists because he knew the Party, which was angry over *Un Cadavre,* would be opposed to it on many grounds. Such things as the cover of the fourth issue of *La Révolution surréaliste* which read, in huge capital letters, "WAR ON WORK!" naturally infuriated Party officials. "This anathema provided a weighty argument to those Communists who opposed any rapprochement with the Surrealists."[7] It should be explained, however, that their glib declaration of war on work had nothing to do with the proletariat; it was merely another expression of their hatred of middle-class values. The idea of making money, or of furthering their careers, was completely abhorrent to them. It was a matter of pride to Breton, Aragon, Eluard, and many of the others, to have dropped out of the university and they preferred on principle to be virtually destitute rather than take a regular job. The offensive slogan, whatever Communist Party officials thought, was not directed against Soviet factory workers building a new society. But this incident was typical of the continual misunderstandings they had and Fourrier was caught in the middle between the disapproval of the Party, and Bernier and Crastre who threatened to leave *Clarté* if the Surrealists were not permitted to join them.

> It required all the eloquence of Bernier, and the obvious good will of Breton who was disposed toward making very great concessions, to convince our friend that the time had come to

risk more subversive operations than the publication of agricultural inquiries and protests against literary prizes.[8]

Finally, Fourrier agreed. *Clarté,* with all its ideological twists and turns, had lost most of its readership and desperately needed to be revitalized, and this decided him.

Turning Point

The *Un Cadavre* polemics had failed to bring about a permanent rift because, in spite of the insults that flew back and forth, *Clarté* and the Surrealists did find themselves side by side on this issue, in opposition to both the bourgeois and the Communist press. Also, the Surrealists had entered a "new phase," according to Breton, in which, "truthfully, a will to subversion possessed us."[9] The word "revolution," which before had conjured up images of Saint-Just and Robespierre, or of Rimbaud and Lautréamont, now meant Marx, Lenin, and Trotsky. Breton declared that reading Trotsky's biography of Lenin had a tremendous influence on him. It had been the first and decisive step toward his understanding of the Russian Revolution.[10]

More important, as Crastre pointed out, the Surrealists had to avoid falling into the Dadaist trap of sterility, continuing their scandals-for-scandal's-sake. Even worse, from their point of view, they were beginning to suffer the terrible fate of becoming fashionable, of being taken up by well-to-do patrons of the arts and in fact, this was a fate Surrealism was never entirely able to avoid. Inevitably, it was rich, cultivated bourgeois intellectuals who were most interested in the *avant-garde,* and who flocked to Surrealist films and exhibits, buying their paintings and even subsidizing the writers, as did the manuscript collector Jacques Doucet. Breton kept hoping that extremist organizations such as the paramilitary *Jeunesses patriotes* or the *Camelots du roi* would attack them, thereby showing the Left unequivocally which side the Surrealists were on. But these organizations remained obstinately ignorant of their existence. The movement had come to a turning point, as Breton himself admitted. "Surrealist activity was driven . . . to ask itself what were its proper resources. [It] had in some way or another to *reflect upon itself* its realization, in 1925, of its relative insufficiency."[11] In short, the *Clartéistes* and the Surrealists needed each other.

A first official joint meeting was held in October 1925 and it had an astonishingly sweeping agenda:

I.   Ideological position. Political level, moral level.
     A) Political. With regard to the Communist International.
        With regard to the French Communist Party.
        With regard to the bourgeois parties.
     B) With regard to the individual, the Revolution, other disciplines (artistic, philosophical, religious).

II. Necessity of a discipline based on trust. Means of assuring it: principle of the ballot.

III. Formation of a Committee. Its duties, powers, censorship of individual activity. Its duration, composition. [12]

With amazing naïveté, they planned to dispose of such problems as their position vis-à-vis the Communist International, the French Party, and the role of art, philosophy and religion, all in one evening. Needless to say, many of these issues were never successfully resolved. The one item, censorship of individual activity, was to be a continuous bone of contention for the Surrealists from then on, not only because of the Communist Party, but because Breton himself often acted as a kind of commissar periodically decreeing the expulsion of those deemed unworthy. Nevertheless, the agenda certainly reflected the good will and the genuine spirit of cooperation that animated the two groups. Crastre vividly described the inevitable strain produced by the decision to merge.

> The two sides demonstrated the greatest willingness for agreement. . . . The Surrealists showed themselves as unliterary as possible, trying to use a "Marxist" terminology that sometimes verged on jargon. We, on the other hand, forced ourselves to show that Surrealist activities interested us in the highest degree, and for some of us—Fégy and Altmann, for example—that required a lot of courage. . . . To formulate it a bit crudely, one could say that the Surrealists turned into Communists, while we, at *Clarté,* turned into Surrealists. [13]

The task of convincing the Party that the artists were worthy recruits was not so simple and a number of articles appeared in *Clarté* arguing that they really were good Marxists. Crastre wrote one in the March 1925 issue called "Le Suicide est-il une solution?"

The title referred to the article of the same name that had appeared in *La Révolution surréaliste* which was an inquiry into the reasons for suicide with responses from various literary figures. He defended the Surrealists' despair in the face of bourgeois society and spoke of the current "crisis of pessimism" among radical young intellectuals, thus trying his best to give a political significance to the Surrealists' fascination with suicide.[14] But his defense earned him the disapproval of the Party for, how could one believe in their revolutionary zeal if they approved of suicide? This was to be a conflict which erupted again in 1930 when Vladimir Mayakovsky, a Soviet poet whom the Surrealists much admired, killed himself.

Crastre, however, continued to write articles favorable to them such as "Explosion surréaliste," in which he contended that, in spite of their preoccupation with dreams and automatic writing, the Surrealists had true revolutionary potential. "The revolutionary qualities of a Breton, for example, simply cannot possibly be doubted," and of the proposed collaboration he said, "these angers and revolts are the points of contact between us and the . . . Surrealists . . . which we find in no other literary group in existence. The essential motivation of Surrealism is a passionate desire for demolition and this desire exists nowhere else."[15] Crastre also wrote about one of their "scandals" that occurred at this time, the Vieux-Colombier incident in which, having come to see a play by Aragon, they had to sit through an opening lecture on Rimbaud by a certain M. Aron. He was soon drowned out by cries of "Down with France" and "Down with the army" from the Surrealists who were angry at his daring to pronounce the name of Rimbaud whom they regarded as their special property. They were so noisy and disruptive that the police were called in to disperse them, and the play was never performed. Crastre called them courageous and managed to give even this incident a revolutionary interpretation. "The Surrealists, on this occasion, have not belied their promise. The tone, violence and profundity of their attacks reveal a truly *revolutionary* activity . . . of which no intellectual could disapprove."[16]

In his self-appointed role as interpreter of the Surrealists to the Communist Party, Crastre explained their motives as a desire to break once and for all with the intellectual bourgeoisie. Their antics had finally earned them the censure of the bourgeois press, which is what they wanted, and they sincerely hoped that the Communists would now consider them serious revolutionaries.

The Party, however, remained dubious and continued to distrust their motives and their orthodoxy.

> The Communist Party remained in its position . . . of . . . mistrust, or at least a certain scepticism—before such antics. This was not surprising since these escapades reeked of anarchism, that detestable abomination in the eyes of orthodox Communists. Besides, the spontaneous individualistic violence shocked the petit bourgeois minds of these militants. . . . In any case, Fourrier had to make great efforts to prevent *L'Humanité* from joining . . . with *L'Action française,* the *Journal* and *Le Temps* in castigating our friends.[17]

The famous "scandals," such as the Vieux-Colombier incident, the Saint-Pol-Roux banquet, and the letter to Paul Claudel, now came to be regarded by the Surrealists themselves as youthful pranks. The movement was becoming serious. The opportunity to prove this had come with the Riff war in Morocco which had provided the artists with their first real occasion to align themselves with the Left. In July, 1925, *Clarté* published a special issue called *Clarté contre la guerre du Maroc: Contre l'impérialisme français.* It contained the document, *Appel aux travailleurs intellectuels: Oui ou non, condamnez-vous la guerre?*, which revealed Barbusse's lingering influence and was reminiscent of the old liberal, pacifist *Clarté.* It denounced imperialism, colonialism and militarism and demanded an end to the war by calling on "the government of the Republic to put an immediate end to the bloodshed in Morocco by negotiating a just armistice. . . . We call upon the League of Nations to justify its existence by an urgent intervention in favor of peace."[18] The document was in the form of a question, and *Clarté* published answers from various intellectuals such as François Mauriac who, it turned out, supported the war, and some of the Surrealists who, although they denounced the war, were critical of the *Appel*. Aragon criticized the tone of the statement because he felt it was an appeal to nationalism and Crevel condemned its reliance on treaties and international conventions which he said are always worthless. Eluard hoped the war would lead to revolution and Artaud, the most apolitical member of the group, said, "as for me, the whole question boils down to a pure panic of massacre."[19] However mild a statement the *Appel* might have been, it did have the effect of producing an indignant reply, *Les Intellectuels aux côtés de la patrie,* which appeared in the newspapers with the signatures of many members of the *Académie française,* and of university professors. The signers assured the government that "the vast majority of writers and scholars remain on the side of the country," and they upheld France's great mission in Morocco "for justice, for civilization, and for peace."[20]

The next issue of *Clarté,* October 1925, published the joint manifesto, *La Révolution d'abord et toujours,* that praised Lenin, and advocated total disarmament and revolution. In a preface the editors, apparently responding to criticism, apologized for the un-Marxist tone of the previous *Appel aux travailleurs* they had just published:

> The political opportunity to act in a way contrary to nationalist activity led us, in spite of ourselves, to sign, along with bourgeois pacifists, the *Appel aux travailleurs intellectuels* of Henri Barbusse. . . . Certain passages of this document, notably . . . those calling on the government of the Republic to negotiate a just armistice, and on the League of Nations to intervene in favor of peace, are—is it necessary to say it—principles which are really unacceptable to us. But, since no other . . . protest against the Moroccan war . . . appeared, we signed this one . . . for the sole reason that it existed. We would have signed it even without reading it. . . . However, we cannot be content with that . . . petty protest which confuses us with the very intellectuals we consider the most dangerous enemies of the Revolution, those whom Lenin called social-traitors. . . . It is perfectly obvious that we have nothing whatever in common with any social democratic, republican, or pacifist organ.

They also said that, whatever ideological shortcomings *La Révolution d'abord et toujours* might have had, were due to the divergent backgrounds of the groups participating in this protest and not to any change in *Clarté's* politics. "One will be able to judge by the results of our future activities which, it goes without saying, . . . will never for any reason differentiate itself from any activity in France led by the Communist Party."[21] Thus, Bernier and Fourrier gave their assurances that they had not deviated and turned into social democrats and had no intention of doing so.

Even Naville, who became so critical of the Surrealists' politics, affirmed the importance of *La Révolution d'abord et toujours.* "The policy of colonization and pacification in Morocco has degenerated into open warfare. . . . In France, no one is even indignant about this. . . . No one, outside of the whole Communist Party, with the exception of *Clarté* . . . and the Surrealist group, has risen in protest directly against the cynical policies of the colonialist pacificators."[22] There had been two other groups, *Philosophies* and *Correspondance,* who signed it but they never again participated in any common enterprise. *Philosophies* wandered far afield, with a new title, *L'Esprit,* eventually became a theoretical Marxist journal whose editors joined the Communist Party. For years *Correspondance* remained a largely apolitical Surrealist journal in Belgium with loose ties to the movement in France. It refused to continue to collaborate and Naville complained that "the anarchism to which it obstinately adheres prevents it, temporarily we hope, from participating in the political activities of our new group."[23] But the Surrealists and the *Clartéistes* sought to reconcile their differences. They emphasized everything they had in common, such as their contempt for Anatole France who symbolized the bourgeois, nationalistic values they were trying to destroy, and their hatred of the imperialist Riff war. The Surrealists, with their newly aroused interest in politics, were being given informal lessons in Marxist theory by the *Clarté* group and were changing their ideas significantly. At the same time, the *Clartéistes,* who were closely allied to the Communists, were attempting to gain acceptance of the Surrealists by the Party. Crastre, in particular, made heroic efforts in this regard by giving a Marxist interpretation to virtually everything the Surrealists did, constantly assuring the Party of their revolutionary potential. Both groups wished to continue the cooperation they had so successfully initiated with *La Révolution d'abord et toujours.*

La Guerre civile

In keeping with their new communal spirit, *Clarté* and *La Révolution surrealiste* agreed to the joint publication of a new review to be called *La Guerre civile.* There were several reasons for this decision. For one thing, it seemed unnecessarily expensive to maintain two separate journals when the members of both groups often contributed to each one. It was always hard to raise the money for printing but, more important, they hoped to create a journal, unlike either *Clarté* or *La Révolution surréaliste,* dedicated to the Revolution. These plans must have been fairly well set since the November issue of *Clarté* carried the announcement that "this is the final number of the review, *Clarté*. On the 15th of February, the first number of the review, *La Guerre civile* will appear."[24]

Meanwhile, the Surrealists made numerous declarations of their wholehearted support for the proletarian revolution in order to reassure both the *Clartéistes* and the Communist Party of the sincerity of their conversion. One such declaration was published in *L'Humanité* on November 8.

> Only a semantic confusion has allowed the persistent misunderstanding that there was a *Surrealist doctrine of Revolution*. . . . There was never a Surrealist theory of Revolution. We want the Revolution; however, we want revolutionary means. Of what do these means consist? Only of the Communist International and for France, of the French Communist Party. . . . When it comes to realizing the Revolution, there can be no question of a "Surrealist group" as such. . . . Their revolutionary point of view in no way differs from that of the Communist International. *They can only conceive of the Revolution in its social and economic form: the Revolution being the totality of events determining the transfer of power from the hands of the bourgeoisie to those of the proletariat and the maintenance of that power by means of the dictatorship of the proletariat.*[25]

To say that Surrealism had always thought of the revolution in strictly social and economic terms, and that there had never been a Surrealist theory of revolution was stretching the truth quite a lot but, unquestionably, it was a true reflection of a profound ideological change in the Surrealists' thinking. It also indicated tremendous concessions on their part, and a willingness to accommodate themselves to what they felt were the requirements of the Party.

Bernier's editorial in the November *Clarté* quoted this declaration as proof that the Surrealists "have adhered without reservation to the Marxist definition of revolution."[26] He praised the zeal with which they had thrown themselves into the study of Marx, and tried to placate those who feared that Marxism was just a passing fancy with them.[27] He also reassured those who were concerned that *Clarté* was becoming unduly influenced by them. Yet he spoke at length in language reminiscent of Surrealism of the "profoundly subjective despair . . . despair verging on defeatism," that the *Clartéistes* felt after the failure of the revolutionary move-

ments in the West and how very difficult it was to "preserve our
faith in the Revolution and to continue to be effective revolutionaries." Perhaps unconsciously, this was the source of the attraction
these young leftists felt for Surrealism with its strain of pessimism
and its suicidal despair. Bernier also spoke of the "crisis" of *Clarté*
caused by its anomalous position as a Communist journal outside
the Party that published political and economic articles better
suited to the official Communist press. He added that the Party
itself was in a state of crisis as to what its basic nature was to be:
whether to adhere without reservation to the International, or to
adopt a wider, more flexible position encompassing different varieties of socialist thought. He complained that this problem
"weighs unceasingly on us in our preoccupation with interior
Communist policies ('line,' 'tendencies,' 'orthodoxy,' etc.), and is
one of the most important aspects of our crisis." He then proposed
a joint program for *Clarté* and the Surrealists to follow.

> For the time being, we propose to undertake the task of
> systematic denunciation of bourgeois thought that, for many
> reasons, the French Communist Party cannot undertake. . . .
> We will have a dual purpose: to demonstrate to our pro-
> letarian readers the ignominious ruin of what is pompously
> called French thought and to expose the insidious influence of
> the writings of counter-revolutionary intellectuals (practically
> all of them are). Eventually, we will sow the seeds of doubt in
> the minds of cultivated bourgeois . . . which, however
> slightly and indirectly, will further the progress of the revolu-
> tionary idea.[28]

In essence, his suggestion was that *Clarté* and *La Révolution surréaliste* embark together on a reformist educational task: the systematic demoralization of bourgeois culture for the benefit of the
proletariat.

In the same number there was an article by Aragon that
Bernier described as "thoroughly Marxist," thus showing how far
Aragon had come. Formerly denounced as an anarchist, he had in
the space of a year undergone a profound transformation. Re-
pudiating his past opinions, he now declared firmly that "anarchy,
the origin and foundation of every kind of fascism, is counterrevolutionary."[29] He wrote a series of articles for *Clarté,* "Le Prix
de l'esprit" (The Price of Intellect), in which he attacked intellectuals as the willing tools of the ruling class and said that their role

in capitalist society is to uphold and strengthen the bourgeoisie. Thought, under capitalism, is a product for sale and when it takes a social form, it becomes a kind of merchandise and

> this merchandise is essentially an emanation of capitalism, the servant of capitalism, its helper. For this reason nothing is more justified than the contempt which the oppressed proletariat has for intellectuals. They are certainly the servile enemies of the Revolution all the more because they sometimes pretend to be its defenders. I have always thought: here is a traitor—whenever I have heard one of them proclaim that he *loves the people*. . . . With the exception of a few poets outside of politics and a few theoreticians of dialectical materialism, all intellectual forces for the past hundred years have undergone a bourgeois evolution. . . . It is high time that intellectuals understood their proper role . . . [which] is to prepare for the revolution, the worldwide Communist revolution as it is defined by the Third International. . . . It is useless for them to argue about the fate of Russian intellectuals in the Soviet Union. . . . Whatever happens in the interior of the Russian Party should not be judged by those still under the government of the bourgeoisie. No comparison can be made between life under the dictatorship of the proletariat and life under the rule of capital.[30]

It is clear from this passage that Aragon, like an eager schoolboy, had learned the correct vocabulary, and he seemed to have completely accepted the teachings of his mentors of *Clarté* and *L'Humanité*. Strangely, his zeal apparently even led him to share the negative feelings of many Party bureaucrats toward intellectuals.

There was also an article by Desnos who made a heroic attempt to give a Marxist interpretation to Breton's famous definition of Surrealism in the *First Manifesto*. He conceded that the idea of psychic automatism, of thought dictation in the absence of all control by reason, outside of any moral or aesthetic considerations, might not seem at first glance to have revolutionary significance. But it really does, as Desnos explained it, because by reason was meant *bourgeois* reason and ignoring aesthetic and moral questions meant disregarding *bourgeois* aesthetic and moral questions. Therefore even this definition, seemingly so irrelevant to political issues, was really "perfectly compatible with the Revolution and I doubt that even Karl Marx would take exception to this."[31] Admittedly, that particular passage is difficult to explain because there was probably never a man so concerned with aesthetic and moral problems as Breton and perhaps Desnos' interpretation, however implausible, was correct. At any rate, it was regarded as acceptable by the editors of *Clarté*.

Articles by *Clartéistes* were also appearing in *La Révolution surréaliste* and, just as the Surrealists tended to adopt a Marxist tone when they wrote for *Clarté,* the *Clartéistes* tended to sound like Surrealists when they wrote for them. Crastre's article, "L'Europe," for example, had as its theme the myth of the free spiritual life of the Orient, contrasted with a dying Europe and he lamented that "we are nothing more than living corpses. . . . Europe is bleeding to death!"[32] Fourrier contributed an optimistic essay in which he drew a connection between the Riff war and an English miners' strike, saying, with more enthusiasm than accuracy, that these two events proved that "the revolutionary cause is becoming more internationalized every day."[33] Many more articles, however, were contributed by the Surrealists to *Clarté* than the other way around. As Crastre said, *La Révolution surréaliste* was, in a sense, a technical journal of a very esoteric nature and it was difficult for a Communist to appear in print next to recitations of dreams, automatic texts and the like.[34] It was also true that the Surrealists had more to offer creatively, in that they were masters of the task *Clarté* set for itself of destroying bourgeois cultural predominance.

The December *Clarté* again carried on its cover the announcement that "*Clarté* will disappear, *La Guerre civile* will succeed it."[35] In this issue Fourrier concluded sadly, as had Bernier, that it would be a long time before the Revolution came to Western Europe. Therefore, the present task could only be the destruction of *l'esprit bourgeois.* Bernier had resigned, so, more than ever, *Clarté* desired rapprochement with the Surrealists. Fourrier announced the forthcoming appearance of *La Guerre civile* and told his readers that even Lunacharsky, Commissar of Education in Russia in the early 1920s, looked with interest upon this project and had praised the revolutionary contributions of the Surrealists. "The pact is now sufficiently solidly cemented so that *Clarté* will become *La Guerre civile,*" he added, although he was wrong in this prediction.[36]

Breton had a significant article in the December issue in which he affirmed his belief in Marx, but also in Rimbaud and Lautréamont. This was a first statement of his life-long insistence upon the essential compatibility of Marxism and revolutionary *(avant-garde)* literature.

> In the revolutionary sense, just as on the social and economic
> plane, one can honorably claim to be Marxist, in the same
> way, on the spiritual plane, I affirm that it is always permissi-
> ble to uphold Lautréamont and Rimbaud. These two strands
> of thought are essentially compatible. . . . I would like to
> believe that there is no true work of the mind that is not
> shaped by the desire for the *real* amelioration of the conditions
> of existence of the whole world.

He added that the famous Surrealist despair would cease on the
threshold of the new society. "We belong, body and soul, to the
Revolution and if, until now, we have never accepted command-
ments, it was in order to keep ourselves at the orders of those who
are making it." But he warned that he was not willing to disavow
Surrealism.

> I do not believe that, at the present time, it would be proper to
> oppose the cause of the pure spirit to that of the Revolution,
> and to demand of us . . . a greater specialization. Even less
> would I comprehend that, for utilitarian reasons, one would
> try to exact from me a disavowal of Surrealist activity. . . . We
> will maintain, over and above everything in the twentieth
> century in France, that irreducible independence of thought
> which implies the greatest revolutionary determination.[37]

His last remarks were actually a warning that the Surrealists had
much to do in their own particular sphere and could not immerse
themselves entirely in politics, even for the noble cause of revolution.

But *La Guerre civile* was destined never to exist. *La Révolution
surréaliste* continued publication and *Clarté* reappeared in June
1926, in a new series. The reasons for this failure are not entirely
clear. Maurice Nadeau stated that "this intransigence of Breton's as
to the strict autonomy of Surrealism, which he was quite willing
to put at the service of the revolution but which he would not
sacrifice to it, ultimately caused the project of the new alliance to
collapse."[38] Yet, that might not have been the real reason. There
had, after all, been a period of close cooperation and many sincere
concessions had been made on both sides. Breton had come to the
conclusion that the failure was due to personal differences and to
the widely divergent backgrounds and political views of the individuals involved, but this, too, seems an inadequate explanation.[39]

Crastre, who took part in the many meetings and discussions of that period made the excellent point that *La Guerre civile* really had no program beyond the vague notion of a "critique of bourgeois society and of its cultural values," and this was clearly a meaningless formula.[40] It was apparent that everyone knew what *La Guerre civile* should *not* be, but no one could agree on what it *should* be.

The editors of *Clarté* themselves might have been partly responsible for the split because of pressure from the Party which was still suspicious of the Surrealists. The evidence for this lies in the numerous articles they published insisting on the Surrealists' revolutionary credentials. But an even more likely explanation was that *Clarté* itself underwent an ideological change. The editors began to veer toward the Trotskyist opposition because of their close relationship with Boris Souvarine, of the French *Bureau politique,* who supported Trotsky.[41] Souvarine had recently been ousted from the Party for "right-wing deviation" as a part of its new "bolshevization" campaign and *Clarté* was being tarred with the same brush. Crastre suggested that the Surrealists had just come to realize that *Clarté* was not identical with the Party so the proposed collaboration may not have interested them as much as before, since they were bent on joining the Party itself. But he also pointed out that the Surrealists never knew how much the *Clartéistes* had shielded them from the real attitudes of the Party. On at least one occasion, two of them, Fégy and Altmann, deliberately caused an article published in *L'Humanité* to be so completely garbled that it was unreadable because it attacked the Surrealists. It was also true that whatever favorable notice they received in *L'Humanité,* such as the two articles praising the Vieux-Colombier and Saint-Pol-Roux incidents, appeared only because Bernier and Fourrier were able to use their influence with its editors.[42]

In spite of the failure of the *La Guerre civile* project, *Clarté* continued to publish the Surrealists, which certainly is an indication that they remained on friendly terms. Among these were a series of essays by Aragon, some violently anti-clerical poetry by Péret, an article in praise of Rimbaud by Michel Leiris, and an essay by Eluard on the Marquis de Sade, whom they held in great esteem. Fourrier, in the June 1926 issue, wrote in their defense that the task for which they were eminently suited was the "destructive denunciation of capitalist civilization," and he added

> I believe I am right in thinking that everything which is
> violently opposed to bourgeois thought, ought to be utilized
> by Communism for revolutionary ends. . . . Not only do the
> Surrealists completely agree with Marxism, but in addition,
> they adhere to the modes of organization and to the discipline
> of Communism. They adhere—those who do support the
> Revolution—because they know very well that the Commu-
> nist International stands for the only principle of revolution-
> ary action in the whole world. When the decisive moment
> comes, they will take their places in the ranks of the Commu-
> nists.

He also defended their desire to continue with their independent
Surrealist activities. "It would be absolutely ridiculous at the present time to demand of the Surrealists that they renounce Surrealism. Have they demanded that the Communists renounce
Communism? . . . I insist that, before anything, one should ask
the question what cause do the Surrealists serve, and what cause
do they betray?" He then assailed their critics. "I have only seen
raised against them criticisms . . . of a contemptible petit bourgeois sort, revolutionary in the shallowest way . . . that reveal a
remarkable sense of social conservatism."[43] It was obvious from
these remarks that Fourrier, at least, did not think they were at
fault.

In 1927, the line of *Clarté* changed again. Naville, having
broken with the Surrealists, took over as editor and announced
that the *Clartéistes* have decided "to make our journal into a real
arm of the working class . . . to really plunge into the struggles of
the proletariat."[44] For some time the review continued to be
attacked in *L'Humanité* for being too "literary," and for being too
much under the influence of the Surrealists. But, in fact, no articles
of theirs had appeared since the end of 1926, and Naville gave
rather half-hearted assurances concerning his former friends that
"if the critics have taken note that recent numbers have not carried
the names of one or another of our Surrealist friends, let them not
draw the conclusion that we have abandoned them."[45] Naville,
however, clearly considered it more important to defend *Clarté*
against the charges of *L'Humanité* than to continue its policy of
alliance with the Surrealists and, in fact, he shortly broke with
them definitively. He never again published Surrealist articles, in
spite of the fact that the following year he himself joined the

Trotskyist opposition and *Clarté,* still under his editorship, became a Trotskyist review with a new name: *La Lutte des classes: Revue théorique mensuelle de l'opposition communiste* (Class Struggle: Theoretical Monthly Review of the Communist Opposition).[46]

Although the two groups failed to maintain their brief period of cooperation, there were some definite achievements. The Surrealists, beginning with their protest against the war with the Riff, had made a real political commitment and they had also received something of an education in Marxism from the editors of *Clarté.* They had become completely convinced of the need for social and economic revolution, and they envisioned a close alignment with the Communist Party, since their "heroes" were now Marx, Lenin, and Trotsky. But they were probably unaware of the implications of the Stalin-Trotsky split and of the need for orthodoxy on this and other questions. They simply assumed that all that was needed to dispel the Party's hostility toward them were repeated assurances of their good will.

4 The Surrealists Join the Communist Party

Did Surrealism in order to survive have to involve itself in a factual revolt concerning the eight-hour day or the fight against inflation? What a joke and what baseness of soul!
—Antonin Artaud, *A la Grande nuit ou la bluff surréaliste*

I cannot understand that on the road to revolt there should be a Right and a Left. I say that the revolutionary flame burns where it lists, and that it is not up to a small band of men to decree that it can only burn here and there.
—André Breton, *Légitime défense*

The "Naville Crisis"

The decision to politicize Surrealism, to join forces with the French Communist Party, was far from unanimous. In fact, it provoked a schism within the group that resulted in the departure or expulsion of several members who disapproved of this step. On the other hand, Naville, formerly a Surrealist, who became a militant Communist and ultimately a Trotskyist, criticized the artists for not becoming completely immersed in politics. He even tried to persuade them to abandon Surrealism entirely and devote themselves to the cause of Revolution. In addition to these internal divisions, Breton still faced the problem of the attitude of the Communist Party, which remained hostile. He found himself attacked on all sides, his position was extremely precarious, and the future of the movement was called into question.

55

The "Naville crisis" was provoked by a pamphlet Naville wrote, *La Révolution et les intellectuels: Que peuvent faire les sur-réalistes?* (The Revolution and the Intellectuals: What Can the Surrealists Do?) in 1926, shortly after the collapse of the *La Guerre civile* proposal, in which he made some fundamental criticisms of Surrealist politics. He began by quoting Lunacharsky on the role of intellectuals in the Communist Party.

> We have need of intellectuals and yet, for the most part, they are still hostile to us. . . . It is not absolutely necessary to extract a complete profession of faith from them . . . [nor] to be very demanding concerning political questions. It would be unreasonable to apply the maxim "he who is not with us is against us" to problems of theory and of discipline. . . . No: "he who is against the bourgeoisie is with us." This is the kind of slogan we need to found an International of Intellectuals.[1]

It was unfortunate from the Surrealists' standpoint that Lunacharsky's position did not prevail. But Naville merely quoted this sensible and flexible view in order to dispose of it by saying that it was now 1926, France is not a socialist country, and therefore our task is different. Tracing the evolution of Surrealism, Naville declared that it began as pure anarchy, but is developing dialectically toward a revolutionary consciousness. However, intellectuals as such are suspect to Communists because they are likely to be counterrevolutionary and this was true of the Surrealists because the various "scandals" they indulged in could accomplish nothing constructive. "They do not force the overthrow of intellectual and social values. The bourgeoisie does not fear them; it absorbs them easily."[2] Even their violent anti-patriotism was only a *moral* scandal and could not contribute to the overthrow of capitalism.

The question was: Can the Surrealists be useful to the Revolution? He replied that they could, but only if they resolved the contradiction between what he called their "metaphysical" and their "dialectical" attitudes. The dilemma was

> 1. Either to persevere in a negative anarchistic attitude which is false *a priori* because it does not justify the idea of revolution it claims to have, an attitude which consists of a refusal to compromise its own existence and the sacred character of the individual to [engage in] disciplined action of *class* struggle.

2. or to march resolutely on the path of the Revolution, the
only revolutionary path: the Marxist path. . . . In this theory,
the struggle is directly against the bourgeoisie, the proletarian
struggle, . . . commanded by mass movements, with the aid
of intellectuals resolved to recognize no field of liberty but
that on which the bourgeoisie will perish.[3]

Naville clearly favored the second alternative and asked, "Do the
Surrealists believe in liberation of the mind *before* the abolition of
bourgeois conditions of material life, or do they comprehend that
a revolutionary spirit can be created only after the Revolution is
accomplished?"[4] Thus far, they have affirmed the possibility of the
liberation of the mind before and independently of the overthrow
of the bourgeoisie, so as of now, they can only be "momentary"
allies of the Revolution.[5]

There were also certain "counterrevolutionary" aspects of
Surrealist thought that must be changed. First, they must abandon
the "Orient myth" because "to want to see the Mongols camping
in our squares, rather than the bourgeoisie and the police, means
nothing; it only indicates a sentimental vision of the Revolution."
Second, they must abandon their cherished individualism. Their
passion for revolution is purely individual, not collective, which is
why they cannot be truly revolutionary. Third, they must abandon
their poetic, Romantic scorn for science and technological progress because this attitude only plays into the hands of the bourgeoisie. The Surrealists have simply refused to face this question:
"Yes or no, this desired revolution, is it of the mind *a priori,* or of
the world of facts? Is it linked to Marxism, or to contemplative
theories about the purification of the inner life?"[6] They cannot
have it both ways. He reminded the Surrealists that "wages are a
material necessity with which three quarters of the world's population are constrained to live. . . . The quarrels of the intellect are
absolutely vain before the unity of their condition."[7]

Naville believed the failure of *La Guerre civile* was inevitable
because the Surrealists were unable to resolve their fundamental
contradictions, and he presented them with two choices: either to
become political revolutionaries or to continue with their "researches" in dreams and automatic writing. There was actually a
third possibility which he refused to consider, and that was to
attempt the difficult task of combining Surrealism and Marxism,
as they were determined to do. But at the time, his pamphlet
caused great agitation and threatened to disrupt their unity. As

Breton said, "these declarations gave rise among us to considerable anxiety," and it was necessary to attempt "for the first time to justify Surrealism's social implications."[8]

Breton was forced to reply in a pamphlet, *Légitime défense,* first printed in the December 1926 issue of *La Révolution surréaliste.* Actually, the text was a diatribe directed at the French Communist Party because of its decidedly lukewarm attitude toward the Surrealists; moreover, while ostensibly answering Naville's criticism, Breton's foremost intention was to defend them against attacks by Communists in general. He began by reaffirming their adherence to Marxism which "has not been received without the greatest reservations as if, ultimately, it had been judged unacceptable." While it is true that, "the Communist program . . . represents in our eyes a minimum program," he explained that this merely meant that they proposed to deal with psychological questions not covered by Marxism as such. "We do not have the impertinence to oppose the Communist program by any other," he added. He also attacked *L'Humanité* as being "childish, declamatory, unnecessarily *cretinizing,*" and "utterly unreadable." This was hardly the issue, since Naville had not undertaken its defense, but Breton seized the opportunity to turn his pamphlet against Naville into a critique of the Party and its publications. He declared that *L'Humanité* was completely unworthy of the role of educating the proletariat, and that "among the services which, by an inconceivable narrowness, it foregoes . . . are our own."

He also criticized Barbusse who, oddly enough, after leaving *Clarté* because it had been taken over by Marxists, had joined the Party and become literary editor of *L'Humanité.* "I should doubtless yield to the desire to submit proposals for a press campaign to *L'Humanité,* if the thought that M. Barbusse is its literary editor did not completely deter me from doing so. . . . M. Barbusse is, if not a reactionary, at least a conservative," in his banal literary taste. And he added, "M. Barbusse should heed what we say, for it would keep him from abusing the confidence of the workers by praising Paul Claudel and Cocteau, authors of infamous patriotic poems, of nauseating Catholic professions of faith, ignominious profiteers of the regime, and obvious counterrevolutionaries."[9] These criticisms were certainly justifiable since Barbusse was nothing if not eclectic in his approach to politics. He must have been the only Communist in history to have written a life of Jesus and the Surrealists were perfectly correct in their assessment of his confused ideology. David Caute remarked that "his utterances echoed variously the Utopian socialists, or even Rousseau, rather than Marx," but his international reknown was so great that the Party was willing to overlook any possible ideological shortcomings.[10]

To the writers favored by Barbusse, Breton contrasted the genuinely revolutionary literature of Surrealism that "belongs to that enormous enterprise of recreating the universe to which Lautréamont and Lenin dedicated themselves entirely" and he explained that they were following in the glorious tradition of the poet–revolutionaries, Rimbaud, Baudelaire, and Petrus Borel. As Surrealists, they had a special task, an "order" which they have received and "something great and obscure tends imperiously toward expression through us." He conceded that there had been considerable criticism in Party circles of their contention that they could be loyal Party members while continuing with their own activities. But he felt this attitude was unjust, especially since they unequivocally declared their desire for the revolution of the proletariat and their support of the Party and the International. After these complaints about the Party, Breton finally brought up the subject of Naville's pamphlet, which "accuses us of still vacillating between anarchy and Marxism and calls upon us to decide one way or the other." He felt that Naville had posed an entirely erroneous dichotomy revealing "a completely artificial opposition which collapses at once upon scrutiny. In the realm of facts, as we see it, no ambiguity is possible; all of us seek to shift power from the hands of the bourgeoisie to those of the proletariat. Meanwhile, it is . . . necessary that experiments of the inner life continue, and do so, of course, without external or even Marxist control." This was simply a restatement of the position the Surrealists had adopted in 1925, but Breton failed to see why repeated declarations of faith in the proletarian revolution should not be sufficient both for the Party and for Naville.

He defended the use of certain "buffer" words like the Orient saying that they have a symbolically revolutionary meaning. As for Naville's criticism of the Surrealists' negative attitude toward technology, his answer was that the world cannot be saved by "machinism."

I am convinced, with the author of the pamphlet, . . . that "wages are a material necessity for three-fourths of the

world's population" . . . but I cannot share his conclusion
that "the disputes of the intelligence are absolutely futile. . . .
Wages cannot pass for the efficient cause for the present state
of affairs. . . . There is no question here of disputing *historical
materialism,* but once again of materialism *tout court.*

Breton reiterated the Surrealist belief that there is no philosophical distinction between the concrete world and the realm of
thought since both are equally real. He also reaffirmed his revolutionary zeal saying "we would not, for anything in the world,
defend an inch of French territory, but we would defend to the
death in Russia, in China, an infinitesimal conquest of the proletariat." Referring to the failure of *La Guerre civile,* he denied that
the cause was the essential contradiction in Surrealist thought,
rather, "the obstacle in our way was the fear of proceeding against
the true intentions of the Communist International and . . . of
attempting to do no more than obey the orders (disconcerting at
the very least) given by the French Communist Party."

In concluding, he acknowledged his audacity in criticizing the
Party.

> I have . . . been assured . . . I am committing an error by
> attacking from outside the Party, the editors of one of its
> organs, and I have been informed that this action . . . is of a
> nature to give arms to the enemies of the Party which I myself
> regard, in terms of revolution as the only force on which we
> may count. This . . . is why I have so long hesitated to
> speak. . . . It is true that such a discussion should have been
> pursued within the Party. But by the very admission of those
> who are there, this discussion would have been reduced to a
> minimum, supposing it were even permitted. . . . In this
> regard, I have known since last year what to look for, and that
> is why I have decided it was useless to be *registered* in the
> French Communist Party.

He did add, at the end, that "I am not ready to turn elsewhere."[11]
Yet the contentious tone of *Légitime défense,* which Breton knew
would be badly received, was a dramatic about-face from the
period shortly before when he had announced he was at the
disposal of the International "body and soul." His eagerness to join
the Party had apparently evaporated. Now, he was most concerned
with staking out a certain ground for purely Surrealist activities
which were to be carried on completely independently while

waiting for the Revolution. But even though he said he no longer wished to join the Party, he still wanted very much to have Surrealism accepted and approved by it as the most revolutionary form of art, and he never ceased to put this argument before Party officials.

As for Naville, Breton remained very bitter toward him for many years. He was convinced Naville had deliberately sabotaged the rapprochement between *Clarté* and the Surrealists because Naville was angry at him for taking over the editorship of *La Révolution surréaliste*. He also claimed that the animosity of the *Fourth International* to the Surrealists in the late 1930s was due to Naville's resentment and, as one of its leaders, he was able to prevent the Surrealists from working with it. Breton declared contemptuously that "there has never been a Naville crisis in Surrealism. There was only a Naville defection . . . and that was all."[12]

Au Grand Jour: Becoming Party Members

Breton's predicament in 1926 was an unhappy one for, after committing the Surrealists to political action and encountering the hostility of Party officials, he found that there were also protests from within the ranks. Edouard Kasyade, the poet, wrote a pamphlet in response to *Légitime défense* entitled *Prétexte à la fondation d'un organe de révolte suivi d'une "Lettre à André Breton"* (Argument for Founding an Organ of Revolt Followed by a "Letter to André Breton"), in which he argued for revolt, but only in the realm of ideas.

> In the pure domain of facts, a great event captured our enthusiasm, the Russian Revolution. It seemed to us, with no profound reason to justify this conclusion, that the Marxists and the revolutionary intellectuals of the West had the same adversaries. . . . [However], a debate concerning the mind cannot, by its very essence, be a part of an economic struggle.[13]

He added the perceptive comment that "the aspect of Marxism which is the most seductive to us is its quality of 'revolutionary sanction.'" In his opinion, the Surrealists had an especially valuable role of their own to play of a literary nature, that of leading youth along the paths of rebellion. "Let us create an organ of intellectual revolt which will *always* be a revolutionary organ," he urged,[14] and insisted that "revolutionary intellectuals, Surrealists and philosophers, follow in essence a different path from that chosen by the Marxists. They do not have the same enemies, . . . and they will meet only in the revolution."[15] Some in the circle agreed, not wishing to become embroiled in and perhaps swallowed up by politics, and Kasyade had convincingly pointed out the incongruity of a literary movement joining a political party. His position was undoubtedly closer to Surrealism as originally conceived; however, as Breton saw it, if the movement persisted in its isolation, it would run the risk of stagnation. Even more important, Breton and many of his friends ardently desired to work for the Revolution because like so many artists of their generation, they were intensely politically committed.

Kasyade's argument had the merit of clarity. It avoided the extreme of purely anarchic individualism by advocating collective action of a literary nature, and it avoided the problems involved in attempting to engage in common action with the Party. But Breton was already committed to follow the latter, more difficult path, and Kasyade's proposal was ignored. However, not everyone acknowledged the necessity of politicizing Surrealism and this issue led to the first of many "excommunications" from the movement. Roger Vitrac was expelled for allegedly pursuing a crassly "commercial" journalistic career, but two others at this period, Soupault and Artaud, who had made vitally important contributions to Surrealism, were forced out precisely for their refusal to follow the movement into its new political phase. A meeting was held in November 1926 at the *Café Le Prophète* which led to their expulsion, the ideological nature of which was clearly shown by its agenda:

I.   Objective report on the present situation by Roland Tual.

II. Examination of individual positions:
    a) Are all these positions defensible from a revolutionary point of view?
    b) There is a common position.
    c) Are certain individual activities of a compromising character?
    d) To what extent are these individual activities to be tolerated?

III. Possibilities of future Surrealist actions.
  a) Outside of the Communist Party.
  b) In the Communist Party.[16]

This agenda revealed Breton's determination to impose his own version of revolutionary discipline on the group, and it reflected the obvious influence of the Communist Party, even to the point of imitating it by instituting "purges" for ideological deviation. The meeting was also significant in that it showed that those who were committed to a political path still felt that their place was in the Communist ranks.

Indeed, in 1927, shortly after expressing his exasperation with the Communists in *Légitime défense,* he and four other Surrealists, Péret, Aragon, Eluard, and Pierre Unik, officially joined the Party. By doing this, they hoped to prove their sincerity once and for all. Breton said later that at this point, he regretted having published *Légitime défense* and had it withdrawn from circulation and destroyed as a gesture of loyalty.[17] A publication, *Au Grand jour* (In Broad Daylight), a series of open letters signed by the five, was issued to explain their decision and to insist that they deserved to be accepted as loyal Party members. Although only the five actually became members, as far as they were concerned, the whole group was thereby committed. Naturally, Breton, Péret, Aragon, Eluard, and Unik could not insist that the other twenty-five or so Surealists join the Communist Party. But they did expect the whole group to support it, becoming "fellow travelers" and cooperating with it in much the same way that *Clarté* had had a working alliance with it. Not all the writers of *Clarté* were Party members but, editorially, it had supported the program of the Party and the International. Similarly, now that Surrealism had definitely embarked on a political course, no Surrealist could remain apolitical and certainly not anti-Marxist. This was demonstrated by the expulsion of Vitrac, Soupault, and Artaud. The five stated that "if . . . as a function of our respective temperaments, we have not all believed it necessary to join the Communist Party, at least none of us has undertaken to deny that a great mutuality of aspirations exists between the Communists and us," and those who disagreed were denounced in the most insulting terms. They were accused of bad faith, of having the most reprehensible motives, and of pursuing "literary" careers which, of course, was the worst thing a Surrealist could do. The vilification of Artaud was especially bitter. "Today, we have vomited up this vile dog," and, greatest insult of all, "we don't see why this stinking corpse waits any longer . . . to declare himself a Christian."[18]

In the collective life of the Surrealists, this kind of anathema was really comparable to a religious excommunication which was usually pronounced by Breton who, in fact, was often called the "pope" of Surrealism. Crastre used this same religious analogy calling the café where they met a sacred place.

> Those who failed to show up regularly for the meetings—and these took place every day—ended by being suspected of being lukewarm. . . . A *good* Surrealist could not refuse the "communion" . . . that was given every day. . . . The excluded Surrealist could not fail to fall into an abyss of desolation because at the same time, he lost his friends, the audience of Breton, and the gathering places they frequented together, and was forced into solitude, or into the mediocre games of the "literary life."[19]

In such a closely knit group, disagreements were intolerable, and had to be dealt with by means of the most violent personal attacks.

Au Grand jour continued with a letter to the Belgian Surrealists of *Correspondance,* who had not become political activists. "We have made . . . a different decision from yours: we have adhered to the *PCF* [Parti communiste français], believing that, before everything, not to do so would imply a reservation on our part which does not exist, a second thought which would be profitable to its enemies (who are the worst of our own)." The writers assured them of their continuing friendship, but added "we summon you to act as soon as possible."[20] The Belgian artists refused to heed the summons, in fact, after they had signed *La Révolution d'abord et toujours,* they made the firm decision to avoid all future political activity. They now issued a statement to that effect, *A L'Occasion d'un manifeste,* in which they insisted that "our activity is not situated on the political plane and is different from that of the parties working for social revolution," and they stood by this decision in spite of the exhortations of their French colleagues.[21]

There was a letter from the five to Fourrier taxing him with being weak in his defense of the Surrealists against elements in the Party that disapproved of them. This was not altogether fair to him because in spite of pressures from Party officials, he did take the side of the Surrealists, but they apparently felt he could have done more. Another, addressed to the "non-Communist Surrealists," stressed the need for action to overcome the contradictions of Surrealist thought. "One can only find the resolution of these contradictions in the idea of Revolution," declared the five. In the world of facts, the Revolution is a concrete reality with its own functioning organization, to which they, as Surrealists, have nothing to offer. "Thus is posed, without . . . abandoning Surrealist activity, the principle of Surrealists joining the Communist Party, a principle that appears to follow the logical development of the Surrealist idea and is its sole ideological safeguard." The non-Communist Surrealists were also told that their conduct was irresponsible because, although they refused to join the Party, they had no alternate plan of action to offer.

> Nothing, neither the taste for independence, nor heroism, nor disrespect for the law (even, in all its beauty, desertion in time of war), could keep you from sinking into anarchy. Between you, who still believe you can give your lives the sense of pure protest, and us, who have decided to submit our lives to an exterior discipline capable . . . of carrying that protest much further, there is, however, no real barrier.[22]

They wanted to make it clear that while they disagreed with their non-Communist colleagues, French as well as Belgian, they did not propose to break with them.

The next letter was to Naville, reproaching him for his "defection," and for the ease with which he could abandon Surrealism entirely for purely political activities. He was also accused of deliberately creating a misunderstanding about the ideology of the movement. "It is regrettable that you have allowed an equivocation concerning the nature of Surrealism to be produced in *Clarté*. . . . This confusion is the one which attempts to pass off Surrealism as an *a priori* deviation from Marxism. . . . It was really not a question of an error in terminology . . . but of a deliberate confusion which, it seems to us, you alone . . . can straighten out." He was then called upon, amicably enough, to correct this misunderstanding, which, however, he did not do.

It seemed that, in spite of their formal adherence to the Party, the Surrealists were still mistrusted. They had assumed that all that was really needed was to make this definite commitment, but it was not as easy as that. The final letter was addressed to their comrades, the Communists. They reiterated their position and protested against the "heated attacks directed against us . . . because such grave confusion exists concerning the nature of Surrealism which is being taken for a political theory . . . which is absurd," and they proclaimed their right to be considered Communists in good standing.

> There is not a single one of these demands we do not support; . . .
>
> The eight hour day
> The struggle against unemployment, against capitalist rationalization and inflation.
> General and total amnesty.
> Down with the Paul Boncour law!
> Down with the militarization of the trade unions!
> Protest against the imperalist war!
> Down with the intervention in China!
>
> There is not one of these slogans . . . for which we are not willing to work.

They added that it was painful to them that the Communist Party would not allow itself "to utilize us in a sphere where we could really be useful and that the only decision it has made concerning us is to regard us as rather suspect." Meanwhile, said the five, *L'Humanité* continues to publish such reactionary writers as Blaise Cendrars and Jules Romains, whose works are nothing but a glorification of crime, stupidity, and cowardice. Wistfully, they concluded, "we are waiting with regret for better days . . . when the Revolution will recognize its own."[23]

Breton and the others were convinced that by formally joining the Party, their sincerity could no longer be questioned and they expected that Party officials would now cease their attacks and welcome them as comrades. They made the naïve assumption that, having joined the Party, they were automatically transformed into orthodox Communists. But, even while loudly insisting they were loyal and obedient Party members, they persisted in their denigrations of *L'Humanité,* of Barbusse, and of Party policies.

Quarrels within the Ranks and with the Communist Party

The announcement by the five authors of *Au Grand jour* that they had joined the Party provoked a schism in the ranks of the

Surrealists. It was not a quarrel between Left and Right, in the usual political sense; instead, it was a division between those who favored collective political action and those who wanted to preserve the independence and purity of Surrealism.

Artaud spoke for the latter when he answered *Au Grand jour* with *A la Grande nuit ou le bluff surréaliste* (In the Middle of the Night or The Surrealist Bluff). He had not yet definitively broken with the group but, stung by their insults, he replied in kind, calling the Surrealists impotent, feeble and hungry for publicity. Nevertheless, he did pose serious questions about their Marxist commitment. "Basically, all the exasperations of our quarrels turn around the word 'revolution,'" he rightly pointed out, and launched a bitter assault on the Surrealists' political pretensions.

> Didn't Surrealism die the day Breton and his followers believed it necessary to rally to Communism? Don't they see that they revealed the inanity of the Surrealist movement . . . when they felt the need to destroy its . . . true internal development . . . by an adherence . . . to the French Communist Party? . . . I deny that the logical development of Surrealism has led it to . . . Marxism. I had always thought that such an independent movement as Surrealism was not susceptible to the ordinary processes of logic. This is a contradiction which, however, will not disturb the Surrealists very much, bent as they are on letting nothing go which could be to their advantage, or anything that can serve them momentarily.

Sounding rather like Aragon at the time of the *Un Cadavre* polemic, he declared that "from the point of view of the absolute, there could only be a slight interest in seeing a change in the social conditions of the world, or in seeing power pass from the hands of the bourgeoisie to those of the proletariat." Artaud, in whom the current of Surrealist despair was very strong, added that "what separates me from the Surrealists is that they love life as much as I despise it."[24] This attitude explained his contempt for political action, and perhaps it is indicative of the severe depressed and suicidal state that overcame him later in life. But he did say that for him, Surrealism would always retain a kind of magic, and would always stand for the complete liberation of the unconscious mind. "I know that in the present debate, I have with me all the free men, all the true revolutionaries who think that individual liberty is a quality superior to that of any kind of conquest obtained on a relative scale."[25]

His argument had evidently made some impression because he was published in *La Révolution surréaliste* of March 28, which indicated that he was, at least provisionally, still in the group. That year, however, the final break came over a supposedly "commercial" production of Strindberg which he directed at the *Théâtre Alfred Jarry*. The Surrealists tried to stop the performance and the management had to call the police to throw them out and restore order so the play could go on.[26] Their objection this time was that Artaud was attempting to make a serious career for himself in the theater, thus compromising Surrealist ideals.

Naville, too, had a brief rapprochement with them in the fall of 1927, but after that their paths diverged completely. *Mieux et moins bien* (Better and Worse), in which he again urged the Surrealists on to revolutionary action, was the last article he ever wrote for *La Révolution surréaliste*. "Surrealism is still an actor without a voice. . . . But one forgets that the dialectic is demanding. . . . It was not *while waiting* that Rimbaud lived his cruel life . . . on the Somali coast, it was not *while waiting* that Lautréamont dismantled logic so magnificently. . . . We have to understand the way in which Lenin did not wait, and in what sense Karl Marx was 'at the command' of a furious impatience." The phrase "while waiting" (*en attendant*), referred to Breton's statement in *Légitime défense* that Surrealist activity should continue "while waiting" for the Revolution. He was really accusing the Surrealists of refusing to engage in genuine political work. But this charge was not entirely justified since they had been demanding to be entrusted with revolutionary tasks by the Party which, while formally accepting their membership, had left them in a sort of limbo.

Speaking of the Surrealists' complaints in *Au Grand jour,* Naville conceded that they had hardly been made to feel welcome by the Party and he explained that it was because most Communists persisted in their attachment

> to a proletarian "cultural" tradition of which, obviously, Surrealism gives no external evidence. This tradition which we know has become thoroughly entrenched since the time of Zola—and which was not without a certain legitimacy at that time—has since become utterly debased . . . by an Anatole France, or a Barbusse who . . . utilized it by paying the price of the worst kinds of compromises, of which the most serious

was becoming the object of the unanimous admiration of a miserably bourgeois nation.[27]

This statement suggested that, at least in terms of aesthetics, he had some sympathy with their position. He then proposed a possible revolutionary path for them to follow, that of systematic pessimism. "This kind of pessimism originated in the philosophy of Hegel, and it is also the source of the revolutionary methodology of Marx." Optimism, he explained, was bourgeois, whereas true pessimism is revolutionary. Despair can be a source of revolutionary inspiration, therefore the Surrealists can play a revolutionary role that would be congenial to their temperaments, athough he felt that "those among us whose capabilities extend to revolutionary practice are the best."[28]

Naville's article failed to solve their difficulties with respect to political action and, soon after, he completely abandoned them to become entirely absorbed in his own political work, while the Party continued to cast a jaundiced eye on almost everything the Surrealists did. Breton observed, however, that his criticisms had nothing to do with the actual objections of the Party. These objections were specific, even mundane, not theoretical. One of the things Party officials did complain of, according to Breton, was the very title of *La Révolution surréaliste*. It sounded suspicious, and even heretical because it seemed to indicate a distinction between a Surrealist and a Marxist revolution. "Neither my complete good faith, nor the ardor of that conviction which threw me into this adherence . . . could calm the anxiety of the 'rational' party officials on seeing the title and the contents of the review which, with astonishment and indignation, they passed from hand to hand." He recalled that he was summoned time and again before the *Commission de contrôle,* in order to justify one or another of his group's actions or manifestoes and he had to give repeated pledges of loyalty. These commissions always had three Party bureaucrats known only by first names, and they were usually foreigners who spoke French badly.

> It resembled nothing so much . . . as a police interrogation. . . . My explanations were judged satisfactory soon enough, but there always came a moment when one of the questioners displayed an issue of *La Révolution surréaliste* and the whole thing started all over again. The funniest thing, looking back on it now, . . . that made them literally beside

themselves, were some of the illustrations, especially . . . the works of Picasso. Faced with these, they would vie with each other to see who could be the most sarcastic: how was one supposed to regard this?, could I tell them what this "represented"?, did I think I had time to waste on such petty bourgeois nonsense?, did I consider this compatible with the revolution?, etc. [sic]. I had the impression that I carried it off rather well: at least, each commission confirmed my membership. But, I don't know why, a new commission would convene soon afterward to give me a hearing and, amidst the general consternation, the review with the orange cover would again be called on the carpet.[29]

In spite of this discouragement, the artists persevered in trying to be both Communists and Surrealists.

André Thirion, a new recruit, explained that the problem was that "the French Communist Party didn't know what to do with the intellectuals who were coming into it." Aside from using "sympathetic celebrities intended for a solemn role as voices of universal conscience [such as] Romain Rolland," the Party failed to take advantage of the potential usefulness of artists and intellectuals. "Permeated with all the bourgeois values, the Communist apparatus felt that Breton and Surrealism were not well known enough to warrant a red-carpet treatment [and] it was in this framework of disappointments and bureaucratic arguments that the 'opposition' ferment sprang up among the Surrealists."[30]

In spite of all the polemics, Surrealism continued to flourish and in October 1927, a new scandal was provoked by the publication of the manifesto, *Permettez!* Signed by the entire group of thirty, it was addressed to the officials of the Ardennes who proposed to honor Rimbaud by erecting a monument to him and it consisted simply of extracts of Rimbaud's writings showing what he really thought of such things as patriotism, religion, and French literature. Rimbaud was venerated by the group and they were furious at the proposed desecration of all that he stood for.

We are curious to know how you can reconcile the presence in your town of a monument to those who died for their country and of a monument to the memory of a man who incarnates the highest conception of defeatism, of the active defeatism that in wartime you put in front of the firing squad. . . . Rimbaud? He did not allow anyone to salute the dead in his presence, he wrote "shit on God" on the walls of churches; he did not love his mother. . . . Rimbaud? A communard, a Bolshevik. . . . He got drunk, picked fights, slept under bridges, had lice [and] he loathed work.[31]

They concluded with the hope that this monument would suffer the same fate as its predecessor and be melted down by the Germans to be used as bullets, a fate, they said, which would have delighted Rimbaud.

Surrealism and Sexuality

To the Surrealists, it was axiomatic that Rimbaud was to poetry what Lenin was to socialism: both were revolutionaries. They believed that revolution was needed in all spheres of human life and the complete liberation of human sexuality was a vitally important aspect of their ideal of revolution. On this theme, Eluard wrote several laudatory essays about the Marquis de Sade. It should be stressed, however, that the reason the Surrealists admired de Sade was that he fought for freedom, both in the French Revolution of 1789, and against the stifling hypocrisy of society. His sexual perversions had no particular appeal for them; they simply admired him as a rebel against all the conventions, as Eluard made clear. "For having wanted to give back to civilized man the force of his primitive instincts, for having wanted to free the amorous imagination, and for having struggled for absolute justice and equality, the Marquis de Sade was shut up in the Bastille, in Vincennes, and in Charenton for almost all of his life."[32] A manifesto on the same theme was *Hands Off Love!* It was a defense of Charlie Chaplin, whom the Surrealists dearly loved, against his "stupid little bourgeois wife" who was suing him for immoral sexual practices. "How is it possible that sexual mores be the subject of legislation? What an absurdity!" was their indignant comment.[33]

While in many areas, the Surrealists were extremely advanced, their behavior toward women tended to be as unrevolutionary as that of the most conservative bourgeois. They were amazingly conventional and even reactionary in their attitudes toward women. Like the nineteenth-century Romantics, they extolled the beauty of a great love, a unique passion and physical union, but unlike them, they deliberately handled erotic themes in a daringly explicit manner. For the Surrealist aesthetic, which in this respect constitutes a new romanticism in the opinion of many authorities, woman was important as muse and inspiration and symbol of the "marvelous." But these men had difficulty in dealing with real women who were creative artists in their own right. Female as symbol was the theme of much of their greatest art, but individual women did not fare as well and for the most part, women among the Surrealists played a very passive role. They were mistresses, wives and mothers, and kept house for their men, but they almost never participated in the daily discussions and they rarely even signed the manifestoes. The perfect Surrealist wife was "Nusch," (Maria Benz), beloved wife of Eluard. She was beautiful, she inspired some of his most extraordinary lyric love poetry, she was utterly devoted to him until her death shortly after World War II, and she kept herself in the background. More assertive women had problems. In the 1940s, Breton explained that he had had to divorce his second wife, Jacqueline Lamda, because she wanted to be an artist herself and for him, this was a perfectly reasonable motive to break up their marriage.[34]

Many of the women Surrealist artists complained that they could not function professionally until they left Paris, physically separating themselves from the group, even though they credit the movement with providing the impetus for their own creative work. Meret Oppenheim, creator of one of the most famous Surrealist objects, "Object Fur Breakfast," a fur-lined teacup and saucer, implied that the men had impeded her growth as an artist and added, "when I met the group, end of 1933, I was twenty years old and I was not at all sure about political opinions. I made my work and did not worry about these discussions. (After the war I met Man Ray again. He said to me: 'But you are speaking!' I asked him: 'Why do you say that?' He answered: 'You never said a word formerly.')."[35] Remedios Varo and Leonora Carrington only became fully productive painters when they moved to Mexico in the 1940s. Frida Kahlo, whose husband was Diego Rivera, had a show in the Surrealist gallery in Paris and was scathing in her vituperations because she felt she had been badly mistreated. "You do not have even the slightest idea of the kind of old cockroach Breton and almost all the Surrealist group are," she said angrily.[36] Elsa Triolet, who had already published three novels when she met Aragon in 1928, despised the Surrealists for their condescending attitudes. She refused to play the passive role demanded of her and resolved to create some distance between the group and Aragon and herself which she felt was important for her survival.

While physical love was celebrated in Surrealist painting and poetry, there is a demonstrable element of brutality in the sexual attitudes they reveal. This is especially clear in some of the work of the visual artists with their depictions of dismembered and distorted nudes, but it is also discernible in some of the poetry. Magritte's "Rape" is a painting in which female breasts and genitals become the eyes and mouth of a face and "it is as much a rape of the spectator's preconceptions as it is of the female face."[37] Bondage is the subject of Ernst's collage series, "La Semaine de bonté," and Dali's "Femme-phallique," a nude with elongated, sharp pointed breasts, expresses a menacing eroticism. His "Young Virgin Self-Sodomized by Her Own Chastity" is a painting of a female nude whose buttocks are about to be pierced by several enormous phallic objects and Jindrich Stýrský's "Collage," in which a knife is thrust between a pair of legs clad in stockings and high-heeled shoes, convey a powerfully sadistic message. Some critics make a distinction between the writers and the painters, arguing that in Surrealist poetry, there are only positive images of women. However, in all the art forms of the movement, one can frequently discern a similar savagery. Aragon's tremendously acclaimed prose poem of 1926, *Le Paysan de Paris,* evinces an obsessive fascination with brothels and prostitutes. Dali and Buñuel's films, *Le Chien andalou,* and *L'Age d'or,* exhibit the same sort of blatantly cruel sexuality and Man Ray's "Monument to de Sade," a nude viewed from the rear and bent over, is clearly an object of violent lust. In a discussion of these images, Mary Ann Caws states that "the woman's exposure is not—and Breton would surely agree—a matter of her own sexuality, but of the sexuality of the observer."[38] It is apparent that woman was object rather than subject in Surrealist art.

The Surrealists held a group discussion on sexuality in 1928, published in *La Révolution surréaliste,* in which the participants were supposed to answer intimate questions about their own sex lives with perfect frankness. In spite of their convictions about complete sexual freedom, it was clear that only heterosexual relations were permissible. Breton was adamant in his moralistic condemnation of homosexuals and said, "I accuse pederasts of proposing to human tolerance a mental and moral deficit which . . . would paralyze all the enterprises that I respect." Naturally, he made an exception for de Sade: "by definition, everything is permitted to a man like the Marquis de Sade for whom moral freedom was a question of life or death." But when some of the others protested that, although they themselves were not homosexual, they did not necessarily find it morally repugnant, Breton indignantly threatened to end the discussion and leave if they continued in this vein.

The participants were asked questions such as when they had their earliest sexual experience, what positions they preferred, and whether they could be unfaithful to a woman they loved. True to their avowed hatred of religion, Breton and Péret said they would like to make love in a church and desecrate it, but the others were indifferent to this idea. The subject of oral and anal sex was raised, which most said they enjoyed, and of simultaneous orgasm, which all thought was desirable. For the most part, however, the responses were limited to "yes," "no," "sometimes," "I approve," "don't approve," and the like, although there was a long argument about female orgasm and whether or not there are objective signs by which one can tell if a woman has climaxed. When Unik said that he always asked his partner what sort of lovemaking she preferred, Breton was astonished. "I think that is absolutely colossal, really phenomenal! Talk about complications!" Unik wondered why he found it so astonishing and Breton replied, "because her preferences have nothing to do with it."[39] Breton was also astonished when Aragon, no doubt influenced by his new companion, Triolet, suggested that "the validity of what has been said appears to me to be in some degree negated because we only have the masculine point of view here."[40] It is obvious that Breton felt that having women contribute to a discussion of human sexuality would only introduce unnecessary "complications," and the Surrealists generally did not share the most progressive ideas on women and sexuality of the 1920s.

They also continued to have great admiration for Freud and to publish articles about him in their journal. One, by J. Frois-Wittman on the unconscious, contained this interesting statement: "I believe that Surrealism, psychoanalysis, and some form of socialism will eventually come together to create a consistent, unified system."[41] This was precisely the synthesis of ideas that the Surrealists were, at least implicitly, groping toward. Indeed, Freudianism was of such importance to them that they were sometimes called "Freud's disciples," who were among the "small number of Frenchmen who paid serious attention to psychoanalysis."[42] The Communist Party bureaucrats could not have been pleased by their emphasis on sex and on Freud. Except for a few brief years just after the Bolshevik Revolution, Communists have generally been rather prudish, even puritanical, in their official attitudes toward sexuality. Freud, with his emphasis on the sexual origins of neurosis, has been condemned by orthodox Communists as the theorist of a decadent and dying bourgeois culture, promoting an unhealthy individualism and overemphasizing sex and irrational motivations. There must also have been some raised eyebrows at headquarters when the Abbé Gengenbach, a defrocked Jesuit priest, briefly joined the movement, claiming he had lost his faith, and that his discovery of Surrealism and Freud had kept him from committing suicide.

But the movement continued to claim for itself autonomous areas of endeavor, above and beyond its commitment to the Communist Party. Although many of their pursuits were not relevant to Marxism, Breton insisted that they were never contrary to its spirit. But the Party had grave doubts about the propriety of many of the Surrealists' concerns and it neither approved of nor understood their claim that they needed to continue with their own independent endeavors. The Party frowned upon any activities conducted by its members outside of Party affairs, especially when they appeared to be contrary to the principles of Marxism as the leadership interpreted them. The Surrealists were often accused of counterrevolutionary tendencies, in spite of their repeated assurances to the contrary. Breton stated their position clearly and, he thought, reasonably.

> Even if Surrealist activity, properly speaking, continued to develop itself in its own sphere, that of *inner* experience and exploration, it is not any the less imbued with the desire to avoid a fundamental conflict with Marxism. This is so . . . because, at least in our time, Marxism offers the greatest chance for the liberation of oppressed classes and peoples.[43]

But his position was to be continually challenged.

The Surrealists, by joining the Communist Party, lost none of their creativity; in fact, they continued to be very productive. In Hugnet's opinion, they made a very real contribution politically as well, because they paved the way for other artists to make a commitment to the revolution. "The Surrealists were the first intellectuals to assert themselves by taking the part . . . of the

Revolution in a political sense and they contributed materially to the spread of that atmosphere which, at present, permits groups of revolutionary writers to unite with relative ease."[44] The importance of the Surrealists to the Party should also be acknowledged because in the 1920s, they constituted its intellectual life.[45] The Party was clearly ambivalent toward them but, at least for a time, it needed them. In the 1920s, prominent intellectuals and artists willing to join or even support it were extremely scarce and, while the Party was determined to be predominantly working class, and organizing workers was its primary task, it needed intellectuals to run its press, its cultural functions, and to be delegates at international congresses and the like. The Party also needed a relationship with the world of art and was cognizant of the many pronouncements on the importance of superstructure being made in the Soviet Union which claimed to be bringing about a cultural renaissance. The role of art in the revolution was greatly emphasized in the 1920s, so the relations between the Surrealists and the Party continued into the next decade despite increasingly bitter conflicts and Party officials' suspicions that they were really nothing but petit bourgeois counterrevolutionaries.

5
At the Service of the Revolution

Today, I would gladly go and see *L'age d'or* and ask you to explain anything I didn't understand. Dali is now becoming famous and if an anti-Semitic league were to be organized again, I would instantly write to the Chief of Police and demand its dissolution.

— de Launay, Provost of Paris

In their progress toward the Communist Party, the Surrealists had formed a group of only five at the decisive point; now, suddenly, there were dozens of revolutionaries.

— André Thirion, *Révolutionnaires sans révolution*

Crisis of 1929: The Trotsky Meeting

The many controversies with the French Communist Party, as well as with his own followers, compelled Breton to try to reaffirm his leadership of the left-wing *avant-garde*. He decided to call a meeting of radical writers and artists for the purpose of creating a common political program. First on the agenda was a protest against the expulsion of Trotsky from the Soviet Union, for he was a man whom Breton continued to admire greatly, in spite of his fall from grace. In many respects, the Surrealists were ideologically closer to Trotsky and to the several Trotskyist organizations than they were to the Communist Party. But, until they were formally expelled from the Communist Party and from the organizations it sponsored, their sympathy for him was only rarely expressed, and no attempts were made to effect a political alignment with any Trotskyist groups.

77

This meeting was comparable to Breton's attempt in 1922, during the Dada period, to organize a congress of contemporary artists. But it, too, failed in its purpose. Invitations were sent to former Surrealists, Dadaists, members of *Clarté,* of *L'Esprit,* the Belgian group and any individuals who, at one time or another, had collaborated with the Surrealists. They were also sent to the editors of *Le Grand jeu,* a Surrealist-inspired review, founded in 1928 and edited by Roger Gilbert-Lecomte, René Daumal, Joseph Sima, André Delons, and Roger Vailland. Everyone was invited to attend a meeting on March 11, at the Bar du Château, to discuss taking action concerning the recent exile of Trotsky. Thirty-two men of very different temperament and ideology came to the meeting where the replies to the invitation were read aloud. Naville, at this time an active Trotskyist, was especially invited to attend, but did not even reply. Some, like Leiris, Masson and Miró, were opposed to any common action. Others like Kasyade, wanted to cooperate in the future but on a purely cultural level. Still others, such as Fourrier and, of course, most of the Surrealists themselves, favored joint political action. But many expressed a distrust of working with certain of the individuals present so the success of the project was, from the beginning, doomed by personal conflicts.[1]

First, the acceptability of *Le Grand jeu* had to be decided upon. The editors were charged with being too mystical, of using the word "God" too much, of frivolously preferring Landru (a French "bluebeard" who had murdered several women) to Sacco and Vanzetti, and of taking part in Artaud's theatrical productions. There was also the question of their role in the *affaire* of the *Ecole normale supérieure.* Eighty-three *normaliens* had signed a statement against the draft but, frightened by the adverse publicity, they withdrew their signatures. Ten of the students thereupon signed an even stronger statement but, when they were threatened with expulsion by the director of the *Ecole* if they published it, they disavowed it. The editors of *Le Grand jeu* were criticized because, having been in contact with these students, they had had the document in their possession, but had returned it to the students at their request. They claimed that they were morally obligated not to publish the protest against the students' wishes, but Breton was furious because a wonderful opportunity to create a scandal was lost.

That these students would sign a protest, then withdraw their signatures because they dared not risk the consequences of publication is not at all surprising. Are they not, after all, students of one of the great bourgeois schools? But, what is serious, is that certain intellectuals, collaborators of *Le Grand jeu* who claim to be revolutionaries, although that is very doubtful, should have had the document in their hands, then returned it to the students without even making a copy!

Aragon added that the greatest service one could render a young revolutionary would be to get him expelled from his university.

Whatever the merits of this question, which was debated at length, there was another more serious issue, the problem of the former Surrealist, Vailland, who was now part of the *Le Grand jeu* circle. He was a journalist who had written a series of obsequiously flattering newspaper articles on Chiappe, the reactionary Paris chief of police. Excerpts were read in which he described Chiappe as "a little like a grandfather who showers his grandchildren with presents," and he had even called him the "purifier of our capital."[2] These sentiments naturally produced cries of indignation and one man, André Thirion, left the meeting in protest, accusing Vailland of being an agent for the police. Most of the others demanded that Vailland leave, although the members of *Le Grand jeu* defended him. Ribemont-Dessaignes also defended him on the grounds that it was necessary to earn a living—a fact the Surrealists generally did not concede—and, after exchanging insults with Breton and Aragon, he too walked out.

"It was immediately clear," said Ribemont-Dessaignes, "that the alleged purpose of the meeting was an artifice, designed to gather together as large a group as possible and pull off a *coup*. Breton and some of his friends merely intended to discredit one of the members of *Le Grand jeu* in order to compromise the whole group and ruin them in the eyes of public opinion. . . . This led to my complete rupture with Breton."[3] The meeting was adjourned when a compromise was reached whereby Vailland agreed to publish a letter disavowing these articles. But in the letter he wrote a few days later, he tried to justify his conduct by saying he was no worse than a worker forced to earn his wages in a munitions plant. He also questioned the motives of everyone who objected to the articles and was indignant that anyone should doubt his revolutionary sincerity. This response obviously did not heal the rift. His apology was judged unacceptable and the meeting was never reconvened. Ironically, the fate of Trotsky, the ostensible topic of discussion, never even came up and Ribemont-Dessaignes blamed Breton and his friends for this fiasco.

> Judgments! Judgments! Judgments! And of what sort! Your revolutionary activity consists of washing dirty linen in public! . . . Are all your attempts at collective action ever anything else but the perpetual personal problems of petty schoolboys? I consider that the self-appointed task of purification that you devote yourself to is absolutely counterrevolutionary. It condemns you to the impotence which is the mark of the Surrealist movement. It justifies the opinion they have of Surrealism in the Communist Party. . . . You are the bureaucrats of purity and judgment.[4]

Breton naturally dismissed these charges; it was not a question of personalities but simply that moral rigor was necessary to weed out elements whose activities would be destructive of the common cause. But in his memoirs, Thirion substantially agreed with Ribemont-Dessaignes: the Trotsky protest was a mere pretext and the point was to discredit *Le Grand jeu* because its editors would never have agreed to work with the Communist Party. He also claimed that he deliberately staged his angry exit precisely in order to break up the meeting.[5] But even though the Surrealists may well have wanted to destroy the reputation of their imitators, the crucial importance of Trotsky in the development of surrealist politics makes it doubtful that his exile was a mere pretext.[6] Yet it could not be denied that the project for common action had failed, nor could it be denied that Surrealism was growing further and further away from the Communist Party. Personal conflicts did play an extremely important role in Surrealism and there were many who rebelled against Breton's attempts to dominate and dictate to them.

Externally, however, Surrealism flourished and was gaining wide recognition. The year 1929 saw a double number of *Varietés,* a prestigious Belgian journal, devoted entirely to Surrealism. In addition to the account of the Trotsky meeting, which had been published as a supplement to this issue, it contained articles on Freud, Surrealist poems and games, and a "Surrealist geography" in which there was no France, only Paris, no United States at all, and the islands of Polynesia and other "primitive" and exotic places were larger than the continent of Europe.[7] There was also an interesting, if unorthodox, article by Thirion, who for several years was both a Surrealist and a Communist Party member, entitled *A Bas le travail!* (Down with Work!). He expressed the Surrealist attitude by saying that to glorify work was really counterrevolutionary. Communist writers tended to romanticize labor without really knowing what it was and the Soviet Union was admiringly called the *République du travail,* which was absurd because "nothing resembles a foreman from Lens as much as a foreman of the Donetz who was often running precisely the same machine as his French comrade." Thus, glorifying work is reactionary because it is part of the value system of Western culture which revolutionaries should reject. The ruling classes have been trying for centuries to instill the idea that hard work is a virtue and conversely, that laziness is sin. The fact is, that work is slavery.

> Go see for yourself, good little bourgeois. Go sit for a few hours beside the worker who spends his days drilling holes in identical plaques of metal. Or go to the printers and watch the motion of the rotary presses. You'll come out eyes blinking and hands trembling, signs of precocious senility. . . . How can a self-styled revolutionary not believe in the immorality of work? What do sayings like "work is healthy" or "work rehabilitates the criminal" mean if not moral forms of oppression we must destroy?

Technological advances would enable man to drastically reduce the need for labor but even the small amount of necessary work remaining will still be slavery so "I say shit on all those counterrevolutionaries and their miserable idol, WORK!"[8] His article was noteworthy for its use of Marxist terminology to question Communist doctrine and, as he rightly pointed out, the attempt to make a virtue out of the necessity of work was actually a Western bourgeois ideal.

Second Manifesto of Surrealism and Un Cadavre Again

Despite external successes, Breton realized the need for a new direction and he published the *Second manifeste du surréalisme* in the final issue of *La Révolution surréaliste,* in December 1929, shortly after the failure of the Trotsky meeting. It was a polemical document in which he settled a lot of old quarrels and re-evaluated some of his original ideas. The goals remained basically un-changed but were more clearly formulated and the movement now encompassed Marxist ideology. He still stressed a "revolution of the mind," as he indicated by saying "Surrealism tends basically to provoke, from a moral and intellectual point of view, a *crise de conscience* of a most general and serious nature and the achievement or non-achievement of that result alone can determine its historical success or failure."

The underlying philosophy of Surrealism had by this time become clarified and he again emphasized its materialist nature. In a significant passage, influenced by Hegel, Breton disposed of the problem of dualism touched on in the *First Manifesto*.

> Everything leads us to believe that there exists a certain point in the mind where life and death, the real and the imaginary, the past and the future, the communicable and the uncom-municable, the high and the low, cease to be perceived as contradictory. Indeed, one would search in vain for a motive of Surrealist activity other than the determination of this point.

Political contradictions remained, however, for the anarchistic ele-ment in Surrealism was also clearly reaffirmed. "The simplest Surrealist act consists of going into the street, revolver in hand, and firing into the crowd. A man who has not had, at least once, the desire to end it all in this manner, to have done with the pettiness and vileness and idiocy of the system deserves a place in that crowd, a gun at his belly." This statement provoked a lot of criticism from the Left which accused him of anarchy and of lacking revolutionary discipline. In the second edition of the *Sec-ond Manifesto,* Breton tried to explain that what he really meant to advocate was spontaneity, not violence. It was also intended to be an expression of despair at the human condition and, he insisted, it was not to be taken literally. Nevertheless, it is more than likely that the original statement reflected the profound influence that anarchism still had on Surrealist thought.

In contrast to the *First Manifesto,* which had contained a long list of Surrealist precursors, he now said that "in matters of revolt, none of us has any need of ancestors." He was no longer an admirer of Baudelaire, de Sade, or Edgar Allan Poe. Even Rim-baud was no longer a Surrealist "hero" because he "is guilty before us of not having made absolutely impossible certain dishonorable interpretations of his thought."[9] This was a reference to recent attempts that had been made to "rehabilitate" Rimbaud's reputation by claiming he had returned to the Catholic Church before he died and, strangely, Breton seemed to blame Rimbaud for this. In addition, a number of fellow Surrealists were now purged from the ranks. He directed insulting remarks to Artaud, Jean Carrive, Joseph Delteil, Francis Gérard, Georges Limbour, Masson, Soupault, and Vitrac, most of whom had been named in the *First Manifesto* as having 'fait acte de surréalisme absolu" (sworn to absolute Surrealism).[10] But these defections were to be expected for, as Breton pointed out, "perfect fidelity to the principles of Surrealism presupposes a scorn of risk and a refusal to compromise of which very few men in the long run are capable."[11] These men had sinned in Surrealist eyes because they had either turned to "vulgar journalism" to make money, or had begun to care about making their reputations, or were immersed in commercial artistic endeavors. One way or another they had all "fallen away" from Surrealist principles. Breton also bitterly resented the *L'Esprit* group, who had become Communists and who now enjoyed the favor of the Party. There were once again pages of insults vilifying Naville, who was accused of betraying his former friends, and against Georges Bataille author of *Story of the Eye*, who had been critical of the Surrealists. All those who had turned to pure politics as well as those who had turned to "art for art's sake" were bitterly denounced. He also reluctantly took leave of Desnos who had played such an important role in the automatic writing discoveries but who now refused to concede the importance of the social questions which confronted Surrealism.

He had to admit to the partial failure of automatic writing which had not lived up to its hoped-for potential because of lack of discipline. It was not sufficient to let the pen run across the paper; the flow of words must be reflected upon, studied scientifically, and discipline must be applied. The mistake was to have confused automatic technique with passivity. Yet the methods of Surrealist creation were not to be essentially changed and he again acknowledged his great debt to Freud and said that even though Surrealism has adopted Marxist ideology on social questions, it still considered Freudian theory of fundamental importance.

Breton also declared that he did not believe in the possibility of creating a truly proletarian art at the present time, "for the excellent reason that such a culture does not yet exist, even in the proletarian state," and he quoted from Trotsky's *Revolution and Culture* in support of this view. He never claimed that Surrealism was actually creating proletarian art for this was to be an achievement of the distant future, as Trotsky had said. Proletarian culture would come into existence only after the transformation of the whole world and it would take totally new unimaginable forms.[12] He made a distinction between proletarian and revolutionary art and if Surrealist art could not be considered proletarian, it was nevertheless revolutionary. He expressed his disappointment, as he had in *Légitime défense* and *Au Grand jour,* at the Communist Party's treatment of the Surrealists. There were still frequent interrogations at Party headquarters where Breton had to defend the movement against absurd charges of being anti-Communist and counterrevolutionary and, in his opinion, this infuriating treatment was totally unjustified. "Our adherence to the principle of historical materialism—there is no way to play with these words—does not depend only on us. I mean, provided that Communism does not treat us merely like curious beasts destined to be gaped at and mistrusted, we will show ourselves capable of doing our duty from a revolutionary point of view."

He was also angry about being given an assignment which he was forced to regard as pure harassment. He was assigned to a gas workers' cell in Paris and they asked him to prepare a report on the economic conditions of heavy industry in Italy, but Breton refused, saying simply, "I just could not do it."[13] It was true that this sort of analysis was hardly his *forte,* but it is possible, as Maxime Alexandre suggested, that this was not an instance of harassment.

> The gas cell of André Breton became legendary among us! Breton couldn't get over it! He believed—or said he believed—that it was pure provocation and the Parisian gas workers never again saw André Breton. But was it really a provocation? I'm not so sure. The good gas workers, having for once an "intellectual" in their midst, certainly must have believed they were doing the right thing by charging him with an intellectual task."[14]

It was significant, however, that Breton believed his assignment to have been deliberately malicious and he was sure that it was merely another proof that his presence in the Party was extremely unwelcome.

As a further indication of the Party's attitude toward him, he quoted a comment by a puzzled Party member, Michel Marty, who remarked that "if you are a Marxist, you have no need to be a Surrealist." This question had been settled, as far as Breton was concerned, in the days of the collaboration with *Clarté* and he was still unwilling to abandon Surrealism and continued to insist that the movement had a unique role to play in the revolution.

> Why say that the dialectical method can only be validly applied to the resolution of social questions? The whole ambition of Surrealism is to furnish possibilities of application on its own grounds to the immediate conscious domain. I really do not see, with all due respect to certain narrow-minded revolutionaries, why we should abstain from raising, provided we view them from the same angle as they—and we too—that of the revolution—the problems of love, of madness, of art and of religion. I do not hesitate to say that before Surrealism, nothing systematic had been done along these lines.[15]

He again asserted that Surrealism was not an ideology which opposed Marxism, but a complementary system of thought and, since the group believed in Marxism, there need never be any conflict between them. The *Second Manifesto* concluded with a discussion of alchemy, astrology and hermeticism. It was important that the movement continue its independent research in these areas and he said that "Surrealism is less disposed than ever toward giving up its integrity," a clear warning that its own principles were going to be upheld whatever the cost.[16]

Breton paid for his harsh dismissal of old comrades by being the victim of an attack himself. Ribemont-Dessaignes, Jacques Prévert, Raymond Queneau, Roger Vitrac, Max Morise, Jacques Baron, Michel Leiris, J.-A. Boiffard, Robert Desnos, Alejo Carpentier and Georges Bataille collaborated on an insulting tract, *Un cadavre,* whose title was taken from the pamphlet written on the death of Anatole France in 1924. The first page pictured Breton crowned with thorns, and the contributions of each writer consisted of scatalogical verse, accusations of betraying friendships, of being overbearing, publicity hungry, hypocritical and disloyal. Limbour questioned the sincerity of Breton's devotion to Marxism and said that he seized upon it only because "Communism has the advantage in that it offers a field of activity less dangerous than anarchism which, if taken seriously, would require immediate violence." Morise declared that if Breton should find that he likes "*pieds de mouton sauce poulette,* you would suddenly see them consecrated revolutionaries. . . . How could the revolutionary opinions of a Breton possibly be anything other than a joke?" Desnos accused him of making a lot of money by peddling art works in the Surrealist gallery he ran, while adamantly condemning others for trying to earn a living. Baron declared that "he was always talking of Marxism because it was a new way to sell the pictures he could call 'subversive.' He sends his friends to the Ballet russe to cry, 'vivent les Soviets!' then, the next day he welcomes Serge Diaghilev to his gallery with open arms because he has come to buy pictures." Leiris accused Breton of being "a corpse who has always lived off corpses," of exploiting the deaths of Vaché and Rigaut, and of failing to protect Nadja, a woman he professed to love who had been put in a mental institution. *Nadja* was in fact the title of a book he had published in 1928. It is a haunting description of bizarre encounters with an elusive woman who tragically loses her mind, and the story may or may not have been based on someone he actually knew. Prévert declared that Breton "took himself for a bishop or the Pope in Avignon," and Ribemont-Dessaignes called him "a cop and a priest," adding that Breton was an "*agent provocateur* who would be there to arrest anyone who acted on his exhortation to fire at random into the crowd."[17] Later, in another pamphlet, Desnos accused him of betraying personal confidences and called him a Jesuit and a reactionary. "Surrealism, as it is formulated by Breton, is one of the gravest dangers to free thought, the most vicious trap into which atheism could fall, and the best ally of a renaissance of Catholicism and clericalism."[18]

Breton tried to have the last word by listing, in the second edition of the *Second Manifesto* two columns, *avant* (before) and *apres* (after). The latter were insults from *Un cadavre* and the former were earlier extravagant expressions of admiration by the same men. This was hardly a satisfactory answer to the attacks, but any damage to his reputation was certainly minimized by the very violence and exaggeration of the tract. Underlying the various accusations against him was resentment at his assertion of complete authority over them all and his insistence that all must equally share in his every enthusiasm. These were charges to which he must plead guilty, and the acrimonious rupture with so many of his old comrades was not really surprising. It is a measure of his great charm and fascination that the group held together as well as it did. But it could not be expected that the thinking of all the others would evolve, politically and ideologically, along the same lines as his. It was also clear that many of these men, who were forceful personalities themselves, could not be content to follow the leadership of Breton indefinitely. For psychological reasons, they needed to break away from him and the highly vindictive quality of *Un cadavre* indicated that this was, indeed, the real motive.

Although there had been a large exodus from the ranks, many new members joined the movement in 1930. Dali, whose "critical paranoic" method of forcing inspiration by artificially inducing a disoriented mental state, was an important new recruit.[19] Luis Buñuel, Georges Hugnet, René Char, Albert Valentin, Georges Sadoul, who like Thirion, also belonged to the Communist Party, and Thirion himself, had all recently joined, while Man Ray and the painter, Yves Tanguy, had returned to the fold. With all these impressive and talented new members, it was clear that Surrealism retained its vitality in spite of the various "excommunications."

Le Surréalisme au service de la révolution

As an indication of the new direction the movement took in 1930, *La Révolution surréaliste* ceased to appear and was superseded by a new review, *Le Surréalisme au service de la révolution*, which was published from 1930 to 1933. The significance of the title change was made clear on page one of the first issue where a telegram received from Moscow was printed along with the Surrealists' reply:

International Bureau Revolutionary Literature Question: What will be your position if imperialism declares war on Soviets?

Answer: Comrades, if imperialism declares war on Soviets our position will be to follow directives of Third International position of members of French Communist Party. If you think in such a case better use our resources possible we are at your disposal for any specific tasks requiring use of us as intellectuals. To submit suggestions would presume too much on our role and circumstances in present situation unarmed conflict. We believe it useless to wait to put at service of Revolution the methods which are particularly ours.[20]

By this statement, the Surrealists clearly placed themselves at the disposal of the Communist International and they hoped that this flattering attention from the International meant that their conflicts with the French party were over.

There was also a declaration of the purpose of the new review and of confidence in Breton.

We express our solidarity on all points with André Breton and are resolved to apply the *conclusions* imposed by the reading of the *Second manifeste du surréalisme*. Having no illusions about the character of the artistic and religious press, we the undersigned, have decided to publish a periodical under the title *Le Surréalisme au service de la révolution* not only to permit us to respond in an immediate way to the idiots who claim to be thinkers, but to prepare for the turning of current intellectual forces toward aiding the inevitable Revolution.[21]

It was signed by Alexandre, Aragon, Joë Bousquet, Buñuel, Char, Crevel, Dali, Eluard, Ernst, Fourrier, Goemans, Georges Malkine, Nougé, Péret, Francis Ponge, Marco Ristitch, Tanguy, Thirion, Tzara, and Valentin.

The new review had many more overtly political articles and published fewer Surrealist poems, dreams, and automatic texts. The themes, however, were similar to those of *La Révolution surréaliste*. Violent anticlericalism was again expressed in such articles as Ernst's *Danger de pollution*[22] which ridiculed the Church's attitude toward sex. Sadoul's *le Bon pasteur* exposed the soldier-priests fighting for France and Church in World War I as bloodthirsty monsters.[23] Anti-militarist sentiment was also expressed in Aragon's *Guerre à la mode* (War in fashion),[24] in Char's *Les Porcs en liberté* (Pigs let loose),[25] in Crevel's *Bobards et fariboles* (Stuff and nonsense),[26] and in the poems of Péret, such as *Vie de l'assassin Foch* (Life of the murderer, Foch).[27] Valentin's *Le Haut du payé* (Behind the walls) denounced the French colonialist regime in Indo-China which he called organized massacre, and condemned the practice of forced labor there.[28]

The Surrealists still characterized patriotism and imperialism in all their forms as great evils which could only lead to war and oppression, even though they well knew that these were extremely unpopular opinions in France, which regarded its colonialist adventures as a great civilizing mission. As Unik declared,

> France of 1931 is the most solid fortress of oppression in the world. When Laval and Briand went to Berlin to negotiate the price of the chains forged with "our" gold, which were to bind the German people, one Parisian newspaper, *Paris-Midi,* didn't hide the fact that they were surrounded by the same security precautions that were necessary before the war when the Tzar made visits to European capitals. One knows, of course, that the conclusion of these visits was the war of 1914 and the information is perfectly symbolic.[29]

Hitler's rise to power was really the fault of France and the other imperialist nations, the Surrealists believed, and they refused to succumb to anti-German, nationalist thinking. This point of view was aptly expressed in the remark that "that country remains for us the country of Kant, Fichte, Hegel, and Marx."[30] They nevertheless supported the *Secours rouge international* (International Red Aid), headed by Romain Rolland, which called for protests "against the fascist terror in Germany, the violence of the Nazi police against the Jews and the working classes, especially those who are Communists." But they also declared that they "condemn French imperialism which, by its intransigent politics and the maintenance of the Treaty of Versailles, has permitted the triumph of the scoundrel, Hitler."[31] They still admired Hegel, whose centennial was celebrated in the third issue of December 1931. De Sade was still honored as an apostle of liberty,[32] and Freud continued to be studied, with more translations of his writing making their first appearance in France in the pages of *Le Surréalisme au service de la révolution.*[33]

The internationalism of the movement was emphasized by the founding of a Yugoslav group of Surrealists who announced the publication in Belgrade, in French and Serbian, of a review called *L'Impossible,* with which the French Surrealists were to collaborate. The editors were Marco Ristitch and Oscar Davitcho and they made a declaration of solidarity with French Surrealist principles in December 1930.

> Our revolt can only take on the character of incessant action, violent and destructive. . . . Our revolt will lead, on the plan

of dialectical materialism, to the erection of a system for the transformation of the real conditions of existence. We affirm that until now philosophers have only interpreted the world. Now it is a question of changing it.[34]

In 1933, Crevel wrote that they had begun publishing a new periodical, *Le Surréalisme aujourd'hui et ici,* which was outspokenly anti-fascist, and for which they suffered political persecution. Davitcho was arrested for organizing a club for Marxist studies and was sentenced to five years in prison and three others, Kostitch, Popovitch and Yovanovitch, were also serving varying terms in jail. Students demonstrated in Belgrade on their behalf but as Crevel said, "their fate depends on the arbitrary nature of a government which is not merciful toward those who believe in free expression of thought."[35] Surrealism in Yugoslavia continued to exist, however, and even survived into the postwar era.[36]

In *Le Surréalisme au service de la révolution,* even the literary criticism was overtly political in nature, as shown by Aragon's article, "Découverte du nouveau monde" (Discovery of the New World), in which he demanded to know how Milhaud could bring himself to collaborate on an opera with the Catholic reactionary, Claudel, and how a Soviet theater could produce Claudel's plays.[37] There was also much criticism of the Communist weekly, *Monde,* edited by Barbusse, whom the Surrealists accused of being reactionary, both in a literary and political sense.[38]

Suicide, however, continued to play a role and Jacques Rigaut, one of the original group, having in 1919 predicted his own suicide in ten years, actually carried out this self-imposed death sentence. His reasons were never known, but he once remarked that "all of you are poets. But I, myself, am on the side of death."[39] Also, Breton wrote an angry article defending Mayakovsky against *L'Humanité.* The poet had killed himself in 1930, and since no true socialist would do such a thing, it meant that he had revealed himself to be a bourgeois reactionary. Breton described his deep disappointment at reading this "miserable sort of argument in the pages of *L'Humanité,* the one place in France where Mayakovsky might have expected to find defenders."[40] He feared that the attacks on Mayakovsky, who was being linked to fascism because he had belonged to the *avant-garde* Russian Futurist movement, were indirectly attacks against the Surrealists. The poet had made several visits to Paris and they knew him personally through Triolet, who was his close friend and the sister of his lover, Lili

Brik. He was much admired as a shining example of a poet-revolutionary and Breton complained that the left-wing press

> had tried to exploit the suicide of Mayakovsky at our expense and generally at the expense of all those who, with Mayakovsky, proclaim the absolute inanity of literature that pretends to be proletarian. Again we say, show us a real work of "proletarian art." More than ever, with Mayakovsky dead, we refuse to weaken. We will not abandon the spiritual and moral position that he took. Let no one expect from us, in this domain, any concession.

Aragon was so angry at the hostile press reaction to Mayakovsky that he went to the home of a critic, André Levinson, who had written an especially insulting article and assaulted him. The critic's wife called the police and accused Aragon of being a Communist terrorist but Levinson, who had cowered behind his wife when Aragon threatened him, was simply made a laughingstock and charges were never preferred.[41]

The first issue of *Le Surréalisme au service de la révolution* also carried the story of "l'affaire Saint-Cyr." One of the Surrealists, Sadoul, and a friend, Jean Caupenne, wrote an inane letter full of ridiculous threats to a student, Keller, who had just won a scholarship to Saint-Cyr, the military academy of France.

> We can imagine what you look like: your face is covered with pimples, with servility, with shit and with abjection. . . . If we fought at all, we'd rather fight for Germany. We spit on the flag you defend. We eagerly await the next uprising of the men you claim to command and who, tomorrow, with our assistance, will put out to dry in the sun the dirty tripes of every French officer and of little four-eyed snotnoses of your type. . . . You have one chance: as soon as you get this, you must hand in your resignation to the director of Saint-Cyr, along with a copy of this letter. . . . If not, we will publicly spank you in the middle of the *Place Saint-Cyr.*

Keller, who obviously had no sense of humor, gave the letter to his superior, whose reaction was equally humorless. A warrant was issued for the arrest of the two young men and both were put under surveillance by the police and interrogated by the military. Officers of the highest rank involved themselves in the incident—even General Herscher, Commandant of Saint-Cyr, and General

Gouraud, military governor of Paris. Caupenne, under pressure, agreed to make a public apology at Saint-Cyr to the assembled cadets, saying he had been drunk and meant no insult to Saint-Cyr, the flag, France, or the army. Sadoul refused to do this, preferring to face arrest and trial. At this point, the other Surrealists sent a message to General Gouraud affirming their solidarity with Sadoul, but this "letter" was ignored, possibly because, as a joke, it had been written with one sentence on each of ten different postcards.

Fourrier, formerly of *Clarté*, was a lawyer and represented Sadoul in court. He was sentenced to three months in prison and a hundred franc fine, in spite of Fourrier's contention that the proceedings were thoroughly illegal and that the threats in the letter were obviously a joke. Sadoul also lost his job at the *Nouvelle revue française* as a result of the publicity and the numerous inquiries by the police about him.[42] The whole *affaire*, with depositions, the trial transcript, police reports, press clippings, and a letter from General Gouraud to Sadoul's parents, was reported in *Le Surréalisme au service de la révolution*. The Surrealists were delighted to have this opportunity to make the authorities look ridiculous and having one of their number sentenced to jail gave them genuine credentials as subversives. The best comment was made by Clément Vautel, well-known journalist of the influential *Le Journal*, who said the army should never have gotten involved in such a ludicrous affair. Keller should never have even shown the letter to his superiors; instead, he should have gone with a fellow cadet to find Sadoul and Caupenne and challenged them to a fight, thus settling the matter once and for all.[43] It was a sign of the growing conservatism of the country that such a silly prank could result in a prison sentence of three months.

L'Age d'or and the *Ligue des patriotes*

More serious was the controversy that raged around a Surrealist film, *L'Age d'or* (Golden Age), that produced a violent reaction from the extreme Right in France. Because of the tremendous political tensions in the 1930s, the Surrealists' vehement anticlericalism and anti-patriotism got a lot of bad publicity. They could now have the satisfaction of knowing that they were no longer considered harmlessly eccentric, but had gone far toward achieving the status of enemies of the state in the opinion of many.

Produced by Salvador Dali and Luis Buñuel, *L'Age d'or* was at once violent, erotic, savage, and funny, and today it is regarded as a masterpiece of early film making. In one scene, "one sees thrown out the window in quick succession a coffin in flames, an enormous agricultural machine, an archbishop, a giraffe and some feathers. . . . One also sees . . . a blind man mistreated, a dog killed, a son almost murdered gratuitously by his father and an old woman slapped."[44] It is easy to see why the film provoked the wrath of reactionary elements in France since its biting wit mocked the traditional values of the Church, respect for the dead, the sanctity of the family, and compassion for the aged and infirm.

    L'Age d'or was first shown at Studio 28, in Paris, on December 3, 1930, but the screening was interrupted by members of the fascistic, paramilitary *Ligue des patriotes,* who invaded the theater, threw ink at the screen, and shouted "death to the Jews!" They threw smoke bombs, stink bombs, attacked the audience, and slashed an exhibit of Surrealist paintings to ribbons (some were stolen intact, however, presumably with the profit motive in mind). They also destroyed the theater and all its equipment. In addition, the *Ligue des patriotes* issued a public protest against the "immorality of this Bolshevist spectacle," and the response of the official censor was to order the deletion of parts of the film such as the irreverent scene that depicted the corpses of three bishops. On December 10, de Launay, the Provost of Paris, wrote an open letter denouncing the film, the Surrealist journal, and protesting against "films of German [*sic*] origin or importation which are shown in the Champs Elysées quarter, a stone's throw from the Unknown Soldier." The premises of the Surrealist journal were sacked by persons unknown, and the *Ligue des patriotes* gave a vote of thanks to the Provost for his stand and congratulated all those who were "arrested in the course of their admirable demonstration against this Bolshevist film."[45] The censor then announced that the entire film was banned, and legal proceedings were begun against the owners of the theater.

    Press reaction was vicious. *Figaro* called for the suppression of Surrealism and praised the banning of the film.[46] The reactionary *Ami du peuple* had a super-patriotic slur on the nationality of the directors: Dali and Buñuel were the "refuse of their countries of origin, protected by their newly acquired French nationality." [47] The frankly anti-Semitic papers fulminated against "Jewish Bolsheviks," and praised the strong-arm tactics used against "these gentlemen of the synagogue," apparently undeterred by the fact that the creators of the film were Spanish Catholic in origin. The Surrealists issued a pamphlet, *L'Affaire de l'age d'or,* describing the whole incident and expressing their horror at the injustice of such censorship. They also voiced their suspicion that the affair was more than simply an abuse of power by the police. They feared that it reflected the growing menace of fascism which, sooner or later, would plunge Europe into another war.

> Is not the use of provocation to legitimize an intervention by the police a sign of fascistization? This intervention is being made under the pretext of protecting childhood, youth, the family, the country and religion. Could one possibly claim that this obvious fascistization does not have as its goal the destruction of all those forces against the coming war? And especially the war against the USSR?[48]

One amusing footnote was that Charles and Marie de Noaïlles, aristocratic art patrons who had financed the film, were subjected to ecclesiastical hearings under threat of excommunication and the count was asked to resign from his club. Another result of greater significance was that Surrealism was actually defended in the pages of *L'Humanité,* a highly unusual event. *"L'Age d'or* is not a film for the proletariat, but one may affirm that—if I dare to say so—it serves the revolutionary purposes of the working class," was the first comment.[49] The following week, after the attacks by the right-wing press and the banning of the film, the report was even more favorable.

> What we must take notice of here is that an exhibition of Surrealist paintings and objects on the walls of Studio 28 was sacked; the canvases of Max Ernst and of Salvador Dali being particularly lacerated and furiously torn to pieces. One could consequently ask if the censors and the police will not soon set themselves to attacking works of plastic art, elsewhere regarded as quite inoffensive in their gold frames, judged to be too revolutionary and pernicious.

The same article singled out the art of Dali for particular praise, which was ironic considering the Party's later attitude toward him and the fact that he was the most politically unorthodox of the group. It said that Dali's work is "extremely touching and troubling," and that it "illuminates the conflict between human conscience and society emphasizing the attitude of revolt that must result from this in our bourgeois society."[50] Because of the *L'Age d'or* affair, the Surrealists gained, for once, the favorable notice of the French Communist Party and they hoped that at last, an era of good will and mutual trust was developing.

They also continued to issue manifestoes and pamphlets against colonialism and war and in 1931, three important ones appeared, signed by all the Surrealists, but noting that the signatures of foreign Surrealists would not be published for their own protection. *Ne Visitez pas l'exposition coloniale* called for a boycott of the Colonial Exhibition that opened in May 1931, and protested "the idea of colonialist banditry." It declared that Lenin was the first to understand that the colonial peoples were the natural allies of the proletariat, and that the whole exhibition was designed merely to serve the purposes of the bourgeoisie.

> The presence on the inaugural stage of the Colonial Exhibition of the President of the Republic, the Emperor of Annam, the Cardinal Archbishop of Paris, of several governors and old soldiers, opposite the missionaries' pavilion, and those of Citröen and Renault, clearly expresses the complicity of the entire bourgeoisie in the birth of a new and particularly intolerable concept: "La Grande France." It is a question of giving to the citizens of metropolitan France the feeling of being proprietors which is needed so they can hear the distant sounds of gunfire without flinching. It is a question of annexing a view of minarets and pagodas to the fine scenery of the French countryside.[51]

A second anti-colonialist pamphlet appeared that year, *Premier bilan de l'exposition coloniale,* when the Dutch East Indies pavilion was destroyed by fire. It suggested the fire might have been deliberately set and declared that the destruction of priceless primitive art which resulted from it was also indirectly a result of imperialism. "Thus is the work of colonization completed, which began by massacres, and was continued by forced conversions, slave labor and diseases."[52] The third tract celebrated the founding of the Spanish Republic and especially applauded the widespread anticlerical feeling in Spain that had produced a wave of church burnings.

One Church still standing, one priest who can still officiate, are so many dangers to the future of the Revolution. To destroy religion by every means, to efface the last trace of those monuments to shadows before which men groveled, . . . to disperse the filthy priests and persecute them in their last hiding places, that is what the people of Madrid, Seville, Alicanti, etc., [sic] themselves have accomplished in their direct comprehension of revolutionary necessities.[53]

It is clear from these tracts, and from the many articles on these subjects in their journal, that the anti-colonial, anti-war, and anti-religious sentiments of the Surrealists had grown stronger since the first manifesto against the Riff war in 1925, reinforced by the principles of Marxism to which the Surrealists adhered. It appeared that the "new direction" begun after the initial failure of the Trotsky meeting, with the commencement of the new periodical, *Le Surréalisme au service de la révolution,* was highly successful. It brought new recruits to the movement, and the *L'Age d'or* incident initiated a brief period of tranquility between the Surrealists and the Communist Party.

6
L'Affaire Aragon and Proletarian Literature

On my return from Russia, I was no longer the same man, no longer the author of *Paysan de Paris,* but of *Front rouge.* Yet, there still remained a thousand ties to be broken and that cost me dear. If I had the strength for it, it was, I know, thanks to the practical work, the political work in which the proletariat of my country involved me. I had to break with these men who always had the word "revolution" on their lips yet, for whom there were things more precious than the Revolution itself.

— Louis Aragon, *Pour un réalisme socialiste*

The Kharkov Congress

The early 1930s were a time of expansion for the Communist Party in France. One reason was the great Depression but the other, especially important for intellectuals, was the growing fear of fascism and it seemed that the Surrealists' position was more secure, in spite of the continuing disapproval of certain Communist officials. The Party had at last come to terms with them and recognized their usefulness, or so it appeared. Among other things, it had assigned them tasks for which they were well suited, such as putting them in charge of artistic arrangements for various Party functions. But as a result of the incident known as *L'Affaire Aragon,* the inevitable ideological conflicts came to a head and

97

eventually, they were forced out of the Party and out of all the left-wing cultural groups it sponsored.

The *Affaire* comprised a series of events that led Aragon, Breton's oldest and closest friend, to break with Surrealism and become a Communist Party militant. After 1932, it became impossible for him to continue to be a Surrealist in an uneasy alliance with the Party and this became clear after his trip to the Soviet Union. A great deal of pressure was brought to bear and it was necessary to make a choice. Influenced by his future wife, the Russian-born writer, Elsa Triolet, he chose to abandon Surrealism completely to fight for the Revolution under the banner of socialist realism. His "conversion" began in the fall of 1930, when he and Triolet decided to go to Russia, accompanied by Sadoul, who was anxious to leave France to avoid serving his prison sentence. According to Aragon he was simply a casual tourist, taking a trip of no importance,[1] yet the visit had obvious political implications. In the Soviet Union, he was introduced to Russian literary circles by Triolet and she used her influence to get him invited to the *Second International Congress of Revolutionary Writers* being held in Kharkov in November 1930. The Surrealists were delighted to hear of this and they hoped that the fact that Aragon was to attend the Congress meant that good relations could be established with the International. This could do much to counteract the distrust with which French Communist leaders still regarded them, especially Barbusse who was by now their implacable enemy.[2] In fact, for a time, the International did appear to be much more favorably disposed toward Surrealism than the French Party.

The French Communists had once more begun voicing their strong disapproval of the movement. Critical notices again appeared in *L'Humanité* which had briefly, during the furor over *L'Age d'or,* given the Surrealists a favorable press. One such article was especially scathing: "Irrefutable evidence of decadence: the Surrealists are tangled up in their own contradictions. One cannot remain a *littérateur,* when one denounces literature; and one does not become a revolutionary while living cut off from the revolutionary class."[3] Three days later, as a consequence of this attack, Thirion, secretary of the Plaisance cell, resigned in protest. The reason he gave was that such articles indicated the existence of an unfair campaign to drive the Surrealists out of the Party. He described a meeting called the previous day to review the membership status of Sadoul and Aragon during their absence in Russia. This meeting "was carried on in an atmosphere of hostility created by some of the comrades who, no doubt, were not acting on their own initiative and who were actually trying to get the Surrealists expelled. . . . It is painful," he concluded, "that the private interests of an intellectual saboteur like Barbusse are allowed to cause such a turmoil as to bring about my own resignation after five years of serving the Party."[4]

For the past year the Surrealists had been very active in the Party. They had organized its tenth anniversary exhibition and, during Aragon's absence in the Soviet Union, they were involved in creating a revolutionary organization for writers and artists. It was to be called the *Association des artistes et des écrivains révolutionnaires* (Revolutionary Artists and Writers Association), and the plan apparently had the approval of several members of the International. Thirion and Breton had drawn up a constitution in which they emphasized the artist's economic relationship to society in such a way as to reveal his affinity with the proletariat. They hoped to create an artists' union which would merge with the Communist trade unions.

> The artist, who by definition cannot submit today to the ideology of the ruling class, is barely tolerated by that class, and his means of survival in the capitalist regime are the most precarious. He does not control the markets, which are almost exclusively in the hands of the *haute bourgeoisie*. It would do the painter no good to enter into competition with the art dealers, who are united in trusts and cartels. But in this transitional period, the proletariat cannot be reckoned as a buyer. Unless he organizes, the artist has no chance whatsoever of improving his economic situation, a situation as bad as, if not worse than, the proletariat's. His only means of safeguarding the independence of his work is to struggle side by side with the exploited workers against capitalist society. His guide in the struggle can only be the organization of the conscious proletariat: the Communist Party. For the artist, it is crucial that he create his own trade union so as to make sure that the destiny of the revolutionary proletariat is linked to his own.[5]

Plans had progressed very far because Eluard even had a membership card dated November 1930 on which he had written "an attempt that failed." They desisted only because Aragon wrote them that the *International Union of Revolutionary Writers,* being founded at Kharkov, intended to create a similar organization. It was necessary, therefore, to leave the initiative to the International and the following year, the *A.E.A.R.,* or the *Association des écrivains et des artistes révolutionnaires,* came into existence. While virtually identical to the one the Surrealists were planning, even to using almost the same name, they were not allowed to join it for almost a year.

At the Congress, Aragon was charged with securing a favorable resolution on Surrealism and also with working to discredit Barbusse and his weekly paper, *Monde.* At first, he sent encouraging letters describing his favorable reception. "I've been officially appointed to represent France at the *International Bureau of Revolutionary Literature,"* he was pleased to report. In another, he told them that the second issue of *Le Surréalisme au service de la révolution,* which had just been sent to the Congress, had been well received, even though it contained two articles critical of *L'Humanité.*[6] The first of these was an attack on Brice Parain, who had worked for a detective magazine, and had just been made a literary editor of *L'Humanité.* The Surrealists had printed a photograph of a man with his face buried in a copy of detective stories and the caption read "a singular evolution! M. Parain, formerly editor of *Détective,* is now in charge of the literary column of *L'Humanité!"* The other was a letter from a worker criticizing the paper for an article on a church fire. The article had said, luckily the fire was put out and the church building was saved, but the worker argued that a good Communist ought to be glad whenever a church burns to the ground.[7] The Surrealists had reprinted this letter as an example of the ideological errors of *L'Humanité;* the comment on Brice Parain was made to indicate their low opinion of its literary level and it appeared from Aragon's first reports that this view was actually accepted by the International.

Aragon played a very important role at Kharkov, even though according to him, he was not even a delegate, but only an observer. However, he was listed as one of the two official delegates from France; Barbusse was the other. The objectives of the Congress were to create an international group of Communist writers who would keep in close contact with each other in order to maintain true revolutionary principles in their work. Their duties were to address themselves directly to the masses, to support revolutionary movements and colonial revolts, and to encourage the development of new writers from the working class. To achieve this, the Congress founded the *International Union of Revolutionary Writers* and made Aragon a member of its Board. The *Union* then began publishing a new journal, *Literature of the World Revolution*.

But most important were the resolutions of the Congress on proletarian literature. To the question of whether it is possible to have proletarian literature in a capitalist state, the answer was yes, although it was conceded that only after the proletariat comes to power will it attain cultural supremacy.[8] To the question of whether middle class writers could hope to produce true proletarian literature, the answer was usually not. "The proletarian literature movement may include writers coming from other classes, but only such as have broken all relations with those classes. . . . However, the fundamental and principal cadres of proletarian literature must be drawn from the working class."[9] Developing working-class writers had, in fact, been a project of *L'Humanité* which had sponsored story writing contests but, thus far, it was a rather dismal failure. Nevertheless, the principal danger to guard against was the "rightist" menace of those who did not believe in the possibility of proletarian literature until after the revolution, and of those who persisted in underestimating the important role of the *rabcors,* or worker-correspondents.[10] These were workers with a literary bent who were to be encouraged to become writers simply because they may have once or twice written a letter to the editor. Those who aspired to be proletarian writers had to understand that "only dialectical materialism can be the creative method of proletarian literature. . . . The proletarian and revolutionary writers of the world look upon their art as a special form of revolutionary activity in the class struggle of the proletariat."[11]

Another resolution rather off-handedly rejected the entire cultural past because it had been the creation of the bourgeoisie. "Proletarian literature discovers new forms in contradistinction to the old literary traditions and in harmony with the class interest of the proletariat. It casts aside the old *genres* and creates new ones," and proletarian writers are "first and foremost revolutionary fighters." Little was said at this Congress about literary style, although the idea of socialist realism was clearly implied. Most important were those novels "in which the proletarian writer engages in revolutionary criticism of the bourgeoisie, or else exposes the petit bourgeois prejudices yet to be found in the working class." Also commendable were short forms such as sketches on current events and poetry with a political theme. "Proletarian literature is nothing more than a weapon in the class struggle," this resolution triumphantly concluded, thereby reducing the role of literature to propaganda.[12] Even Roger Garaudy, an important Marxist theoretician in the French Communist Party until 1970, conceded that the Kharkov Congress took an extreme left stance. "This negative position, in regard to bourgeois literature in its entirety, led to a complete rejection of the whole cultural heritage and made it impossible for professional writers to write. This 'gauchisme' of the *RAPP* (Russian Association of Proletarian Writers) dominated the conference."[13] Indeed, the *RAPP* was dissolved a year later because its extremist attitudes were contrary to the spirit of the new united front policies that began with the Amsterdam Peace movement.

One would assume that a Congress that passed such resolutions would have severely denounced Surrealism, but this was not the case. At first, it was far more critical of Barbusse and *Monde* than of the Surrealists: "one must guard against opportunism, the clearest example of which is *Monde*. . . . The agents of Trotskyism have been contributing to this journal."[14] "Barbusse, in his creative activity [is] a writer who has not fully transcended his petit bourgeois limitations"[15] and, worse, as editor of *Monde,* he had been allowing social democrats and even fascists to appear in its pages.[16] The resolution on *Monde,* which Aragon helped to write, declared that it "at once took up a false anti-Marxian viewpoint of 'above class' objectivism," that made it a "petit bourgeois journal which was in reality reactionary and hostile to the revolutionary proletariat. . . . Comrade Barbusse, without realizing it, became an instrument of the bourgeoisie."[17] Individual delegates were even more harsh. One declared that he "is a seeker of God, trying to reconcile revolution with religion, and I fear that Comrade Barbusse will never become a real Communist revolutionary writer."[18] His editorial views were also called clear examples of "right-wing deviation in the realm of literary policy, with which our organization must wage a ceaseless struggle."[19] By the tone of these pronouncements, it would seem that Aragon had managed to make the Surrealist position on Barbusse prevail. Because of his worldwide fame, however, Barbusse was simply too valuable a recruit to lose, and in the end he was appointed chief editor of

Literature of the World Revolution, and he remained an ornament of the French Party.[20]

The Surrealists, whatever their reputation in the French Party, were clearly considered important in international Communist circles. They, too, were the subject of much discussion and a resolution by the Congress that was critical, but without animosity. In fact, it expressed a certain guarded optimism about their revolutionary potential. Coming as it did, from serious professional Communists, it was a most interesting document.

> Surealism [*sic.*] This tendency is the reaction of the younger generation of highly qualified petit bourgeois intellectuals to the contradictions of the third stage in the development of capitalism. Not having been able at first to make a profound Marxist analysis of this period of cultural reaction against which they revolted, the Surealists sought an escape in the creation of their own peculiar literary method. The first attempts to fight against bourgeois individualism by this creative method, while not departing from idealism in substance, facilitated the passage of several members of the group to a Communist ideology. This ideology has been reflected, though not very clearly, in a number of political declarations made by the Surealists. In this group, the general intensification of the class struggle expressed itself in the expulsion of certain elements which had been gravitating towards the bourgeoisie.
>
> The reactionary character of this "internal opposition" became manifest when, after the split, the oppositionists passed into the camp of the bourgeoisie, while the fundamental nucleus, retaining the name "Surealists" continued gropingly and falteringly to evolve in the direction of Communism.
>
> This process encourages the hope that the better part of the present group of surealists, continuing its evolution towards dialectical materialism, reconsidering its theory of "the decomposition of the bourgeoisie by intensifying its internal contradictions," and correcting the flagrant errors contained in its "Second Manifesto of Super-Realism" [*sic,*] will finally find its way to the real proletarian ideology.[21]

Individual delegates, however, were much more judgmental than was the official resolution. One *RAPP* writer objected vigorously to them on the grounds that they were linked with the most decadent and reactionary elements in art. Another doubted that the Surrealists had any connection with the working class, "what practical work are they carrying out," he demanded to know, "for the organization of revolutionary literature and the proletarian movement?" Writers, he added, should do more than keep in close contact with the worker, they should be members of his party, his revolutionary organizations, and his trade unions.[22]

Aragon, who made a number of speeches, rather half-heartedly defended his friends "We are not here as Surrealists but as Communists," he said, and added that those who think the movement is linked with reactionary elements must understand that conditions in France are very different because of the strength of the bourgeoisie. He was careful to say that the Surrealists do not claim to be proletarian writers but, he insisted, "we are supporters of every literary form having a truly proletarian class-content. In the first place, we are for the development of propaganda literature . . . everything from the pamphlet to the revolutionary poem."[23] We also favor "carrying out propaganda in harmony with the line of the Third International," and revolutionary literature "cannot have any other purpose than systematic preparation for the speedy establishment of the proletarian dictatorship."[24] He then declared, in the name of the Surrealists, that the only basis for the creation of proletarian literature was the systematic development, along the lines laid down by the International, of the *rabcors*.[25] This assertion was so extreme that, not only were the Surrealists stunned when they learned of it, it did not even win approval at Kharkov. "To declare that the worker-correspondent movement constitutes the *only* source of proletarian literature is to formulate an assertion which is extremely leftist," admonished a delegate from the International.[26] Aragon, of course, had no authority to make such assertions in the name of the Surrealists. He had not only exceeded his mandate, he had placed himself squarely in the hands of their enemies who, if the Kharkov theses were to be taken literally, had acquired ample ammunition to destroy them. "What ideological rubbish did he think he was pulling off at Kharkov?" was their furious comment.[27]

Barbusse had the final word in his message to the Congress and it was his opinion of the movement that was ultimately accepted. "Too often, over-refined intellectuals try to push their way into the pure movements of our revolutionary literature, bringing with them all the unhealthy complications of decadent virtuosity and giving their own meanings to the word 'revolution,' as in the case of the Surrealists."[28] In spite of the crushing judgments of *Monde* and the long list of Barbusse's faults, in the end, he was appointed head of *Literature of the World Revolution*. This sudden reversal took place because his prestige was needed for the peace congresses that were being planned. According to Thirion, they should have seen what was coming because of the sudden coolness of the representative from the International. But "our two friends weren't politically experienced enough to gauge the influence of Barbusse's defenders in the Comintern and the Soviet leadership. Barbusse and Rolland were a source of pacifist propaganda, which the "politicals" valued more highly than the ideological content of *Monde* and the anger of the Surrealists." Their enemies in the French Party also exerted their influence even to the point of refusing to give Thirion permission to attend the Congress, he added.[29]

In December 1930, just before leaving the Soviet Union, Aragon and Sadoul signed their names to an astonishing document that was published by the *International Union of Revolutionary Writers*. Judging by the purely internal evidence of its bureaucratic style and use of terminology, one must doubt that Aragon and Sadoul actually wrote it. It repented of numerous Surrealist sins and, as Pierre Daix said, "it was almost certainly written by a French hand, using French information, that is, the results of an exchange of views on the issue between the French Party and the Soviets."[30] In it, Aragon apologized for his condemnation of Barbusse, and Sadoul apologized for his "ideologically unsound" letter to the Saint-Cyr student. They also said they regretted that *Le Surréalisme au service de la révolution* had printed the two items previously mentioned that mocked *L'Humanité,* and they promised to make no more derogatory comments in public about the Party press. But the apology went even further.

> We must make clear that we do not support all of the individual works . . . published by members of the Surrealist group. However, insofar as these works bear the name "Surrealism" and "Surrealist" we are responsible, especially for the *Second Manifesto of Surrealism* by André Breton insofar as it contradicts dialectical materialism. We wish to make clear that we believe strictly in dialectical materialism and repudiate all

idealist ideologies, notably Freudianism. We also denounce Trotskyism as a social-democratic and counterrevolutionary ideology, and we are committed to combatting Trotyskyism at every opportunity. Our only desire is to work in the most efficacious manner following the directives of the party to whose discipline and control we submit our literary activity.[31]

Breton was astounded to learn that Aragon had signed such a statement which was nothing less than a repudiation of Surrealism, and later Aragon insisted that he and Sadoul had only done so under duress. It would appear that Aragon was vacillating and easily influenced and that he required the presence of a dominating, forceful personality to give direction to his life. This need was filled first by Breton, then by Triolet, and finally by the discipline imposed by the Communist Party. His peculiar upbringing could certainly have accounted for this aspect of his character because he was an illegitimate child raised to believe that his grandmother was his mother and that his mother was his older sister. Only after he grew up did he learn the truth about his parentage. Triolet is either praised or blamed, depending on one's point of view, for persuading Aragon to abandon Surrealism, but it is generally believed that she was responsible. Her convictions about literature and politics had been learned from the Russian Futurists and, although at first she admired the Surrealists because they too, professed to be revolutionaries, she soon realized that their art, with its emphasis on fantasy and its flagrant eroticism, was unacceptable to the Party. She knew of the bitter campaign waged against Mayakovsky in the Soviet Union and since similar attacks were being made against the Surrealists, she feared that they, too, would become completely isolated. She also disliked them personally and thought that she and Aragon ought to work directly with the Communists, even though she herself was not a Party member.[32]

Once back in Paris and confronted with the anger of the Surrealists, Aragon again reversed himself. He and Sadoul issued a manifesto, *Aux Intellectuels révolutionnaires,* which was both an apology to the Surrealists and a defense of their revolutionary character.

Surrealism implies the adherence, totally and without reservations, to the principle of dialectical materialism; its goals are those of the proletariat. . . . In the hands of the Surrealists, the psychoanalytic method is a weapon against the bourgeoisie . . . and it has helped them avoid an individualist position. . . . Also, none of them has the slightest connection with Trotskyism and it is insulting . . . to interpret certain phrases of André Breton to mean that he has ever taken the part of Trotsky against the International.[33]

Aragon would seem to have completely vindicated himself here but the Surrealists apparently thought the statement was inadequate and quite ambiguous.[34] In an article for *Le Surréalisme au service de la révolution,* he enlarged upon his apology and hinted at pressures being put on him revealing that since his trip to Russia, "I have been urged over and over again to break with you." But he vowed his continued fidelity to the movement which, he said, had betrayed its class of origin to throw in its lot with the proletariat and as proof of their revolutionary convictions, he cited the many persecutions the Surrealists suffered. Sadoul had been sentenced to three months in prison, Eluard was not permitted to leave France, censorship was imposed upon Dali and Buñuel, and many publishers refused to print or distribute Surrealist books.[35] In addition, Alexandre was dismissed from his teaching post because of his revolutionary opinions.[36] Yet, one does sense his feelings of frustration because of the Surrealists' difficult relations with the Communist Party. At this time, Dali displayed an amusing new "Surrealist object," a smoking jacket hung with glasses of milk, but to the consternation of all, Aragon reacted with anger at the waste of milk needed by hungry children.[37] He was no longer amused by their jokes and clearly wished they would stop acting like Surrealists and start behaving like Communists.

Front Rouge: **Arrest and Defection**

Aragon's transformation from Surrealist poet to militant Communist writer was marked by the appearance of *Front rouge* in *Literature of the World Revolution,* although at the time of its publication he still considered himself a Surrealist. "This poem is his first genuine revolutionary work," said the Introduction,[38] but it was really less poetry than propaganda and even Garaudy, Aragon's Communist Party biographer, admitted it was not a good poem.[39] Its tone was shrill and savage, as these verses show:

Feu sur Léon Blum
Feu sur Boncour Froissard Déat
Feu sur les ours savants de la social-démocratie
. . . .
Gloire à la dialectique matérialiste
et gloire à son incarnation
l'armée
Rouge.[40]

(Shoot Léon Blum
Shoot Boncour Froissard Déat
Shoot the trained bears of social democracy
. . . .
Glory to dialectical materialism
and glory to its incarnation
the Red
Army)

After the review had been on sale for several months, the French police suddenly seized the remaining copies and in January 1932, Aragon was indicted on two charges. One was incitement to murder, the second was provoking insubordination in the army and if convicted, the penalty could be five years in prison.[41]

Horrified, the Surrealists immediately launched a petition in his defense called *L'Affaire Aragon* in which they asked intellectuals to sign whether or not they agreed with the politics of the poem. It was vitally important to protest, they explained, because the indictment of a poet for his verses was a repressive measure completely without precedent in France. "Is lyric poetry . . . suddenly to find itself the object of persecutions reserved until now to those forms which constitute *exact* expressions of thought? . . . We protest against any attempt to give legal significance to a poetic work and we demand the immediate withdrawal of the charge."[42] The petition ended by expressing solidarity with the revolutionary sentiments of *Front rouge* and by a pledge to go on working for the proletarian revolution. Sixty thousand members of *Secours rouge international* signed, as did about three hundred of the most famous artists and writers in Europe, among whom were Braque, Picasso, Honegger, Matisse, Brecht, Thomas Mann, Le Corbusier, and García Lorca.[43] There were also two petitions for Aragon by the Belgian Surrealists denouncing the hypocrisy of a bourgeois state which proclaims freedom of speech but relies on police repression and these brought approximately sixty more signatures.[44]

The reactions of some of those who did not sign were also reported. Many refused because to sign would be indirectly to support the Soviet Union. Others, like Rolland, thought it was important "for the honor of Surrealism" for Aragon to face trial because "we are fighters; our writings are our weapons, and we are responsible for our arms just as are the workers for theirs." This argument was undeniably logical, and Breton did not succeed in disposing of it except to say that one must fight repression in any form. Gide's reasons for not signing sounded less than sincere. Presumably, because he had encouraged the Surrealist movement in its early days and knew Aragon personally, he felt obliged to explain himself at great length. He said he did not want to precipitate more serious action against Aragon, he thought the proceedings might be dropped and pressure might make the government more intransigent, but he ended on a completely different note. "Why demand impunity for literature? . . . You don't protest when a worker is jailed for passing out anti-militarist tracts."[45] This was unjust since they frequently did protest such incidents and, to their dismay, *L'Humanité* was equally unsympathetic to Aragon's plight and took the same line as Gide:

> We vigorously denounce the utilization of this *affaire* by the Surrealists for their own ends. Far from combatting bourgeois repression, the Surrealists only protest against repression when it is being exercised against a lyric poem. They demand political immunity for poets and for poets alone. . . . We don't accept the position of these pretentious intellectuals who don't budge when repression strikes the workers, but who move heaven and earth when it touches their precious person. . . . Instead of defending the content of the poem, they beat a hasty retreat all along their "red front."[46]

The Surrealists, however, did have some defenders in the Communist Party, to judge from a letter signed unanimously by the members of the cell to which Aragon had belonged, and addressed to *L'Humanité*.

> Cell 638 having taken note of "L'Inculpation d'Aragon," protests indignantly against the unfair content of this article. We too are familiar with the petition, *L'Affaire Aragon,* which we support, especially the final declaration where the Surrealists pledge to work for the proletarian revolution with all their

> forces. . . . We also remember having read in *L'Humanité* the
> signatures of the Surrealist writers on an appeal for the life of
> our Comrade Ruegg. . . .[47] We therefore consider that this
> article in *L'Humanité* is absolutely contrary to the facts and
> that it expresses an extremely sectarian viewpoint in regard to
> intellectuals defending one of their number, which is dan-
> gerous to the very life of our Party.[48]

The issue was even raised in the Chamber of Deputies by Aragon's
lawyer, the Communist deputy André Berthon, and he reported
to Aragon that because of all the bad publicity, he doubted the
government would actually dare to bring the case to trial.[49] Meanwhile, embarrassed because of the Party's attitude toward all the
attention the case was receiving, Aragon wrote to those who
signed the petition that his friends, the Surrealists, had been misin-
formed. He probably would not be tried, and he begged them not
to concern themselves further over such an "unimportant personal
affair."[50] The case was just one example of the increasingly repressive measures the French government took against Communists in the late 1920s and early 1930s. In 1929, all Communist
street demonstrations were banned, Vaillant-Couturier was
charged with sedition and, a year later, some of the Party leadership were arrested. Many of the rank and file were fired from
their jobs and the offices of *L'Humanité* were frequently ran-
sacked.[51] Eventually, the government was persuaded to drop the
charges against Aragon, but only because it had become a *cause
célèbre* with international repercussions.

Aragon still thought of himself as a Surrealist, at least as late
as January 1932, because he defended the movement when it was
again attacked by *L'Humanité* as "the extreme of individualism,
interested only in pure experimentation, and art for art's sake."[52]
He retorted that, on the contrary, "Surrealism was a violent reaction *against* the art for art's sake theory. Furthermore, it is not
individualistic since it takes part in social struggles . . . and its
evolution has led it into active participation in the class struggle
under the direction of the Communist Party." But *L'Humanité*
dismissed his arguments and simply reiterated its position: "We
appreciate the efforts already made by the Surrealists but these
efforts are not complete, not with regard to membership in the
Party *which we do not insist upon,* but with regard to an activity
which must correspond exactly to revolutionary goals, and make
of artists and writers fellow travelers of the proletariat."[53]

With these articles and the one denouncing the Surrealists for their petition in defense of Aragon, it must have become clear that the Party was not going to change its attitude. Yet, Aragon was still not ready to make a definitive break. Alexandre recalled that he, Aragon, Sadoul and Unik, were summoned to headquarters later that year and told they must repudiate Dali because of his pornographic contribution to the latest issue of *Le Surréalisme au service de la révolution*. Entitled "Rêverie," it described his fantasies as he masturbated in front of a little girl in disturbingly graphic detail and it must have been shocking to the Party official who said disgustedly, "you stink of bourgeois rottenness!"[54] The four were threatened with expulsion if they did not break with Dali but they indignantly refused, Aragon more vehemently than the others. According to Alexandre, Aragon actually intended to send a telegram of protest to Stalin himself but was persuaded to be content with sending one to the *International Union of Revolutionary Writers*.[55] The same official, no doubt genuinely troubled, had also complained that, "you are only trying to complicate the simple and healthy relations between men and women." Breton, when he heard of this remark retorted, "who dares to maintain that in bourgeois society these relations are simple and healthy?"[56] There was never to be a meeting of the minds on this question, and Dali's work continued to appear in the Surrealist review.

Breton stoutly defended the Surrealists' part in the *Affaire Aragon,* especially against the criticisms of *L'Humanité*. In a long pamphlet, *Misère de la poésie: "L'Affaire Aragon" devant l'opinion publique,* he summarized their position. He argued, as he had in the petition, that a poem ought not to be subject to legal penalties because the poet was not responsible for his creation, he was merely an *appareil enregistreur* (copying machine) for his unconscious, as he had phrased it in the *First Manifesto*.[57] He did concede, however, that Aragon's poem was not an example of Surrealist automatic writing; on the contrary, it was "poetically regressive" in form. It was a *poème de circonstance,* an occasional poem, a *genre* the Surrealists held in contempt. But, even a poetic text like *Front rouge* must not be taken literally, for how could a line like "shoot the trained bears of social democracy" be construed as a literal provocation to murder? Yet, the Surrealists always maintained that poetry is revolution, a weapon in the struggle for the total liberation of man. This inconsistency cannot have escaped Breton's logical mind and perhaps it was simply that the need to defend a friend overrode all other considerations. It was true that Aragon's indictment was without precedent and for that reason had to be fought, and also, as Breton concluded, "we are *professionally* charged with defending poetic liberty, the necessary condition for the existence of all poetry."

As for the accusations made by *L'Humanité,* Breton simply said that he should not have had to point out that they have always opposed all forms of repression, not just the persecution of poets.[58] He also complained that, in spite of the resolution of Kharkov which had described the Surrealists as a significant revolutionary group, they had been denied membership in the *A.E.A.R.,* which had just been organized.[59] It was obvious to him that they were victims of Party intrigues and that certain people were trying to discredit them by maligning their works as pornographic and therefore counter-revolutionary. He described the Dali incident and emphatically demanded an end to this sort of treatment, adding that the Party's demand that they expel Dali was as reprehensible as the government's threat to prosecute Aragon.[60]

Aragon did not oppose the sentiments expressed in *Misère* and, according to Breton, he would have agreed to its publication except that he wanted no mention of the Dali affair because it was wrong to air conflicts with the Party in public. But Breton would not hear of this. Aside from the fact that uninhibited sexuality was a vital part of Surrealist thought, Dali had to be publicly defended even, if necessary, against the Party and he refused to delete the incident. Aragon remembered it differently, according to Daix. In his version, Breton had agreed to remove the references to Dali because he did not want to cause Aragon trouble with the Party. But when Aragon saw the pamphlet, with nothing deleted, he felt he had been horribly deceived. But, as Daix said, even if this particular misunderstanding had somehow been resolved, there was still no way for Aragon to avoid making the choice between the Party and Breton.[61]

One way or another, it was this issue that brought about the final rupture and, after *Misère de la poésie: "L'Affaire Aragon" devant l'opinion publique* appeared, the Surrealists never heard from Aragon again. He did not even see fit to communicate his decision personally to his former friends and they only learned of it in the pages of *L'Humanité.*

Our Comrade, Aragon, has informed us that he has absolutely no connection with the appearance of a brochure entitled *Misère de la poésie: "L'Affaire Aragon" devant l'opinion publique.* . . . He wishes to state clearly that he disapproves in its entirety of the contents of this brochure and the commotion it has caused in his name must be condemned by any Communist as incompatible with the class struggle. Therefore, the attacks contained in this brochure are objectively counterrevolutionary.[62]

With this terse pronouncement a friendship, begun in the early days of Dada, came abruptly to an end.

Surrealists, Communists and the Problems of Proletarian Literature

The Surrealists collectively produced a pamphlet, *Paillasse! (Fin de "L'Affaire Aragon")* [*Clown! (End of the "Aragon Affair")*], that accused him of the most wretched acts of betrayal. They noted that by breaking with them, he had been permitted, unlike them, to join the *A.E.A.R.* and had been given a privileged position working for *Commune,* its cultural journal. We have "finally unmasked the real motives for his continual *volte-face,* his endless evasions and procrastinations," they announced.[63] *Paillasse* detailed Aragon's byzantine maneuvers from the Congress of Kharkov where he was supposed to have spoken for them all, through all his changes of heart, to the final notice in *L'Humanité.* But what they considered most reprehensible was that he should have allowed them to defend him against legal charges only to reject them a short time later. Eluard, who had been very close to him, wrote his own angry leaflet, *Certificat.* He accused Aragon of monstrous hypocrisy and dishonesty and ended with a favorite quotation from Lautréamont: "all the water in the ocean is not enough to wash away an intellectual bloodstain."[64]

Breton, stung by Aragon's treachery, immediately demanded that the group, gathered as usual at the Café Cyrano, sign a text he had prepared committing them all to accept no other discipline but that of Surrealism. Alexandre and Unik refused because "even the Communist Party had never demanded quite that much," but Breton sternly retorted, "in that case, your place is no longer among us." Unik and Alexandre, although still Party members, continued for a time to be involved with the Surrealists. Their articles still appeared in *Le Surréalisme au service de la révolution* but they also published in *Commune,* the organ of the *A.E.A.R.,* which Aragon now edited. The two, assuming that they were in the best position to see both sides of the question, wrote a pamphlet, *Autour d'un poème:* "Why? An attempt at reconciliation? No, we had no such illusions. But we hoped very much it would be a synthesis," said Alexandre.[65]

They declared their faith in "the sincerity of the Communist convictions of Breton" in spite of the purely personal and vindictive tone of *Paillasse* and *Misère.* As for Aragon, they simply regretted that he, furthest along the road to Communism, had seen fit to break with Surrealism rather than help its evolution toward Marxism. *Autour d'un poème* was also intended as an answer to the manifesto against the Surrealists launched by the *A.E.A.R.:* "The resolution of Kharkov which rightly condemns the idealist base of Surrealism, has been confident that certain Surrealists will abandon their conceptions and rally to dialectical materialism. But Surrealism, insofar as it constitutes a comprehensive method and conception of the world, will not be acceptable to the proletariat, nor welcomed into our ranks." Alexandre and Unik refuted these assertions, pointing out that Surrealism doesn't pretend to have a "comprehensive method" in opposition to the Party, nor does it claim to have its own philosophical conception of the world; it has simply a materialist conception. They asked for an honest recognition of its achievements and said the Surrealists are the only ones to discern

> a domain essential to human life in questions of suicide, dreams, sex, love and madness. It would be a betrayal of proletarian culture in the process of formation . . . to abandon these conquests of human thought simply because they were born under the rule of the bourgeoisie. . . . It would also be a dangerous error to limit the field of intellectual investigation by excluding everything that does not serve the cause of immediate agitation.

They ended by expressing confidence that the Surrealists will correct their errors and continue to serve the cause of revolution.[66]

Apparently as a result of their efforts and those of Crevel and Thirion, the Surrealists were finally permitted to join the *A.E.A.R.* Eluard had a membership card of the organization made out to him dated December 1932, indicating that the Surrealists had had to wait ten months before being allowed to join.[67] Meanwhile, Breton continued his endeavors to maintain the strictest control over his followers. According to the minutes of a meeting held in December, Tzara was guilty of having written articles for the "counterrevolutionary" and "anti-poetic" Belgian *Journal des Poètes.* A public apology was demanded and Tzara complied, issuing one that very day.[68] The question of whether a Surrealist could ever write for the bourgeois press was discussed and it was agreed that, assuming the approval of a majority, one could write for a special number of a review devoted to Surrealism and it was permissible to comment on Surrealist art but oddly, not on poetry, in specialized art journals. These minutes were signed by most of the remaining faithful, Tzara, Crevel, Eluard, Péret, Tanguy, Giacometti, Dali and Breton.[69]

Aragon's break with Surrealism was not only political, it was also stylistic. He left Surrealist aesthetics behind him to devote himself to proletarian literature with very unfortunate results, in the opinion of most critics. Typical of his new style, written for the Party paper, *La Lutte anti-réligieuse et prolétarienne* (Anti-religious and Proletarian Struggle), was "Complainte des chômeurs" (The Strikers' Lament).

> Chômeurs, que les flics ne vous disent plus: circulez!
> Chômeurs, que les flics ne vous chasse plus de sous les
>   ponts?
> Chômeurs, qu'on ne vous fasse plus attendre sous la pluie?
> Chômeurs, qu'on vous foute la paix sur les bancs?
>
> Strikers, if only the cops wouldn't say: move on!
> Strikers, why can't the cops let you sleep under bridges?
> Strikers, why must you wait in the rain?
> Strikers, won't they damn well let you sit on the benches?

Eluard had a clipping of this poem and at the bottom, he has written the wry comment, "l'activité d'Aragon en 1932," with the obvious implication that Aragon's poetry had badly deteriorated.[70] With his propensity for going to extremes, Aragon even wrote a poem in favor of the Soviet Secret Police: "I sing of an OGPU of nowhere and everywhere/ I demand an OGPU to prepare the end of the world. . . ." At its most extreme, this sort of writing—which Aragon soon abandoned—is really "agitprop," not poetry; nevertheless, he continued to work within the framework of this style. Garaudy summed up the situation very well when he said that the literary critics, if they are Communists, regard Aragon's Surrealist phase as youthful folly. If they are not, they see his Communist period as devoid of literary accomplishment.[71]

From his point of view, Aragon merely resolved a conflict of many years' standing, dating from his first glimmer of social consciousness to his joining the Communist Party and breaking definitively with Surrealism. He explained his devotion to the style of proletarian literature by saying "apolitical works are militant weapons for the preservation of the regime in power."[72] By becoming a "proletarian writer," he satisfied a need for immediate usefulness in serving the revolution and overcame what he regarded as a great limitation: the separation between the writer and his public, which had been aggravated by the Surrealists' esoteric preoccupations and style. He announced that, after his trip to Russia, although he agonized over breaking with his old friends, "I finally came to see that the most urgent, in fact, the only thing worthy of a man and a poet, was to put his art entirely at the service of this new world, . . . to shout out the glory of the new world to come."[73] With a certain defensiveness, he complained that, in spite of all his efforts, the Surrealists persisted in their idealistic errors. "They were not able to accept Marxism, except to pay lip service to it. Nothing changed in their methods. Even worse, they claimed the right to enter into Marxism dragging all their poetic baggage with them, and tried to bend Marxism to fit the theories of Freud, with no regard for economic or social considerations." He ended by expressing his impatience with them saying "let us have done with hallucinations, the unconscious, sex, dreams, etc. [sic] Enough of fantasy! I hereby proclaim the return of reality!"[74]

According to Garaudy, Aragon had hoped to lead the Surrealists to Communism, but Breton sabotaged his efforts because he wanted the Party to accept and assimilate the most irresponsible and adventurous ideas of his movement.[75] It is true that Breton was more than ever concerned with keeping Surrealism intact, even while plunging the movement into politics, as he himself admitted.

The Surrealist front would not for ten years have maintained itself unbroken had it not been for such continuous resistance to driftings towards "right" or "left." A drift to the left was, some months ago, seeking to crystallize itself around a poem by Aragon. . . .

This poem, deliberately conceived outside the sphere which Surrealism believes should, at present, be allotted to expression, at once brought up the question whether a social purpose which we pursue in common with others can justify relinquishing methods peculiar to ourselves. However much it has cost me to appear to have, in this matter, parted company with Aragon . . . I was nevertheless obliged to answer the question negatively.[76]

Speaking later at a conference of the *A.E.A.R.*, Breton pleaded for the widest possible interpretation of the resolutions of Kharkov on proletarian literature, quoting Lenin in *What Is to Be Done?* on this question. He pointed out that Lenin himself chastised intellectuals who wanted to create art for the proletariat by using such subjects as life in the factories which the workers already knew only too well. On the contrary, the workers must master the whole heritage of the past, and not be enclosed within the limitations of a special culture of their own. He also proposed that, in addition to courses in Marxist literature, a Marxist-oriented course in general literature be instituted at the *Université ouvrière* (Workers' University), which would survey such writers as Balzac who, though a monarchist, was important for his devastating depiction of society and was much admired by Marx. Such a study would have the advantage of counteracting the influence of the *lycées* where the teaching of literature emphasizes bourgeois conceptions of the family, religion and patriotism.[77] Breton had said earlier that the Surrealists would be "the first to defend that conception of art called useful, provided it is not defined in a way that would be the slightest bit narrow and restrictive."[78] In effect, such a statement was almost a rejection of the concept of proletarian literature. It amounted to saying that he was willing to agree in principle, though not in practice. For Breton, the revolutionary value of a work of art could be subtle and indirect. Its subversive character could reside in the originality of its style, and in the intent of the artist. But for Aragon, once he became convinced of the ineffectuality of Surrealist forms of protest, both style and content had to change because they had to be subordinated to "the writer's first duty," which was to serve the Revolution.[79]

The issues raised by *L'Affaire Aragon* were far-reaching, and had profound political consequences. The two camps, however, were not as yet irrevocably divided since the Surrealists had, after all, been permitted to join the *A.E.A.R.* Breton had even been elected to its board, although he said he found himself in a minority position, relegated to its "left" opposition. Proletarian literature did not yet have the official status that socialist realism was to achieve from 1934 on, although the two were similar in many respects. There was still a certain latitude and tolerance that permitted Surrealism to flourish internationally while officially linked with Marxism. It was important for the growth and influence of Surrealism in other countries, as well as for its survival in France, that it was the one truly *avant-garde* group which could claim legitimate connections with Communism. In many countries, young artists proudly called themselves revolutionary Surrealists, consciously patterning themselves after Breton and his group, and adopting the same politics. One young English Surrealist poet gave his opinion of the issues stemming from *L'Affaire Aragon:*

> The Surrealists are helping to lay the foundations of a new, universal culture, and should not be expected to be immediately concerned *in their researches* with the practical facts of political struggle, though they have always shown themselves to be deeply concerned with it in their "outside" declarations. . . . Personally, I think that the Surrealists should be regarded as desirable "fellow-travelers," and that the Communists are making a silly mistake in treating them either with scorn or suspicion simply because their work does not happen to be about strikes, hunger marches, or life in the distressed areas. They can in their own way do just as much good for the Revolution, ultimately, as the propaganda writers are doing in theirs.[80]

The Surrealists, however, never achieved the status of "desirable fellow-travelers" in the French Communist Party which, at best, barely tolerated them, nor was the "synthesis" hoped for by Alexandre and Unik ever to be a reality. Given the choice between Barbusse, universally honored because he had risked court martial to tell the truth about World War I, and the still relatively unknown Surrealists who were liable to perpetrate untold outrages at any moment, the Party chose Barbusse. His egregious ideological errors were simply ignored and no attempt was ever made to force him to submit to Party discipline because he had such symbolic importance. But the Surrealists were not so fortunate. They were constantly being sternly reproved for not obeying Party directives and their many enemies were apparently working tirelessly to force them out, denying that they could have any possible usefulness to the revolution.

7 Final Rupture and the Doctrine of Socialist Realism

Is Surrealism spreading among the masses?
That is the whole question from the revolutionary point of view. Indisputably no.
—Claude Spaak, *Libération de l'esprit*

How many times have we heard that since poets call themselves revolutionaries this ought to be evident in their works?
—Tristan Tzara, *Initiés et Précurseurs*

You do not reject the philosophy of Marx because it is impossible for every workman to understand. Why, then, should you reject a revolutionary art because, for the moment, it is difficult to understand?
—Herbert Read, *On the Social Aspects of Surrealism*

Surrealism and Ilya Ehrenburg

When the Surrealists were finally permitted to join the *A.E.A.R.*, they became very involved in it. They signed a protest against Nazi terror, demanded freedom for writers imprisoned in Germany[1] and took part in auctions of paintings for the benefit of several anti-fascist committees. They also helped organize a conference headed by Rolland, Barbusse, and Gide entitled "Le fascisme contre la culture," at which Eluard and Crevel spoke.[2] When

119

an accident at one of the Renault plants caused the death of eight workers, the Surrealists signed an *A.E.A.R.* protest against "this latest crime of . . . capitalism in the service of war"[3] and Breton himself wrote a protest condemning the appalling lack of safety devices as the cause of many needless injuries in the Renault factories.[4] They were also involved in the revival of the international peace movement in 1933, although they had serious reservations about its effectiveness.

The shock of Hitler's seizure of power and the ease with which he destroyed the German Communist Party led the International to re-examine its previous policy of noncooperation. The new policy of "la main tendue" (the extended hand), begun by Thorez acting on instructions from the International, had as its purpose the creation of a united front against fascism, and especially against the threat of Hitler's Germany. This initiative was entirely new and even Thorez had been caught off guard and had to make a hurried trip to Moscow to be briefed. "For the man who had believed that, in escalating the struggles against the socialists, he was applying the line of the International, this was a shock," but he returned to Paris prepared to launch the united front.[5] The French Communist Party first implemented it by organizing the Amsterdam-Pleyel Peace Congresses under the leadership of Barbusse and Rolland. Now, the International adopted a new slogan, "mass movements" and began to play down its previous one, "class against class." Amsterdam-Pleyel was an appeal to a wide range of world opinion to join in the struggle against fascism which was finally, after Hitler came to power, seen to be a worse evil than social democracy.

The Surrealists, however, distrusted what seemed to be the old brand of pacifist humanism again being evoked by Barbusse and Rolland, just as in the early days of *Clarté*. They criticized the movement because these leaders were calling for class unity and conciliation and they denounced the counterrevolutionary tendencies of "official pacifism," which could only be the tool of imperialism. Instead, they proposed a variation on the Leninist slogan, "in response to the hypocritical imperialist formula, 'if you want peace, prepare for war,' we say 'if you want peace, prepare for civil war.'" Even though they disagreed with the tactics, they wanted to take part in the Congress because they had "complete confidence in the ability of the masses and the revolutionary workers' organizations to triumph over the confusionism of the intellectuals," and some good might come of it in spite of the leadership.[6] This view was understandably resented by the organizers and was one of the many causes for ill will toward them.

Breton had complained that, although he had been appointed to the board of the *A.E.A.R.*, the Surrealists had been relegated to the "left opposition" and treated so badly that it was clearly only a question of seizing the first opportunity to get rid of them.[7] A letter by Ferdinand Alquié published in the last number of *Le Surréalisme au service de révolution* was the final pretext for their expulsion.[8] In the letter he praised Breton's stand against propaganda literature and criticized "the wind of systematic imbecility that blows from the U.S.S.R." He attacked the Soviet film, *Road of Life,* for its moralistic view that work is the only worthwhile goal and ridiculed the heroes of the film who enter a brothel only to wreck it and abuse the women. With heavy-handed symbolism, they tear down a sign that read "here one can drink, sing and kiss the girls," a motto, said Alquié, that he would gladly take for his own. Worst of all, he dared to contrast *Road of Life* with the Surrealist film, *L'Age d'or,* which he praised lavishly calling it a revolutionary artistic achievement.[9]

The Surrealists were warned that they must disavow him if they wished to remain members of the *A.E.A.R.*, but they refused to do so, in spite of tremendous pressure.[10] Paul Nizan castigated them severely in *Commune,* organ of *A.E.A.R.*

> The profound separation between Surrealism and the revolutionary masses is increasing. Social and political themes are being abandoned in favor of premature experiments on "the irrational knowledge of the object." For the rest, there is a particularly repugnant letter from F. Alquié which is sufficient proof that in the eyes of the Surrealists, revolutionary exigencies weigh lightly compared to their individual desires. It is aggravating that the editors of the review have not broken relations with this personage.

Nizan ended by accusing the Surrealists of moving in an "intemporal universe" and of being concerned with "post-revolutionary problems" of a kind which certainly cannot be solved, and should not even be posed, until after socialism is achieved. He seemed to have tacitly conceded the validity of Surrealism, while simply attacking its sense of timing.[11] His point of view was that of the committed and thoughtful Communist intellectual who, even though drawn to Surrealism, felt its preoccupations were frivolous in the light of the current fascist menace and the threat of war. Guy Mangeot, a Belgian Surrealist, indignantly retorted, "how could there be such things as postrevolutionary problems? . . . As if all problems should not be envisaged even before the revolution in order that those who will make it will be completely free!"[12] But freedom, in the Surrealist sense of the word, was evidently a "post-revolutionary" problem, and the rift between the Communists and the Surrealists was growing wider.

While the Surrealists were being pressured to break with Alquié, Ilya Ehrenburg wrote a widely publicized essay, *Vus par un écrivain de l'U.R.S.S.* (Views of a Writer from the U.S.S.R.), denigrating contemporary French literature. French writers were described as being in the pay of big business and of avoiding the really important social questions in their work.[13] But, aggravated by Alquié's letter, Ehrenburg reserved his greatest malice for the Surrealists. "I am not sure whether they are mentally ill or merely very clever, these young fellows who make a trade of insanity. . . . These young revolutionaries will have nothing to do with work. They go in for Hegel and Marx and the Revolution, but work is something to which they are not adapted. They are too busy studying pederasty and dreams." They would not go out and demonstrate for the unemployed because they might be beaten up by the police. Instead, "they have another program to unfold consisting of onanism, pederasty, fetishism, exhibitionism, and even bestiality."[14] Years later, Ehrenburg explained the exaggerated severity of his attack by saying, "I had been infuriated by the Surrealists organizing discussions on the sex, character, and potential behavior of a scrap of velvet at a time when the fascists just across the Rhine were burning books and killing people."[15] Predictably, the Surrealists were enraged. They fired off angry telegrams to the *A.E.A.R.* demanding that it publicly condemn Ehrenburg's "intolerable" statements and threatened a collective resignation if this were not done.[16] However, Ehrenburg's article was not condemned; instead the Surrealists were ousted from the *A.E.A.R.* because of their refusal to denounce Alquié, and also because of their dissident views of the peace congresses.[17] Ehrenburg enjoyed great prestige as spokesman for the Soviet Writers' Union, and if he held the Surrealists in such low esteem, it was obviously necessary to break with them. Even those who were not happy about his opinion of French literature could agree on that.

Anti-fascist Action: 1934

The break with the *A.E.A.R.* at the end of 1933 did not signify the end of the Surrealists' collaboration with Communist organizations. This was not the final rupture. A few months later, Crevel—the only Surrealist who still had good relations with the Party—began to write for *Commune,* and both Crevel and Tzara joined the *Maison de la Culture,* a cultural organization for professional groups founded by the Party.[18] Also, the exclusion cannot have been strictly enforced since Eluard gave a speech to the *A.E.A.R.* in 1934. He warned of the dangers of the new policy of the united front because in directing it solely against Germany, the French Left would be likely to find itself the tool of nationalism. It is important to remember that imperialist France had crushed the Spartacist and Hungarian revolutions and supported White Terror in the Balkans, and that it was "French imperialism which was responsible for that exacerbation of German nationalism confronting us today." He proposed instead that the *A.E.A.R.* fight against French imperialism, as the Surrealists had begun to do in 1925, and he advocated a "true united front," composed of workers of all countries and supported by intellectuals. This was the only kind of united front that could succeed in defeating fascism in every country, he concluded.[19] It was a lucid presentation of the Surrealists' position because they were consistent in their opposition to the slightest resurgence of nationalism, even that implied by an appreciation of the unique qualities of French culture. They refused to accept the idea that Hitler's Germany was the only enemy. On the contrary, they pointed out that fascism was not an isolated phenomenon, but that all the Western imperialist countries shared responsibility for its rise and that this had been precisely the line of the International until 1934.

But virtually all opposition to the united front melted away as a result of the Stavisky scandal and the February riots that toppled the cabinet. Stavisky himself was merely an audacious crook who floated phony stock issues whenever his earlier swindles threatened to catch up with him. Eventually, his shady deals were exposed and while under arrest, he committed suicide, or so the police reported. It was generally believed that he was murdered because highly placed government officials were involved in his criminal activities and accusations of an official cover-up were made. The affair has never been fully investigated, but Prime

Minister Chautemps, whose own family was implicated, was forced to resign.

On February 6, when Daladier was being confirmed as the new prime minister, a huge angry mob, taking advantage of the government's embarrassment, rioted in the Place de la Concorde, across from the *Chambre des Deputés.* It was an extreme right-wing demonstration composed of the *Croix de feu,* the *Jeunesses patriotes* and the *Camelots du roi,* who engaged in bloody clashes with Communist workers and with the police and a number of people were killed. While there was no actual attempt to seize control of the government, the whole country was extremely shaken and Daladier was forced to resign and a new ministry was formed. Although it is said that the French Right had less in common with Nazism than with Boulanger, the *Action française* and the royalist tradition, the Left was in no mood for such subtle distinctions. Most likely, the February 6 riots were not even intended to over-throw the government, but considering that Hitler had so recently come to power in Germany, the Left was apprehensive about the future of the Republic and it was by no means clear at the time that the French Right posed no real threat. On the contrary, anti-republican sentiment was growing stronger every day. Mem-bership in the *Croix de feu* had more than tripled in 1934 and this alarming fact alone helped to forge anti-fascist unity. The massive counter-demonstration of February 12 was crucial. There had been more rioting on the 9th, but February 12 was the day of the first mass action by all the Parties of the Left and it proved to be the beginning of the *Front populaire.* Almost overnight, the mutual recriminations of Communists and socialists ended and a new era of cooperation began.

Leftists everywhere reacted quickly to the fascist threat. The Surrealists immediately launched *Appel à la lutte* (Call to the Strug-gle), signed by many prominent intellectuals, which warned "to-day, fascist riots, tomorrow, dissolution of the Chamber," and called for a general strike.[20] They also marched side by side with the workers in the exhilarating demonstration of February 12 that had been jointly sponsored by the Communists, Socialists and Radicals. Because of the *Appel,* Breton had been one of those delegated to meet with Léon Blum to plan it and for once, the Surrealists could feel a satisfying sense of solidarity with the workers and with the parties of the Left.[21] Hoping to preserve this sense of unity, they issued a questionnaire, *Enquête sur l'unité d'action,* which asked for opinions on how best to maintain the spirit of February 12.[22] In response, some of its signers founded the *Comité de vigilance des intellectuels antifascistes* in March 1934, so indirectly, the Surrealists were also among its founders. The purpose of this organization was to unite intellectuals, Communist and non-Communist alike, in the fight against fascism. Its chairmen were the scientists, Paul Rivet and Paul Langevin, and its members included such prominent figures as Picasso, Gide, Pierre Joliot-Curie, André Malraux and Julien Benda.[23] Its manifesto, which the Surrealists signed, took a position similar to theirs on the question of Germany, emphasizing the complicity of the bourgeois democracies in the rise of Nazism. "We cannot persuade the German people that Hitler alone of all the capitalist and fascist governments wants war." It cannot be a question of France against Germany; instead, fascism must be fought equally on all fronts, at home as much as abroad.[24]

The Surrealists were not yet completely isolated in spite of having been expelled from the *A.E.A.R.,* but they issued another, more controversial, manifesto against the expulsion of Trotsky. Trotsky had earlier been given permission to reside in France but, after the February riots, a panicky government forced him into exile once more. This manifesto had the effect of further dividing the Surrealists from the mainstream of the Left, even though they were careful to point out that they were "far from sharing all of his current opinions," but that his expulsion must be protested as a blatant instance of political repression.[25] They seemed fated to hold unpopular opinions and, while there were no immediate repercussions from the Trotsky pamphlet, it was certainly added to the list of Surrealist "errors."

Socialist Realism

In August and September 1934, the first *Soviet Writers' Congress* officially adopted the doctrine of socialist realism. In some respects, the line of the Congress reflected the general shift in policy to the acceptance of a united front, since writers were no longer obliged to be members of the Communist Party or even of the Writers' Union. As first defined, it appeared to grant considerably more latitude to the artist than the doctrine expounded at Kharkov and socialist realism was very appealing to many French intellectuals. It differed from the previous concept of proletarian literature in several ways which, in theory, made it less narrow and rigid. Now, it was no longer almost a necessity that the writer come from the proletariat[26] and the achievements of the past were no longer to be rejected as the cultural products of capitalism. "The bourgeoisie has squandered its literary heritage; it is our duty to gather it up carefully, to study it and, having critically assimilated it, to advance further."[27] Speakers at the Congress repeated Stalin's dictum that writers were "the engineers of the soul" and proclaimed that they could now "participate directly in the construction of a new life, in the process of changing the world."[28] While it may seem surprising that left-wing writers and artists in the West, under no sort of compulsion, would willingly place themselves under the constraints of socialist realism, it was a seductive idea because it made them feel that they too could play an important role in fighting for the revolution. They would no longer be merely marginal figures as they were in bourgeois society, and intellectual life and revolutionary activism would no longer be in conflict.

Socialist realism, however, was not identical with objective realism, in the nineteenth century sense. Instead, it was "revolutionary romanticism," as Zhadnov put it. It was not intended to hold up a mirror to society, but rather to depict a glowing future and to use heroic themes. "Socialist realism is distinct from other realisms in the fact that it inevitably focuses attention on the portrayal of the building of socialism, the struggle of the proletariat, of the new man, . . . of the great historical processes of our day."[29] As opposed to the naturalism of Zola, for example, "socialist realism dares to dream!" Yet the Congress condemned Surrealism by implication because "socialist realism is the enemy of everything supernatural and mystic, all other-worldly idealism,"[30] and "while the literature of dying capitalism invokes the aid of the irrational, of the unconscious and of the subconscious, the literature of socialist realism demands a consciousness of the fate of humanity."[31] Finally, in a key statement by Gorky, it was made clear that it was not the aim of the doctrine to preserve and cherish artistic freedom.

> It goes without saying that the Revolution and the Party do not exist in order to insure to all members complete liberty. . . . The Party . . . knows whither it is leading the masses . . . and if a writer finds it hard to give up his most

intimate individual shades of opinion, let him study the experience of the Soviet Revolution and he will then see if he wants to fight against capitalism, against imperialism; if he wants to fight hand in hand with the masses, then he must march in the ranks of these masses.[32]

Unfortunately for the Surrealists, the new policy turned out to be more than ever in conflict with their own principles because socialist realism had to be realist in form, socialist in content. It had to portray idealized working-class heroes, convey a mood of optimism, be party-minded and conform to the current political line. Humor and satire were usually discouraged as subversive of its didactic purposes and, as a statute of the Soviet Writers' Union states, "it is representative of reality not as it is, but as it ought to be."[33] This rigidity soon became apparent; yet, many Western writers continued to be bound by its tenets, imposing it voluntarily upon themselves. Only later was it carried to the extreme of Aragon's pronouncement that the task of the writer was to "write the Stalinist truth." In 1934, it was possible to hope that the new policy heralded greater freedom for the artist. Breton had welcomed the Congress in the belief that it was ushering in a more liberal era. The over-zealous *RAPP,* with its shock troops of writers in the factories, had been dissolved and he was gratified that a high official like Bukharin should have personally presented a report on poetry because it meant that the importance of art was being acknowledged by the central government itself.[34] The Belgian Surrealists were also optimistic. They felt that the Congress had initiated an open debate on artistic principles and that now "our voices will be able to be heard."[35] But the Surrealists were not willing to accept the slightest compromise on the question of art and they hailed the Soviet Writers' Congress only because it appeared to have taken a step toward their own position. They were simply waiting expectantly for the International to broaden its theories of art sufficiently to include them, but their hopes were to be disappointed.

In the same year, the Czech Communist poet, Vitezslav Nezval, made an unsuccessful attempt to get a serious official appraisal of Surrealism. As one of the founders of the Czech Surrealist group, he went before the International and tried earnestly to convince the leaders that Surrealism was a truly revolutionary art form compatible with historical materialism. But, according to Ehrenburg, he was simply laughed at for his naiveté and came to be considered dangerously unorthodox.[36] The attitude of the International had become much more hostile since the Kharkov resolution of 1930. But the Surrealists continued to be deeply involved in the anti-fascist struggle which they wholeheartedly supported. A Belgian review, *Documents,* devoted a special issue to the movement in France and Belgium, and reprinted all their anti-fascist tracts, praising them for their stand. Several articles and manifestoes, including one by the painter, René Magritte, stressed its natural antipathy to fascist repression and insisted on the desirability of its direct revolutionary participation.[37]

A book by Breton, *What is Surrealism?* appeared in 1934 in which he spoke of the "disease of fascism."

> Hitler, Dolfuss, and Mussolini have either drowned in blood or subjected to corporeal humiliation everything that formed the effort of generations straining toward a more tolerable and more worthy form of existence. . . . Is it not the evident role of fascism to re-establish . . . the tottering supremacy of finance capital?[38]

He made still another plea for acceptance by the Communist Party on the grounds that the Surrealists are worthy of the revolutionary role they desire to play, and reminded his readers that "the very next day after the first fascist coup in France, it was they amongst intellectual circles who had the honor of taking the initiative in sending out an *Appel à la lutte.*"[39] But he also underlined his objections to any restrictions on the artist.

> We hold the liberation of man to be the *sine qua non* condition of the *liberation of the mind,* and we expect the liberation of man to result only from the Proletarian Revolution. These two problems are essentially distinct and we deplore their becoming confused. . . . There is good reason, then, to take up a stand against all attempts to weld them together and, more especially, against the urge to abandon all such researches as ours in order to devote ourselves to the poetry and art of propaganda.[40]

His aims were still to claim freedom from any outside control while at the same time supporting Marxist revolutionary goals.

But even the new united front against fascism ultimately failed to produce a more tolerant view of Surrealism.

It is certainly significant that no one on the Left should have taken exception to Ehrenburg's viciously insulting remarks about Surrealism. In fact, several more critical articles appeared in the left-wing press. In *Documents,* Claude Spaak wrote that despite their great talent, Surrealist writings remained "closed, incomprehensible, and without the slightest utility. . . . It would not be difficult . . . to prove that the majority of those who are touched by their rich productivity are, and what is more serious, remain bourgeois." He concluded that the Surrealists made extremely bad revolutionaries, lacking the discipline of the true militant and lacking "a certain necessary abdication of the personality."[41] Louise Périer in *Commune* also reflected the prevalent opinion of Surrealism on the Left. "The noisy publicity he endeavored to give to his 'disagreements' with revolutionary organizations and the certitude he has of being in possession of eternal verities permit us to doubt the good faith of M. André Breton." He was also chastised for his role as leader of the movement. "For the petty satisfaction of being *chef d'école* and being able to say 'we, André Breton,' for the proud illusion of constituting an historical force within himself, he wanted to remain before all and above all the representative of Surrealism." There was even a crude attempt to link Surrealism with fascism in the statement that "scorn for the satisfaction of immediate material interests and the exaltation of the revolution as a fundamental spiritual necessity figure today in fascist manuals." Other writers, who were genuine in their revolutionary beliefs, rallied to the proletariat, giving their writings a new, revolutionary content. Yet, this the Surrealists refused to do, so "we will leave M. André Breton in peace to enjoy his bourgeois monopoly."[42] These two unfavorable commentaries revealed the extent of the Surrealists' isolation. *Documents* had formerly been favorable to them but had recently moved closer to the Communist Party, while *Commune* was the organ of the *A.E.A.R.* from which they had been expelled. They seemed to have no more allies on the Left.

Surrealists Barred from the *International Congress of Writers for the Defense of Culture*

The Surrealists had by now been forced out of all organizations on the Left. Officially, however, the "excommunication" was to come in 1935, precipitated by their reaction to the Franco-Soviet Pact of May 1935 and to the Writers' Congress, the *Congrès international des écrivains pour la défense de la culture,* that convened in Paris that June. They had denounced the Pact as a setback for international socialism because the alliance of imperialist France with the Soviet Union could not be condoned on grounds of expediency. It was a dangerous move that could only lead to ultra-patriotism and militarism; moreover, it was contrary to "revolutionary defeatism," the Marxist idea that the proletariat has no country and therefore, will refuse to fight in a capitalist war. It should be said that this view was shared by many orthodox Communists. The Pact was quite a shock even to officials of the Party and its advantages had to be explained at great length in *L'Humanité* to an outraged rank and file.

The Writers' Congress was sponsored by the International and was devoted to the spread of Soviet culture and especially to furthering anti-fascist sentiment. Among the French luminaries at the Congress were Gide, who had a brief pro-Soviet phase, Barbusse, Rolland, and Malraux. Foreign writers included E. M. Forster, Aldous Huxley, Heinrich Mann, Bertolt Brecht, Anna Seghers, Michael Gold, Isaac Babel, Boris Pasternak, and Ehrenburg. The vague formula "defense of culture" really meant an anti-fascist cultural alliance that would be pro-Soviet and put its stamp of approval on socialist realism. Differences of opinion were discouraged and the organizers made it clear that they did not want the Surrealists to participate. Virtually the only dissident voices were those of Magdeleine Paz (Magdeleine Marx) author of *Woman*, who protested the imprisonment of Victor Serge in the Sovet Union and, obliquely, of Breton. "Malcontents were maneuvered into the background. . . . For example, the Czech delegate and poet, Vitezlav Nezval, waited his turn for two days in the wings and suddenly discovered the Congress was over." He was treated this way because he was known to favor the Surrealists and to oppose socialist realism and, in fact, he had recently invited Breton and Eluard to Prague for a series of lectures.[43]

The Surrealists suspected, because of its timing, that the real purpose of the Congress was to win acceptance of the new Pact. They also feared that it would deliberately avoid all controversy and produce nothing more than a broad, meaningless declaration against war and fascism, but they still wanted to take part. Tzara was on the program, but it was known that he would not really speak as a Surrealist and the sentiments he expressed in calling on poets to aid the proletarian revolution were not at all controversial. Soon after, he broke with the group and, while his poetic style changed to reflect his new Communist militancy, he never went to such extremes as Aragon, nor was his defection as acrimonious.[44] Crevel, universally respected, was actually on the organizing committee, but only by exerting the greatest pressure did he succeed in getting permission for Breton to read a statement. This was the only concession the planners were willing to make and the Surrealists were not even listed on the program. It was feared they would try to disrupt the proceedings but all they wanted to do was to provoke serious discussion.

Even this minimal participation was made impossible by an incident that occurred just before the Congress began. Breton saw Ehrenburg on the street and, still smarting from his outrageous insults, Breton slapped him in the face. The Soviets were furious at this treatment of one of their official delegates and, because of Breton's inexcusable behavior, the Congress withdrew its permission for him to speak.[45] He explained that he had meant no offense to the Soviet delegation and was only responding to a personal insult, but to no avail. Crevel worked desperately to get him reinstated but did not succeed. Tragically, after this failure, Crevel committed suicide. No doubt he had personal reasons that had nothing to do with politics. He was in poor health and, in the early days, had been especially preoccupied with suicide, but it was generally believed that the cause of his death was the exclusion of the Surrealists from the Congress.[46] Out of respect for his memory, Eluard was finally allowed to read Breton's paper to the Congress, however, this gesture was less magnanimous than it appeared. Eluard was not given the floor until after midnight when the hall was half empty and the audience was noisy and hostile. Even worse, the lights were turned off immediately afterwards and no discussion of Breton's text was permitted.

In *Discours au congrès des écrivains,* Breton denounced the Franco-Soviet Pact on the grounds that any war with Germany on one side and France on the other would have to be an imperialist war. He added that the function of this Congress was to reconcile people to the Pact, and he warned that revolutionaries should be suspicious of the new rapprochement between France and Russia since the French bourgeoisie seemed to favor it. Because the Pact was clearly directed against Germany, it would promote an unhealthy nationalism and it was an insidious trap to which even Communists were falling prey. "It was absolutely dismaying, to read in *L'Humanité* that 'if the proletariat, to use Marx's phrase, has no country, it does have . . . something to defend: the cultural patrimony of France.'" "For us Surrealists," he continued, "it is not a question of French culture," but of a "universal legacy" which includes the great heritage of Germany. "We remain firmly opposed to any claim . . . of the cultural patrimony of France alone [or] to any exaltation in France of French sentiment."[47] Breton also reiterated the Surrealists' stand against art as propaganda, saying that mechanical declarations against fascism are not the way to "defend culture," which can only be defended by upholding the complete freedom of art in form and content. The speech ended with a phrase which has since become famous: "'Transform the world,' said Marx: 'Change Life,' said Rimbaud; for us, these two commands are the same."[48]

After the speech had been read and no riot occurred, "disappointed reporters went off to the refreshment room—everything had ended peacefully: we realized that the trouble was not Breton, but Hitler," Ehrenburg recalled.[49] But at the time, press reaction was extremely negative. *L'Humanité* declared, in what must have been a deliberate distortion, that the Surrealists "came out against cultural exchanges between France and the U.S.S.R."[50] *Commune* simply remarked that "the petit bourgeois mentality of some of the Surrealists was an object of scorn or pity for everyone."[51] *Documents* also criticized them. One article granted the wisdom of Breton's belief in a universal cultural legacy but defended Ehrenburg against him. Another writer said that to be against the Stalin-Laval Pact was to take a counterrevolutionary stand because it meant opposing the Communist Party and he complained that the Surrealists, although they called themselves revolutionaries, persisted in their "bourgeois sense of liberty." He granted their importance in destroying capitalist culture, but they should now disband and move on, as had Aragon, to the task of perfecting socialist realism.[52] Clearly, there was a "united front" against Surrealism. The Left confronted the movement with two choices as Naville had done: to cease to exist and merge with the Party, or to continue to exist independently at the price of abandoning political activism.

Angry at their shabby treatment by the Congress and at the refusal of the Left to consent to a genuine dialogue, the Surrealists published a manifesto of defiance, *Du Temps que les surréalistes avaient raison* that signaled the end of any formal association with Communist organizations, either in France or abroad. As Breton remarked sadly, "this was . . . the crushing of the hopes that we had for years, in spite of everything, for reconciling Surrealist ideas with practical revolutionary action."[53] They accused the Congress of refusing to permit any real debate, and pointed out that Nezval and the defenders of Victor Serge had also been denied a hearing. They denounced the "frenetic need for orthodoxy" displayed by the Congress and affirmed that the "permanent confrontation of all tendencies constitutes the most indispensable ferment of the revolutionary struggle." They insisted that their ideological position was, until recently, identical to that of the International, but that they could not agree with its recent compromises. They were unwilling to give up the tactic of "revolutionary defeatism" and they condemned the propaganda that portrayed Germany as solely responsible for the new militarism because this could only discourage any hope of fraternization if war came. They also denounced what they believed to be a deliberate stirring up of patriotic feeling among the French workers and praised the *Comité de vigilance des intellectuels antifascistes* which was also against the encirclement and isolation of Germany. They ridiculed the cult of personality being created around Stalin, along with such signs of *embourgeoisement* as the rehabilitation of the family and resurgence of patriotism. "It only remains to re-establish religion and—why not?—private property. . . . To this regime, to this chief, we can only formally declare our defiance."[54]

The Surrealists had now become completely isolated. It was ironic that, at a time when the Left was welcoming all varieties of antifascist intellectuals, they should be expelled from every leftist organization the Party sponsored. Their opposition to the Franco-Soviet Pact was obviously a major factor in their "excommunication." Yet, the *Comité de vigilance des intellectuels antifascistes,* and even a number of Party members, also opposed the Pact. In reality, the Surrealists were expelled not primarily because of political disagreements, but because of their stubborn, and public opposition to socialist realism, and to any constraints whatsoever upon their artistic freedom. They had even dared to propound the view that their "research" had great revolutionary value, and that their poetry was a real contribution to the Revolution. But such audacity was intolerable. As one writer put it, Breton's mistake was that he kept trying to *se mettre d'accord* (come to an agreement with) with the Communists in open debate.[55] While other intellectuals had joined the Party as individuals, the Surrealists came as a group, equipped with their own ideology although, as George Lichtheim pointed out, even this was not unique. Another group, the editors of *L'Esprit* (formerly *Philosophies*), had been allowed to join the Party *en bloc,* and were not expelled even though they sometimes "deviated" from the line. But *L'Esprit* dissented in silence, unlike the Surrealists who were most vociferous critics of Party policies.[56] As bourgeois writers and artists, they were obviously lacking in the proper humility.

One of their few defenders on the Left, P. O. Lapie, pointed out that they alone had had the imagination to see the revolution as an expansion of poetry and that, with the increase in leisure and education of a liberated proletariat, poetry would no longer be the province of a privileged few. He also said that they were the first group of artists to become Marxists and their example would be an important influence on French youth.[57] Another left-wing writer, Claude Cahun, defended Surrealism at the *A.E.A.R.* Commission on Poetry. He contrasted them with Aragon whom he found contemptible because his work had become "regressive" since he joined the Communist Party. Aragon was now writing "blue, white, and red verses of propaganda,"[58] clearly demonstrating that "ideological conformity is the negation of all poetry."[59] He was now nothing but "a parasite of the revolution," rigidly clinging to a "false interpretation of Marxism . . . utopian and reactionary." Since he had abandoned Surrealism for the Communist Party, he was no longer either a revolutionary or a poet. In Cahun's opinion, Surrealism was "the most revolutionary poetic experience of any capitalist regime. . . . The Dadaist-Surrealist experiment . . . has tended to destroy all the myths about art that for centuries have permitted the ideological as well as economic exploitation of painting, sculpture, literature, etc. [sic]. . . . This experiment can and should serve the cause of the liberation of the proletariat."[60] But these sentiments merely caused him to be lumped together with the Trotskyist opposition within the *A.E.A.R.* To defend Surrealism from a revolutionary point of view was to risk one's own expulsion.

Surrealism Abroad and *Contre-Attaque:* 1935–1936

Although in France the Surrealists were a small, isolated circle, rejected by the Left, they had a large following abroad. Surrealism was always an international movement and in 1935–36, Breton and Eluard had a very successful lecture tour of Belgium, England, Czechoslovakia, and the Canary Islands. There were Surrealists in Yugoslavia, Denmark, Switzerland, New York, Tokyo, and Mexico City; but the Czech, English and Belgian groups were especially active and they published a *Bulletin international du surréalisme* in collaboration with the French group.

Nezval, who had attempted to defend Surrealism before the International, had previously expressed a desire to collaborate because the Czech movement had the same difficult relationship with the Czech Communist Party as the French Surrealists with the French Party.[61] When Breton and Eluard arrived in Czechoslovakia, they were very well received, lecturing to *Left Front* and to various student groups, and the Czechs issued a manifesto that took the same line as the French group.

> In founding the Surrealist group of Prague, we have not hesitated to let the Central Agit-Prop of the Czech Communist Party know that our intention is to examine and develop, in all senses, in a revolutionary manner and from the materialist dialectical point of view, human expression in all spheres. . . . We will always proclaim our solidarity with all those ready to fight in the ranks of the revolutionary proletariat. On the other hand, we will always claim our right to maintain the independence of our experimental methods.[62]

The Belgian group issued a manifesto expressing its opposition to the Franco-Soviet Pact, just as the French Surrealists had done.

> Until now, our attitude with regard to the international policies of the U.S.S.R., since the death of Lenin, has been one of reserve. We considered that it was necessary to avoid . . . criticizing the leaders of a people who had accomplished a considerable revolution and in whom we had the greatest hopes. But today, we find ourselves forced to ask if the present chiefs of the U.S.S.R. are not dangerously removed from the greatest and the best Marxist tradition, that of the First International, that of Lenin, and that of the Congresses of Zimmerwald and Kienthal.[63]

The English Surrealists, headed by Herbert Read, took their inspiration from Lewis Carroll and Edward Lear, English "pre-Surrealists," but also from Marx, and in a talk given to the Artists' International Association in London, Read said

> It seems paradoxical that I should be expected to speak in defense of revolutionary art. Indeed, . . . it is for others to explain why in this one domain of thought and feeling, we who are revolutionaries should respect the established order of things. . . . I do not intend tonight to . . . expose the pitiful banality, the vulgar ineptitude of so-called socialist realism. But . . . no good service is done to the cause we all serve by reducing art to the lowest common denominator of the understanding.

He made it clear that the English Surrealists considered themselves Marxists and pointed out that "the Surrealist is naturally a Marxian socialist, and generally . . . a more consistent Communist than many."[64] Artists of other countries who found inspiration in the movement also adopted its politics. The one notable exception is the United States where Surrealism has been enthusiastically received on the aesthetic plane but stripped of its ideological content.

It must not be thought that Breton contented himself with expressions of solidarity from abroad. He continued to be involved with politics in spite of his rupture with the Communist Party. Unlike many intellectuals who became disenchanted with Communism and then drifted to the far Right, Breton and his friends stayed on the Left, never ceasing to consider themselves Marxists, even though orthodox Communists refused to concede the validity of their revolutionary sentiments. At the end of 1935, Breton was preoccupied with the problem of action, for he still believed in the principle of political commitment. "Confronted with the bankruptcy of the parties of the Left, and the impotence of their slogans on the occasion of the Italian-Ethiopian conflict and its possible generalization, the question of what action to take must receive . . . an unequivocal response."[65] The answer was found, briefly, in organizing *Contre-Attaque, Union de lutte des intellectuels révolutionnaires.* The idea for the new venture came from Georges Bataille, at one time a critic of the Surrealists, whom Breton had denounced in the *Second Manifesto of Surrealism.*

They had, however, become reconciled. Many former Surrealists such as J.-A. Boiffard, and new recruits such as Henri Pastoureau, joined, as did Claude Cahun, defender of Surrealism before the *A.E.A.R.*

Its "position paper" of October 1935 declared that it was open to Marxists and non-Marxists alike but stressed that "none of its essential points is in contradiction to the ideas of Marx." *Contre-Attaque* favored socialization of the means of production and recognized class conflict as an essential historical force. It pointed out the need for new revolutionary tactics to deal with the Western countries since the tactics of the Communist parties in Germany and Italy had clearly been disastrous. It also predicted the failure of the Popular Front since its program was really intended to prevent revolution and preserve capitalism. The signers added that they were opposed to all of the so-called Marxist parties which, out of expediency, were temporarily supporting the bourgeois parties. "Our cause is that of the workers and the peasants," they said, yet they denounced all "demagogic attempts to make the workers believe that the only truly good and human values are found in the working class." Recognizing that the working class can be led astray by fascism, *Contre-Attaque* vowed to oppose all reactionary and nationalistic tendencies within it, and to work for a "universal revolution . . . of men of all colors all over the world."[66]

Two issues of the review appeared with articles on various aspects of political theory such as Hegel's dialectics, the Utopian socialism of Fourier, the revolutionary implications in the work of de Sade and the possibility of creating an autonomous peasant movement to aid the revolution. The group also held a protest rally in January 1936 whose theme was international human solidarity in opposition to the concepts of family and country and the speakers included Bataille, Breton, Maurice Heine, and Péret. They also issued a "call to action" against fascist elements in France saying "Colonel de la Rocque [head of the *Croix de feu*] is the only one who is actively trying to change the order of things—the revolutionary parties are merely upholding the status quo." Noting the panic that followed Hitler's occupation of the Rhineland, *Contre-Attaque* criticized the French Communist Party for having no constructive policies. On the contrary, "the Communists are reduced to the role of defenders of everything established at Versailles." The group went on to declare that "we have nothing

in common with the senile dementia of French nationalism. . . .
We belong to the human community betrayed today by Sarraut as
by Hitler, and by Thorez as by La Rocque."[67]

Contre-Attaque dissolved after a year and a half because of
dissension among its members, its extreme isolation, and its obvious ideological confusion. Needless to say, it remained unknown
to the workers and peasants whose cause it claimed to support, but
it even failed to attract other intellectuals. It attacked both Right
and Left, sometimes making very astute criticisms and was often
correct on such issues as the Versailles Treaty, the Popular Front,
and the resurgence of nationalism and militarism which even
infected the Left. But insofar as the group kept aloof from all
parties, it could not hope to become an effective political force.
One historian has even claimed that it had fascistic tendencies and
was "potentially pernicious" because it was so utterly irresponsible
in equating the kinds of political repression that occurred under
the Third Republic with Hitlerism.[68] Certainly, Contre-Attaque had
no desire to support fascism, but it is clear that its essential
negativism doomed it to failure and it did not meet the Surrealists'
need for political action.

They still vigorously opposed the trend toward militarism
and nationalism and a successful art exhibition in London, in
which Surrealists from all over the world participated, emphasized its
internationalist tradition. An anthology written for the exhibition
explicitly stressed the political significance of Surrealism. "Its
weapons are still poetry and direct political action," declared an
English Surrealist,[69] and Hugnet affirmed that "in addition to its
poetry, Surrealism has its social and political function: complete
adherence to dialectical materialism, its revolutionary position and
its struggle against patriotism and the bourgeoisie."[70] The artists
had not ceased to be politically conscious and even after their final
break with the Communist Party, they still thought of themselves
as Marxist revolutionaries. But their insistence on "liberation of
the mind" was an impossible formula for the Communists to
accept. The Surrealists had their own special view of revolutionary
art which had nothing in common either with proletarian literature or with socialist realism. At best, their search for "absolute
reality," that union between the dream and the waking world, was
irrelevant and at worst, it was counter-revolutionary. Even more
serious, from the Communists' point of view, the Surrealists re-

fused to dissent in silence and therefore had to be considered a harmful and divisive element. They could not be tolerated in an era when fear of the spread of fascism made ideological unity imperative. Yet they continued to search for some form of political action, trying to find a movement whose principles would be compatible with theirs.

8 Trotsky and the Surrealists

The style of official Soviet painting is called "socialist realism." The label could only have been invented by a bureaucrat at the head of an art department. The "realism" consists in imitating provincial daguerrotypes of the previous century; the "socialist" style in using tricks of photography to represent events that have never taken place.

—Leon Trotsky, *Art and Politics*

True art is unable *not* to be revolutionary, *not* to aspire to a complete and radical reconstruction of society. The *opposition* of writers and artists is one of the forces that can usefully contribute to the discrediting and overthrow of regimes which are destroying every sentiment of human dignity.

—Leon Trotsky, André Breton, *Pour un art révolutionnaire indépendant*

Breton and Trotsky

With the outbreak of the Spanish Civil War and the advent of the Moscow trials, Breton and his followers were more than ever convinced that a new world war was inevitable. Lacking a forum of their own because there was no longer a Surrealist review, they could only watch helplessly as events unfolded, feeling more isolated than ever. Péret, the most active revolutionary of the group, went to fight in Spain, as did Buñuel, Miró, and the English Surrealists, Roland Penrose and David Gascoyne. Péret had a long history of political activism and in spite of the fact that he faithfully signed all of the Surrealist tracts, he was not in Paris during the early thirties. He was living in Brazil and was involved with the Brazilian section of the Trotskyist Fourth International and had been jailed and finally expelled from the country for his leftist activities.[1] With this background, it was natural that, upon returning to Europe, he should volunteer to fight with the Spanish revolutionaries. Breton, on the other hand, rather lamely explained that he could not volunteer because he had just become a father. He felt he could not jeopardize the future of the baby girl dependent on him for support—clearly, his hatred of war was personal as well as ideological.[2]

The Surrealists did publish several tracts on Spain, however. One angrily demanded the arrest of the Spanish fascist, Gil Robles, leader of the Catholic *Confederación Española de Derechas Autónomas (Confederation of Autonomous Right Parties),* who had taken refuge in France. It denounced the Popular Front government for being oblivious to the dangers of the spread of fascism to France and its title quoted Robespierre's celebrated cry, "no liberty for the enemies of liberty!"[3] While it was true that Robles, as leader of the Catholic Party, was not technically a fascist, he had conferred with Hitler on several occasions, presumably to win his support, and seems to have toyed with the idea of creating a clerical fascist state in Spain on the model of Dollfuss's Austria.[4] Another protest, *Neutralité? Non-sens, crime et trahison!* bitterly assailed the French policy of nonintervention in Spain and warned that a wave of fascism would engulf all of Europe if France did not act.

> Wake up, *Front populaire!* Help the heroic *Frente Popular!* Not just with speeches and resolutions, but with volunteers and guns! . . . Create a workers' army without which you are nothing but a sham! The time has come to make use of the old argument of your enemies that the concrete assertion of force is the best guarantee of security.[5]

The Surrealists supported all the left groups in the Spanish struggle except the Stalinists and Péret's letters from the Front angrily denouncing Stalin's intervention in Spain only confirmed and clarified their position. Péret, a delegate from the Fourth International in charge of liaison, gave radio talks in Portuguese for the *P.O.U.M.* (Unified Marxist Workers' Party), which was close to the Trotskyists, and also fought alongside of them in Catalonia. In a letter of August 1936, he said that the Communists had already announced their intention of "sabotaging" the Spanish revolution by their insistence that there could be no question of bringing about a proletarian revolution but only of fighting for the preservation of the Republic.[6] As early as September, he wrote that he feared a defeat for the revolutionary forces. The Madrid government was sending fewer arms and supplies to the radical Catalan government and already, cooperation was breaking down. He blamed the dissension between the various revolutionary forces on the U.S.S.R. which was pursuing a "politics of bluff, intrigue and cowardice," in trying to gain control over the leftist parties. He was furious at Eluard, Aragon, Ernst, Tzara, and Desnos for signing an open letter of congratulations to Russia for her role in the Spanish conflict because in fact, the U.S.S.R. was betraying the Spanish revolution.[7] In mid-1937, having decided it was impossible to work with the *P.O.U.M.,* Péret joined the Anarchist forces. Again, he railed against the "villainy" of the Communists "who are openly sabotaging the revolution with the aid of the petite bourgeoisie."[8] The letters vividly described his frustration and exasperation at the infighting among the parties of the Left that weakened and ultimately destroyed them. He also continued to denounce, in equally strong terms, the intervention of the Soviet Union and the non-intervention of France and his position was the one the Surrealists adopted.

Driving them still further away from the Communist Party and from Stalinist Russia were the Moscow trials which had led many intellectuals to break with the Party. The French Section of the Trotskyist *Parti ouvrier internationaliste,* held a meeting on "The Truth of the Moscow Trials" in September 1936. The Surrealists attended and read their own statement saying that the trials were "an abject police enterprise which far surpasses that of the Reichstag fire." By this act Stalin had become "the great negator and principal enemy of the proletarian revolution. Now, instead of the watchword, 'defend the U.S.S.R.,' we urgently demand that 'defend revolutionary Spain' be substituted for it, especially the magnificent and revolutionary elements of the *C.N.T.* (National Confederation of Labor), the *F.A.I.* (Federation of Spanish Anarchists), and the *P.O.U.M.*" They also said they wanted to work with the *Comité de vigilance des intellectuels anti-fascistes* which was conducting an investigation of the trials and they ended with a declaration of support for Trotsky. "We salute this man who has been for us an intellectual and moral guide of the first magnitude and whose life, now that it is threatened, is as precious to us as our own."[9] Certainly, this statement was the strongest expression of pro-Trotsky feeling the Surrealists had yet made. Most likely, it does not reflect a significant change of opinion but rather the fact that, no longer tied to the Communist Party, they could freely express their admiration for him. Yet in spite of these sentiments, Breton said that the Surrealists were not welcomed by the *P.O.I.,* a fact which he attributed to the old feud he had had with Pierre Naville, now one of its officials. The intervention of Victor Serge, now in exile from the Soviet Union and living in Paris, was required before they were allowed to read their statement but their desire to collaborate with the *P.O.I.* was simply ignored.[10]

Breton also wrote a declaration of his own on the Moscow trials, *Déclaration d'André Breton à propos des seconds procès de Moscou,* expressing his disbelief that such faithful old Bolsheviks as Zinoviev, Kamenev, and Radek could be guilty of treason. No more than was Trotsky, he added. He also denounced Soviet action against the *P.O.U.M.* and the whole non-Communist Left in Spain in the strongest terms.

> It is necessary for Stalin to prevent at any price a new revolutionary wave from engulfing the world. It is a question of aborting the Spanish revolution, just like the German and Chinese revolutions. If one objects that [Russia] supplied arms and planes? True, first because it is necessary to save face and then because these arms have another purpose: to destroy those in Spain who are not working for the restoration of the bourgeois republic, but for a better world.[11]

There could be no more hope of working with the French Communist Party, yet, unlike so many disillusioned ex-Communists, the Surrealists never turned to the Right. Breton's next political move was to align the movement with Trotsky whom he visited in Mexico and with whom he established close personal ties.

In 1938, being in especially difficult financial straits, Breton accepted a cultural mission from the French government to lecture on French art and literature in Mexico. But his chief motive for accepting was that it would give him the opportunity of meeting Trotsky and, because of his great admiration for the exiled revolutionary, his trip to Mexico was virtually a pilgrimage. He complained that his political enemies in France had conducted a campaign to turn Mexican artists and intellectuals against him before he had even arrived. According to him, the *A.E.A.R.* circulated a letter among their Mexican counterparts that said

> M. André Breton has always taken a stand against the *front populaire*. He has allied himself with the most dubious political elements and his actions against the Spanish Republic have taken the most perfidious forms. Avowed admirer of Trotsky, he has always denounced the *International Association of Writers* and because of this, was not allowed to speak at the *First International Congress of Writers for the Defense of Culture*.
> (signed) René Blech.

He also said that Aragon sent a letter to the Mexican *A.E.A.R.* asking for a "systematic sabotage of all Breton's activities in Mexico."[12] However, in spite of these attempts to discredit him, Breton reported that he was very warmly received in Mexico when he arrived in February 1938.[13]

Through Diego Rivera, at whose house he stayed, he was able to meet Trotsky who was then living in Coyoácan. He vividly portrayed the tense atmosphere of Trotsky's existence; the heavy guard surrounding the house and the constant threat of assassination with which he had to live.[14] He also spoke of his overwhelming joy at meeting Trotsky, whose profound mind, breadth of learning, and great love of art impressed him immeasurably and he was very moved by the spectacle of the heroic, lonely figure of Trotsky in exile:

> I saw him as that man who placed his genius in the service of the greatest cause I know. . . . I saw him at the side of Lenin and later, as the only one continuing to defend Lenin's ideas. I saw him standing alone among his fallen comrades . . . accused of the greatest crime possible for a revolutionary, threatened every hour of his life, delivered up to blind hatred. . . . And yet, what self control, what certainty of having lived in perfect accord with his principles, what great courage! . . . Be assured, comrade, that the capitalist countries are quite right to have unanimously forbidden Trotsky asylum. Trotsky free, here in Paris today, speaking to the masses, would create a new wave of revolution everywhere.[15]

His admiration was so boundless, it bordered on hero-worship. In a letter to the former Bolshevik leader, written as he was leaving Mexico, Breton said he had felt inhibited in the presence of such a great man. A "Cordelia complex" gripped him when he was face to face with Trotsky whom he regarded as the greatest man alive and it was difficult for him to express his thoughts. "I need a long process of adjustment to persuade myself that you are not beyond my reach," he declared fervently.[16] His effusiveness was so great, it embarrassed Trotsky who admonished him in his reply, "your eulogies seem to me so exaggerated that I am becoming uneasy about the future of our relations."[17] But Breton's admiration had begun when he "discovered" him in 1925, after reading his biography of Lenin and it continued to grow long after Trotsky's assassination in 1940.[18]

Breton reported that the two had intensive discussions about art and that Trotsky was especially interested in current *avant-garde* movements. He found him to be very sympathetic to the special problems of the artist and was gratified to discover that he shared the Surrealists' concern for the freedom of art and that he approved of their stand against socialist realism. Trotsky was indeed interested in Surrealism, as he was in all such movements, although he had reservations about certain aspects of its philosophy. He was skeptical of the Surrealists' Freudian emphasis on dreams and the subconscious and "shook his head over a strand of mysticism in the work of Breton and his friends," as Isaac Deutcher put it.[19] But he was not entirely anti-Freud. He approved of the materialist basis of psychoanalysis, namely, the stress on physiological drives, and said that while Freud's hypotheses were sometimes fantastic and too much emphasis was given to sexual factors, Marxists should not totally reject Freudian theory.[20] Some aspects of Surrealist thought seemed too metaphysical to Trotsky yet, on the whole, he was favorably disposed toward it and believed in the revolutionary character of *avant-garde* art movements in general, as he had said in 1934: "Cubism, Futurism, Dadaism [and] Surrealism have all superseded each other without any of them coming to fruition. . . . It is impossible to find a way out of this impasse by means of art alone. . . . If society does not succeed in reconstructing itself, art will inevitably perish. Hence, the function of art in our era is determined by its relation to the Revolution."[21] Moreover, his views of socialist realism coincided with those of the Surrealists: "One cannot without revulsion and horror read the poems and novels or view the paintings and sculptures in which bureaucrats armed with pen, brush or chisel, supervised by bureaucrats armed with revolvers, glorify the 'great leaders of genius.' . . . The art of the Stalinist period will remain as the clearest expression of the decline of the proletarian revolution." He concluded, in words which could as easily have been written by Breton, that "a genuinely revolutionary party cannot and will not wish to 'guide' art, let alone command it. Only an ignorant and insolent bureaucracy run amok with arbitrary power could conceive such an ambition. . . . Art can be the Revolution's great ally only insofar as it remains true to itself."[22]

During Breton's stay in Mexico, he and Trotsky agreed to collaborate on a manifesto to be called *Pour un art révolutionnaire indépendant*. Since Trotsky was forbidden by the Mexican government to engage in any political activities, it appeared under the names of Breton and Diego Rivera. But after Trotsky's death, Breton revealed that Rivera contributed nothing more than his signature and that it was really the work of Trotsky[23] and himself and Deutcher, Trotsky's biographer, has confirmed that Trotsky was the real co-author.[24] The manifesto developed the convictions that he and Breton held in common about artistic freedom. It began by damning both the fascist and Stalinist regimes for stifling and destroying art, but it also condemned the decadence of the bourgeois democracies. Freudian theory was used to illustrate the psychologically damaging effects on the artist of the conflict between his ego and the hostile environment in which he must live and "this fact alone, insofar as he is conscious of it, makes the artist the natural ally of revolution." The young Marx was quoted as saying that "the writer by no means looks on his work as a *means,* it is an end in itself," and the authors added that "it is more than ever fitting to use this statement against those who would regiment intellectual activity."

The manifesto was emphatic in demanding freedom for art: "In the realm of artistic creation, the imagination must escape from all constraint. . . . To those who would urge us . . . to consent that art should submit to a discipline which we hold to be radically incompatible with its nature, we give a flat refusal, and we repeat our deliberate intention of standing by the formula *complete freedom of art*."[25] On this point, according to Breton, the text originally read "complete freedom of art, *except against the revolution,"* but Trotsky insisted on striking out the qualifying clause because he feared it would lead to new abuses.[26]

In a key statement on the role of the state in regulating artistic production, the text was somewhat ambiguous. It was conceded that occasionally, for a limited period of time, some censorship might be necessary.

> We recognize, of course, that the revolutionary state has the right to defend itself against the counterattack of the bourgeoisie. . . . But there is an abyss between those enforced and temporary measures of revolutionary self-defense and the pretension to lay commands on intellectual creation. If, for the better development of the forces of material production, the revolution must build a *socialist* regime with centralized control, to develop intellectual creation, an *anarchist* regime of individual liberty, should from the first be established. No authority, no dictation, not the least trace of orders from above.

However, the authors were strongly opposed to an "art for art's sake" philosophy: "It is far from our wish to revive a so-called pure art which generally serves the extremely impure ends of reaction. No, our conception of the role of art is too high to refuse it an influence on the fate of society. We believe that the supreme task of art in our epoch is to take part actively and consciously in the preparation of the revolution." The dilemma of the artist, as Trotsky and Breton saw it, was that, choked and stifled by decadent capitalist society, he turns to the Stalinist organizations to escape his isolation. But he cannot remain in them without becoming utterly demoralized and subservient. "He must understand that his place is elsewhere," they declared.[27]

The purpose of the manifesto was to provide such an alternative. It concluded with an appeal to the artists of the world to unite in forming a new organization, a "popular front" for artists to be called the *Fédération internationale de l'art révolutionnaire indépendant,* or F.I.A.R.I.

> The aim of this appeal is to find a common ground on which may be united all revolutionary writers and artists. . . . Marxists can march hand in hand here with anarchists provided both parties uncompromisingly reject the reactionary police patrol spirit represented by Joseph Stalin. . . . Every progressive tendency in art is destroyed by fascism as "degen-

erate." Every free creation is called "fascist" by the Stalinists.
Independent revolutionary art must now gather its forces for
the struggle against reactionary persecution.

In order to bring the *F.I.A.R.I.* into existence, Breton and Trotsky
called for the creation of local committees in different countries
and eventually, for an international congress of artists to decide on
a program of action. They ended with the slogan, "Our aims: the
independence of art—for the revolution. The revolution—for the
complete liberation of art!"[28] It was published in *Clé,* an
F.I.A.R.I., organ that appeared in France, in the *Worker's International News* in England, and in *Partisan Review,* in the United
States.

    Although Trotsky did not admit authorship, he did write a
letter to Breton that was published in *Partisan Review* giving his
enthusiastic endorsement to the project.

> My dear Breton,
>
> With all my heart I congratulate Diego Rivera and yourself on
> the creation of the *F.I.A.R.I.*—an international federation of
> truly revolutionary and truly independent artists. And why
> not add of *true* artists?. . . The sheep-like servility of the
> intelligentsia is . . . a not unimportant sign of the rottenness
> of contemporary society. . . . Why speak of the Aragons, the
> Ehrenburgs and other *petites canailles?* Why name those gen-
> tlemen (death has not absolved them) who compose, with
> equal enthusiasm, biographies of Christ and of Stalin?

The last reference was, of course, to Barbusse, and it is significant
that Trotsky should have singled out the three writers, Barbusse,
Ehrenburg, and Aragon, whom Breton most detested. Trotsky's
letter shows such familiarity with the aims of the new organization
that it provides further proof that he co-authored the original text.
"Properly understood, the *F.I.A.R.I.* is not an esthetic or political
school and cannot become one. . . . [But] in our epoch of con-
vulsive reaction, . . . truly independent creation cannot but be
revolutionary by its very nature. . . . To encourage such attitudes
among the best circles of artists—this is the task of the *F.I.A.R.I.*
I firmly believe that its name will enter history."[29]

    Both the manifesto and Trotsky's letter emphatically under-
lined the artist's right to, and need for, complete creative freedom.
But the problem of counterrevolutionary art was not adequately

resolved. One cannot demand complete freedom for art on the one hand, and concede the possibility of suppressing reactionary art on the other. This inconsistency did not escape an art critic who heard Breton read the tract at a Trotskyist meeting in Paris in 1939. "The authors of this manifesto . . . claim complete liberty for all artistic production . . . yet they are careful really to postulate this independence of art *only insofar as it would not go against the coming of the dictatorship of the proletariat.*"[30] While this critic was admittedly hostile, he did point to an important contradiction. To say that the artist is a natural revolutionary, to equate the "true" artist with the revolutionary artist, did not solve the problem. It would still presumably be the task of some authority to evaluate art in terms of its revolutionary content. The authors declared their opposition to "so-called pure art" because, in reality, it was art in the service of reaction. Yet they did not say how reactionary artists should be dealt with. The manifesto was emphatic only in its demand for a new role for art, different from any that it had played in Stalinist Russia, the fascist dictatorships, and the bourgeois democracies. Although the authors did not entirely reject censorship for political reasons, they were aware of the dangers and stated that it should be severely limited. As envisaged by the manifesto, it would certainly be far less onerous than that exercised by totalitarian regimes. Breton's own expulsions of various men who had failed to live up to Surrealist ideals suggests that he himself could not have been completely opposed to censorship. But as Breton and Trotsky tried to make clear, such interference by the State would be an unfortunate and temporary expedient rather than a fundamental characteristic of government policy.

The manifesto clearly rejected the doctrine of socialist realism, as well as the reactionary bourgeois "art for art's sake" school of aesthetics. It called upon a broad coalition of left-wing artists who had also rejected both these alternatives to come together, and specifically extended an invitation to anarchists to join the *F.I.A.R.I.* thus emphasizing the libertarian nature of the project. This last point may well have been Breton's contribution because, mindful of his frustrating experiences with the French Communist Party, he was determined to define revolutionary art in the broadest possible way. In spite of its shortcomings, the manifesto was a definite assertion of the necessary connection between creativity and artistic freedom. It also included a constructive plan of organizing to achieve its goal, namely, the *F.I.A.R.I.*

The interesting question of why Trotsky should have desired to collaborate with Breton on this venture was asked of him by a friend who was formerly a French Communist Party member. "I pointed out my surprise at the collusion existing between the rationalism of Trotsky and the increasingly publicized unreason of the Surrealists. . . . [Trotsky] told me he could not afford to be sectarian in ideological matters when allies were so hard to come by. Since the Surrealists accepted unity of action, he could not see why he should refuse an alliance with them."[31] To his admission of isolation should be added the fact that Breton, already famous, could not have been unknown to him. He must have also been aware of the several tracts written in his defense by the Surrealists and thus been favorably disposed towards them, and Breton's high regard for him may also have been a factor. But most important was the striking similarity of their views on the question of artistic freedom, as shown by their earlier writings. On this subject, at least, Breton and Trotsky were of one mind, and both worked to bring the F.I.A.R.I. into existence.

Surrealism in 1938

On Breton's return to Paris in May 1938, he was determined to organize a French branch of the *F.I.A.R.I.* but first, there were problems within the Surrealist ranks that required his attention. He learned to his utter dismay that Eluard had been writing for *Commune,* the *A.E.A.R.* journal, which had tried to sabotage his Mexican mission. When he told Eluard that contributing to *Commune,* was, in his opinion, an act of personal as well as political disloyalty, Eluard retorted that such collaboration implied no political adherence on his part and shocked Breton by adding that he even contributed to right-wing journals.[32] He then felt he had no choice but to break relations with Eluard who had been one of his closest friends and one of the original founders of the Surrealist group. "We never again saw one another. Thus, abruptly ended a friendship which for years had never stopped growing," said Breton sadly.[33]

Eluard began moving closer to the Communist Party, which he formally joined in 1942.[34] Whatever his reasons, there is no question that the rewards for a writer in the mainstream of the Left were far greater than if he remained attached to one of the many marginal splinter groups. In fact, this was the interpretation some of his contemporaries gave of his actions. "It has been a shock that Eluard's sense of expediency has made so brilliant a poet prefer continuation of his connection with the Stalinist *Commune* to signing the *F.I.A.R.I.* manifesto," said Sean Niall, Paris correspondent of *Partisan Review*.[35] But perhaps Eluard simply hoped to reach a larger audience through the publications of the one revolutionary party with a mass base. Perhaps he needed to participate more directly in the political events of the day, a need which Surrealism, isolated as it was, could not adequately fulfill. This is all the more likely since he joined the Party in 1942 and immediately became active in its Resistance organizations. However, there was never an "affaire Eluard" comparable to the "affaire Aragon," which had involved the international artistic community in vehement protests and petitions.

By 1938, events in Europe were moving too rapidly and grimly toward war for Eluard's defection to be given much publicity and his break with the Surrealists passed virtually unnoticed. The only reference Breton made to their former friendship came years later when he protested the treatment of the Czech poet, Zavis Kalandra. In 1950, he wrote a "Lettre ouverte à Paul Eluard" reminding him of their trip to Czechoslovakia where they had been so well received. "Nothing separated us then. From the political point of view, we were far from claiming orthodoxy." He also reminded Eluard that together, they had signed the document, *Du Temps que les surréalistes avaient raison,* that had hurled defiance at the Stalinists, and he pleaded with him to come to the defense of their old friend who had been one of the chief supporters of Surrealism in Czechoslovakia. Kalandra had just been sentenced to death on what Breton believed were trumped up charges. But Eluard refused to come to Kalandra's aid because, "I have too much to do with the innocent who proclaim their innocence to occupy myself with the guilty who proclaim their guilt."[36] Breton's appeal to past friendship could not prevail over the politics of the Cold War.

Another defection, or rather expulsion, was that of Salvador Dali. He had been given the insulting epithet "Avida Dollars" (Greedy for Dollars), an anagram of his name because, as it implied, Dali had "sold out to café society, General Franco, and Roman Catholicism."[37] Naturally, his commercialism was a grave sin in the eyes of the Surrealists. He had gone so far as to design window displays for Bonwit Teller and to Breton and his friends this was an inexcusable vulgarization of Surrealism.[38] But even more objectionable were Dali's bizarre political attitudes. He had painted an insultingly scatological portrait of Lenin which the Surrealists had forced him to alter.[39] He had even painted the portrait of the Spanish ambassador to France which meant that he had been so unprincipled as to accept an official commission from a fascist government.[40] Worst of all, he apparently felt a strange mystical attraction for Hitler although, with Dali, it is hard to tell what was sincere and what was mere publicity seeking. It is clear, however, that his political opinions were inseparable from his sexual fantasies.

> I was fascinated by Hitler's soft, round back always so tightly encased in his uniform. . . . The softness of the Hitlerian flesh, squeezed into the military tunic brought me into a state of ecstasy. . . . I considered Hitler a complete masochist possessed by the idea of provoking a war in order to lose it heroically. In fact, he was preparing one of those gratuitous acts which were at the time very much appreciated by our group.

Dali was quite well aware of how these remarkable reflections would be taken for he commented that "my insistence on considering Hitler's mystique from the Surrealist point of view, . . . as well as my insistence on the sadistic element of Surrealism, . . . ended in a series of breaks and intermittent rows with Breton and his friends."[41] He could hardly be said to have had rational political views. His peculiar fascination with Hitler, whom he described as a Wagnerian tragic figure, might best be called a form of "aesthetic fascism." Dali apparently even developed a theory of the inherent superiority of the Latin race, although this may have been only a questionable form of humor.[42] His ideas scarcely endeared him to the Surrealists who, in the tense and troubled times of the late 1930s, felt compelled to expel him, even though he was their most celebrated painter, more famous even than Miró or Ernst.

Breton, in the late 1930s, tried desperately to publicize the plight of the victims of fascism. Mindful still of the great debt he owed to Freud's work, he hurriedly published a moving protest against his alleged arrest in Vienna by the Nazis. Trying to marshal world opinion to come to Freud's aid he said,

> We learn with deep misgiving of the arrest at Vienna of Sigmund Freud. An entire life of shining understanding, of

exclusive devotion to the cause of human emancipation . . . is practically bound to end in one of Hitler's concentration camps. . . . A symbolic guard of honor must be organized around his person to secure his . . . immediate release and assure a peaceful and glorious end . . . to a life of inspiration which we hold as dear as our own.

As it turned out, his protest on this occasion was unnecessary because, happily, Freud had been able to flee to London. But Breton did not forget the countless other less fortunate victims. "We are also aware . . . that, with a daily increasing despair of being heard, other appeals fly about our heads . . . on behalf of people who ask nothing except to be left free, but are suddenly accused of monstrous crimes."[43]

One other pre-war tract that was extremely pessimistic, *Ni de votre guerre, ni de votre paix* (Neither your war nor your peace), was issued on the subject of the Munich talks. The Surrealists were not deluded into thinking that the Munich settlement meant "peace in our time," and they spoke sadly of the "coming war which is threatening to erupt out of the inextricable conflicts of imperialism." It "will not be a war for democracy, nor a war for liberty," they predicted. The countries of the West and their accomplices in the Third International, had allowed Italy to swallow up Ethiopia, aborted the Spanish revolution, and delivered China into the hands of imperialist Japan. They firmly declared their opposition to the fascist countries, to Russia, but also to the Western capitalist countries. After condemning all sides, they ended with a pathetically vague formula of faith in the "new forces which will build a completely new Europe through the proletarian revolution."[44] This manifesto was signed *Le Groupe surréaliste,* rather than with individual signatures, because of fear of reprisals by the government, especially against foreign Surrealists residing in France, and perhaps also to conceal from the public the defection of Eluard, one of their most prestigious members.[45] The political atmosphere in France in the late 1930s was becoming increasingly repressive. Even before World War II began, the Communist Party was banned, many of its leaders jailed or forced into exile, the Party press was censored, foreign Communists and socialists were denied asylum, and the Surrealists shared the despair over the fate of Europe that gripped anti-fascist forces everywhere.

"Toward an Independent Revolutionary Art"

In spite of their pessimism, the Surrealists had no intention of abandoning their political activities. On the contrary, they threw their energies into the creation of the new international artists' organization, the *Fédération internationale des artistes révolutionnaires indépendants,* that had been proposed by the Trotsky-Breton manifesto. The "new forces" mentioned in the tract on Munich were, they hoped, to be marshalled with the help of the *F.I.A.R.I.* that came into being when Breton returned to France and founded the French section. Its membership included the Surrealists, and some of the people from *Contre-Attaque.* Some Trotskyists also joined, although the French Trotskyists as a whole did not support the *F.I.A.R.I.* A national committee was formed whose members were Yves Allégret, André Breton, Michel Collinet, Jean Giono, Maurice Heine, Pierre Mabille, Marcel Martinet, André Masson, Henri Poulaille, Gérard Rosenthal, and Maurice Wullens.[46] In addition, those who agreed to collaborate with the *F.I.A.R.I.,* in response to a questionnaire by Breton included Jef Last, Francis Vian, Read, Serge, Paul Bénichou, Albert Parez, J. F. Chabrun, Nadeau, Cahun, Nicolas Calas, Michel Carrouges, Roger Blin, Marcel Duhamel, Marcel Jean, Ignazio Silone, Thirion, and Henri Pastoureau.

True to its internationalist principles, *F.I.A.R.I.* groups were simultaneously organized in Mexico, where Diego Rivera published a new review, *Clavé,* based on the ideas of the Trotsky-Breton manifesto, in Buenos Aires, where a group called *Liborio Justo* published the manifesto, and in England, where the editors of the Surrealist *London Bulletin* founded a London section of the *F.I.A.R.I.*[47] There was also an American section organized by *Partisan Review,* which had originally published the manifesto as well as Trotsky's letter advocating its formation. *Partisan Review* had recently broken with the Communist Party and welcomed the anti-Stalinist revolutionary artists' group. Niall felt that the *F.I.A.R.I.* would provide a rallying point for those artists who, because they cherish their independence, have grown more and more disillusioned with "Stalinism's increasingly hypocritical betrayals of Communism." Yet, he did have certain reservations. He thought it unfortunate that Breton felt it necessary to confuse the issue by praising Freud in the manifesto. He was afraid that "many honest writers . . . will hesitate to sign a manifesto which seems to imply adhesion not only to revolutionary liberties, but also to cult limitations." However, the project of organizing the revolutionary artists' group was a "courageous action which cannot be too highly admired." He also pointed out that "the admirable *F.I.A.R.I.* has already made excellent progress: more than fifty signatures of leading artists have already come in. The Moscow frame-up trials are having their delayed but certain result."[48]

The Paris group, the most numerous and best organized, began to publish its own review, *Clé: Bulletin mensuel de la F.I.A.R.I.,* but after only two issues, it inevitably became one of the many casualties of World War II. A flyer announcing its appearance declared optimistically that "*Clé: Bulletin de la F.I.A.R.I.,* . . . will serve the closely linked causes of art, of revolution, and of man."[49] *Clé* was primarily a political journal and was not devoted exclusively to artistic questions, although freedom of art was naturally one of its dominant themes. Its first editorial denounced the new decree laws against foreigners residing in France which even affected some of their own members. These laws, said the editors, were "the politics of panic." To deny the right of asylum was a fascist measure and they protested that for generations Paris had been the home of the international *avant-garde:* "Art has no country any more than does the proletariat. . . . To try to bring about a return to "French art" . . . is to bring about a deliberate historical regression, as the fascists and Stalinists have done. Our foreign artist comrades are being threatened today just as much as our foreign worker comrades." They furiously denounced the French government for arbitrarily creating a whole category of people, foreigners residing in France, with no legal status or protection.[50]

The resurgence of French nationalism and militarism even among the Communists, was especially alarming to the *F.I.A.R.I.* In one article, Pastoureau chastised a Communist for a bellicose speech calling for a renewal of French patriotic values to defeat "the Huns of the twentieth century." "We conclude," said Pastoureau, "that the intellectuals on the Left are ready to throw themselves without conscience into war. . . . Our most urgent task will be to expose these aggressive motives."[51] Giono, the pacifist novelist, took an even stronger anti-war stand saying, in words reminiscent of Ribemont-Dessaignes in his Dada period, "all men fight because they are forced to fight. But it requires more courage to say 'this is not my *métier*' than to obey and be mobilized. It requires a lot of courage to be an avowed pacifist, . . . more than to be an avowed warrior."[52] *Clé* was as much opposed to French government policies as to Stalinism and fascism. It criticized Daladier for ordering strikers back to work and for forgetting that these workers were the very same ones who, in February 1934, had marched in his support.[53] It denounced Léon Blum for "strangling the Spanish revolution with the garrot of non-intervention,"[54] and the Popular Front in general because "its goal is not to satisfy but to deceive the masses."[55] In demanding that the French government intervene in Spain against Franco, they may have seemed inconsistent, but they made a distinction between a popular revolution, such as the Left in Spain was trying to bring about, and an imperialist war.

Just as *Contre-Attaque* had done, *Clé* denounced Stalin and the French Popular Front government as equally counterrevolutionary and of practicing a politics of deception.

> We accuse Stalin and Litvinov of breaking the existing ties between the Russian workers and their foreign comrades. More particularly, they break these ties by practicing the policies of the Popular Front which, like all reformist politics, delivers the proletariat over to its enemies. In effect, under the false pretext of social peace, the democrats have disarmed the working class. . . . Blind is he who does not see that to fight for anti-fascist democracy means to fight for imperialist oppression: British imperialism in India, French imperialism in Indo-China and Morocco, [and] legal assassination of the true revolutionaries in the Spain of Négrin.

As for Stalin, "all revolutionary action is abhorrent to him as . . . has already been proven by his policies in Germany, in China, in Spain, and in France."[56]

The journal also took issue with those intellectuals, such as Julien Benda and Jean Schlumberger, who asserted that in these times of crisis, normal liberties must be suspended because dissent against the government was irresponsible and dangerous. The editors announced that "we will maintain freedom of expression from all constraint and . . . we are dedicated to working . . . for the achievement of an authentic peace, sole guarantee of human civilization. . . . To this end, we maintain our solidarity with the working class which we hope will retain its great organized strength."[57] *Clé*'s concern with individual liberties was not re-

stricted to the cultural sphere. In a collective protest signed by the
F.I.A.R.I., Persécutions démocratiques, Clé came to the defense
of Spanish civil war veterans exiled from their own countries and
ordered expelled from France, an order which in some cases was
tantamount to a death warrant.

> One of the most important and shameful effects of the wave
> of xenophobia which today washes over this country is re-
> vealed in the attitude of the French government with regard
> to the wounded and sick former fighters for the Spanish
> Republic. . . . These men are condemned to death in their
> own countries (Germans, Italians, etc. [*sic*] . . .). Yet, the
> French government finds it expedient to expel these men.
> This gesture of hypocritical complicity with international
> fascism is . . . monstrous.[58]

In an article for *Clé*, Péret, a veteran of the Spanish Civil War,
blamed the failure of the Spanish Revolution on the Stalinists just
as he had done in his letters to Breton from the Front. "The results
of the Stalinist policies . . . are now evident. The *coup de grâce*
given to the proletarian revolution in May 1937 was followed by
an uninterrupted series of defeats. . . . The policy of Negrín,
increasingly revealing its counterrevolutionary character, has led
to a crushing demoralization . . . of the entire working class." He
concluded sadly that "the civil war had become more and more an
imperialist war . . . for the defense of Anglo-French capital as
opposed to Italo-German imperialism."[59]

The second and final issue of the review struck a profoundly
pessimistic note. As Péret had noted, the revolution in Spain had
failed. Intellectuals were being ruthlessly purged in the Soviet
Union, as well as in Nazi Germany.[60] France itself was becoming
less free and more militaristic, suspending the recently guaranteed
forty-hour week in munitions factories.[61] Even in Mexico, revolutionary artists were being persecuted. A collective protest,
N'imitez pas Hitler, denounced the Mexican government for
destroying some politically controversial frescoes of O'Gorman:
"Destroying works of art was until now the infamous privilege of
fascism. . . . The first Manifesto of the *F.I.A.R.I.* called for complete liberty of art. It follows from this that any persecutions of
artists lead us to oppose the perpetrators who, at the same time,
become enemies of culture and of the proletarian revolution."[62]

Several articles explored the possibilities of action for revolutionary artists and intellectuals but failed to reach any positive conclusions. Diego Rivera demanded that "the *F.I.A.R.I.* serve to reassure artists . . . that they will not become what they were in 1917: victims, accomplices, and dupes. . . . It is necessary that the *F.I.A.R.I.* succeed in its work of giving us a clear and precise position in the revolutionary movement. It is no longer a question either of . . . shining a light on the road to revolution nor of being charming, irresponsible children . . . buying the goodwill of capitalist whores."[63] The same pessimism was voiced by Michel Collinet who declared that the intellectual in capitalist society is necessarily either a whore or a slave. He must be on the side of revolution, yet both "the Germany of Hitler and the Russia of Stalin show us that the intellectual has become a simple cog in the military state machine."[64] Herbert Read had also become utterly disillusioned.

> In our decadent society . . . art must enter into a monastic phase. . . . Art must now become individualistic, even hermetic. We must renounce, as the most puerile delusion, the hope that art can ever again perform a social function. . . . This is equally true in Russia and in the West. Art has become nonsense [because] it matters little whether your army is military or industrial; it is still an army and the only art appropriate for an army is the music of a military marching band. . . .[65]

The general consensus was that neither liberty nor the creative spirit can prevail against the power of the state. *Clé* was tending, whether consciously or not, toward anarchism in its politics and one article did advocate the study of the anarchist classics: "Kropotkin's idea that the state is always incompatible with liberty and must be destroyed is most relevant today. . . . The disasters of the first two Internationals and the perfection of the capitalist military machine make it imperative that radicals thoroughly reexamine the problems of the Revolution in the light of Kropotkin's analysis."[66] Yet this anarchist theme was not enlarged upon and apparently was not then considered as a possible direction for the *F.I.A.R.I.* One last manifesto, *A bas les lettres de cachet! A bas la terreur grise!* (Down with arrest orders! Down with secret terror!) appeared in February 1939. It indignantly protested the incarceration without charges of three French leftists: a student, a professor, and a worker. "Until now, in this country, individual liberty enjoyed a relative protection. But the French government is beginning to fight the totalitarian states with their own weapons, chief among which is the suppression of individual liberty." *Clé* feared this was only a first step toward a general detention of suspects for the sake of national security and concluded with the warning that "it is not a question of their liberty alone, but of liberty for all of us."[67] This was the final publication of the short-lived *F.I.A.R.I.,* whose members were soon dispersed by the war.

According to Nadeau, who was himself a member, even this small group was not free from dissension. Hugnet was expelled because of his continuing friendship with Eluard, and Marcel Martinet and Henri Poulaille caused bitter antagonism by trying to take control of the group from the Surrealists. However, its failure cannot be blamed primarily on internal conflicts, but rather on external events. The role of *Clé* as guardian of liberty in all spheres, political and artistic, was an admirable one given the increasingly repressive atmosphere of France in the late 1930s. But it was completely ineffectual. Compared to the enormity of the approaching world war, such injustices as the jailing of the three leftists, or the expulsion of Spanish Civil War veterans, mattered little. The destruction by government officials of a certain artist's work mattered even less. The voice of *Clé* could not possibly be heard and Breton comented that "the unity necessary for the success of the *F.I.A.R.I.* was lacking by a great deal, so that *Clé* disappeared after its second number. Yet this failure, at such a moment, was compounded by so many others: intellectual activity in general came to a halt because thinking men had already decided that nothing could turn back the scourge of war."[68]

"Thinking men" had obviously become anachronisms and the *F.I.A.R.I.*'s policies, as Breton suggested, were simply irrelevant. They were merely an elaboration of the ideas of *Contre-Attaque* and of the Surrealists at the time of the Spanish Civil War and the Moscow trials. *Clé*'s members were anti-Stalinist as well as anti-fascist. They also opposed the Western European bloc because of its imperialist and militarist character and continued to proclaim their solidarity with the proletariat against capitalist governments. They were against the Popular Front because it was aimed at preventing revolution in Spain and deceiving the workers at home, and the Stalinist parties cooperated in this deception because they, too, wanted to prevent further revolution. Stalinism had become counterrevolutionary and desired only to preserve the status quo. The *F.I.A.R.I.* articulated its demand for a genuine world peace, its belief in the international character of culture in opposition to nationalism of any kind, and for freedom of the individual, as well as freedom of artistic expression. The impetus for its formation had been provided by Trotsky and his views on revolutionary art, yet, as has been shown, its members were left with the apparently insoluble problem of how the revolutionary artist was to function as such. It was doubtless inevitable, given the political circumstances of 1939, that they failed to resolve this problem. The grandiose, or at least wildly optimistic, notion of bringing into being a "third force," anti-fascist, anti-militarist, and revolutionary, was obviously doomed to failure and, after the war, the social and political climate had changed so much that it proved impossible to revive the *F.I.A.R.I.*

2
The Revolutionary Legacy

Breton in the United States and Haiti

The impact of Surrealism has been so great that it gave rise to a whole new international generation faithful to its artistic conceptions and often to its political ideology. But by 1939, even though its influence continued to grow, its major contributions had already been made. Although the group reconstituted itself in postwar Paris with new members and continued in existence after the death of Breton in 1966 under the leadership of the writer, Jean Schuster, it was no longer the pre-eminent *avant-garde* movement. Existentialism had taken its place.

World War II and the Resistance are not really germane to the history of Surrealism because most of its members were noncombatants in exile from Europe. Former Surrealists who remained in France, like Aragon, Eluard, and Tzara, took part in the Resistance, but they joined as Communists, not as Surrealists, having long ago broken with the movement. The three lived underground, built Resistance units, worked for the *Comité national des écrivains,* the organization for writers in the Resistance, and contributed to a number of clandestine publications. Both Aragon and Eluard were decorated after the war and both are sometimes given the unofficial title of "poet of the Resistance."

Char fought in the French army, then worked for the Resistance, as did Thirion, who also took part in the liberation of Paris. Unik was killed by the Nazis and Desnos, arrested by the Gestapo, died in Theresienstadt, but none of these men were active in Surrealist circles at the time of the war. Of the remainder, most left the country.

Despite his vehement anti-militarism, Breton found himself back in uniform after the general mobilization of September 1939, assigned as a medical corps instructor to an aviation school in Poitiers.[1] Ernst was interned in France as an enemy alien but, with the help of Peggy Guggenheim, who later married him, he was able to go to New York.[2] Péret was jailed for his political activities by the Nazis, but was released after paying a ransom. He then fled to Mexico where he remained for the duration.[3] After the fall of France, many of the Surrealists had gone south to the Unoccupied Zone and found temporary refuge at the Villa Bel-Air, maintained by the American Committee of Aid to Intellectuals in Marseilles. From there, they went to the United States or to Latin America. The Vichy government censored Breton's books and even put him under arrest, but the American Committee intervened on his behalf, succeeded in getting him released, and he and his wife also went to New York.[4] In France, Surrealist activity virtually ceased, with the exception of a few clandestine works put out by a group of younger followers of Breton. They were "secret messages in a bottle floating in the sea from people (many of whom are now dead or disappeared) who were forced to write "POETRY" to mean "REVOLUTION.""[5] Nöel Arnaud was the leader of this short-lived imitator of Surrealism, called *Surréalisme-Révolutionnaire* that tried to work with the Communist Party and attempted to carry on the movement's identification of poetry with revolution. But it disbanded in 1947,[6] and this was the only Surrealist, or Surrealist-inspired writing to appear in France during the war.

Once in New York, the artists were welcomed by various patrons—in particular, Peggy Guggenheim and Julien Levy—and they threw themselves into the work of staging a large exhibition for the benefit of French relief organizations. Breton founded a new review *VVV,* which he edited with Duchamp, Ernst, and the American sculptor, David Hare. *VVV* had four issues that appeared from 1942 to 1944, but despite its title (V for Victory), it made very few references to the war or to contemporary politics. He also did broadcasts for the Voice of America and gave a very moving lecture at Yale where, conscious that he was addressing young men soon to be drafted, he stressed the Surrealist commitment to liberty.

> Liberty: whatever gross abuses some have tried to make of it, this word is not in the least corrupted. It is the only word which could burn the tongue of Goebbels, it is the one word that his colleague, Pétain, could not stand to see carved on public monuments. . . . From one war to the other, one can say that the passionate quest for liberty has constantly been the motivation of Surrealist activity.[7]

But Breton's most significant political activity in the New World occurred on a visit to Haiti where he unintentionally touched off a revolt that overthrew the government. The visit was meant to be a cultural mission, like his previous trip to Mexico. He was to give lectures and establish good relations with intellectuals in Haiti and the French Antilles and was warmly welcomed when he arrived in Port-au-Prince in December 1945.[8] He gave his first lecture to a packed hall speaking of the grandeur of the Haitian past and the African patrimony which had given the Haitian people the will to throw off the yoke of oppression and win its independence. He also spoke of the philosophy of Surrealism, the essence of which was freedom, and of the word liberty, which he loved more than any other. His audience, consisting largely of intellectuals chafing under censorship restrictions, was electrified. The newspaper *La Ruche,* organ of young liberals in opposition to the regime, devoted a special number to Breton and Surrealism, and quoted extensively from his lecture. As a result, it was immediately suspended by the government.[9] The next day, what became known as the "Revolution of the Seventh of January" began.[10] In protest against the suspension of *La Ruche,* students demonstrated in the streets. The following day, they were joined by workers who declared a general strike because the government, headed by President Elie Lescot, had become increasingly unpopular. Postwar inflation had added to the misery of the people and Lescot was generally suspected of being too friendly with the hated Trujillo.[11] In three days, he was forced to resign and flee the country, as a result of a revolt touched off by—of all things—a lecture on Surrealism.

While the revolt would seem a perfect vindication of the revolutionary character of the movement, Breton had no illusions about his own role in the uprising: "Let us not exaggerate it. . . . At the end of 1945, the misery of the Haitian people was at its height: Imagine that, on the island of Gonave, off the coast of Haiti, a day's work paid less than one American cent, and that . . . children on the outskirts of Port-au-Prince kept alive by fishing in the sewers."[12] René Bélance pointed out that "naturally, Breton had no intention of disturbing the political order of a country which was not his own . . . [but] the banal fact was that to speak of liberty—at that moment—was certainly a subversive act."[13] A new assembly was elected, a new constitution drawn up, and a new president, Dumarsais Estimé, took office, but unhappily, no lasting improvement in Haitian conditions took place. It was merely a "palace revolution." There was, for a while, however, greater freedom of expression, and the year 1946 marked the beginning of the "Haitian Renaissance," an extraordinary flowering of Haitian art and literature, influenced in part by Surrealism.

Postwar France: Surrealism under Attack

After his trip to Haiti, Breton returned to France only to find himself greeted with coldness and hostility both by former Surrealists and by younger poets and artists. Tzara, in a book called *Le Surréalisme et l'après-guerre,* objected to the Surrealists' presumption that they could simply return from their safe wartime haven in America, and resume their former activities just as if World War II had never happened.

> What is Surrealism today and how does it justify itself historically when we know that it was absent from this war, absent from our hearts and from our activities during the Occupation? . . . History has passed Surrealism by because the world cannot be fixed upon immutable positions. Ideological currents move and change in the wake of social transformations.[14]

Tzara criticized the movement's opposition to *poésie de circonstance* and argued that the necessities of clandestine life in the Resistance required this *genre.* "How," he asked, "could we divide ourselves in two, thinking and acting on the one hand for the liberation of our country, and thinking and writing on the other according to a disembodied ideal? . . . The problem of *poésie de circonstance* could not pose itself to us, any more than could the dilemma of dream and reality. These questions were resolved by acting. In the Resistance, we found our unity."[15] He then complained that in the one Surrealist publication of the war years, *VVV,* "one cannot find the slightest allusion to the war and the Occupation." It was clear, in spite of Tzara's protestations to the contrary, that he could not forgive Breton and the others for having been in America during the war.

> It is far from my intention to reproach those who left France at the time of the Occupation. But one must point out that Surrealism was entirely absent from the preoccupations of those who remained because it was of no help whatsoever in their struggles against the Nazis. . . . I fail to see how Surrealism can simply begin playing its old role again, at the point where it left off, just as if this war and all that resulted from it was nothing more than a quickly forgotten dream.[16]

The movement was also attacked by an old enemy, Roger Vailland, whom Breton had severely denounced years earlier for writing laudatory articles on the Paris chief of police. Vailland, now a Communist Party member, wrote *Le Surréalisme contre la révolution,* in which he complained that the Surrealists were never really politically committed. The "purest" of them fought and died in the Resistance—but not Breton. "He continued to live on the margins, in exile, in New York. The Revolution has no need of Surrealism: it needs coal, steel, atomic energy, and above all, that virile energy that makes great scholars, far-sighted leaders and heroic thinkers." The Revolution also needs poets, he conceded, but the Surrealists are not real revolutionaries. The real ones, Picasso, Eluard, Aragon, and Tzara, have broken with Breton, "who has lately revealed a mystical and religious streak and rehabilitated the notion of the sacred."[17] As a Party member, Vailland had a special reason to denounce the Surrealists. They had just issued their first postwar manifesto, *Rupture inaugurale,* announcing their refusal to cooperate with the Communists because "these heirs of Marxism are guilty of class collaboration and because of their fanatically vengeful attitude toward Germany. . . . It is inconceivable that one could, without endangering all the other peoples of the world and without shame, keep the German people quarantined and cut them off from the world community."[18] This criticism came at the period of the Party's greatest prestige and popularity because of its heroic role in the Resistance, and it resulted in what one Surrealist, Jean-Louis Bédouin, called "a powerful offensive against Surrealism in general and against its founder in particular."[19]

But it was not only the Communists who denounced the movement; the younger generation of intellectuals, too, were either opposed or indifferent. One of the young *avant-garde* writers, Isidore Isou, leader of the new *Lettrist* group, declared that he had interviewed Breton and that the meeting was a waste of time because he had nothing new to say about literature. "There remains only a rather vague gentleman with failing memory who chews over the poor fodder of André Breton."[20] The Existentialists, who were now the intellectual leaders in France, also assessed Surrealism and found it wanting. Camus dismissed it as purely negative revolt, merely a manifestation of what he called "metaphysical rebellion." "In reality, revolution for André Breton was only a particular aspect of rebellion. While for Marxists, and in general for all political persuasions, only the contrary is true. . . . Breton made use of revolution to further the Surrealist adventure."[21] Camus's dismissal of Surrealism was, if at all, applicable only to the period of trances and séances, but Sartre had similar, though more subtle, criticisms. "I recognize in no uncertain terms that Surrealism is the *only* poetic movement of the first half of the twentieth century; I even recognize that in a certain way it contributes to the liberation of man. But what it liberates is . . . pure imagination."[22] The famous "systematic destruction" of Surrealism never went any further than provoking *scandales,* so the Surrealists were merely rebels, not revolutionaries. As such, "they were right in the bourgeoisie's line," and "even became their accomplices."[23] According to his reasoning, their very success was ultimately counter-revolutionary because it made people content with the status quo: "If Breton thinks that he can pursue his inner experiences on the margin of revolutionary activity and parallel to it, he is condemned in advance, for that would amount to saying that a freedom of spirit is conceivable in chains, at least for certain people, and, consequently, to making revolution less urgent."[24] The movement was condemned to futility, he added, because one of its many paradoxes was the contradiction between its need for violence and destruction and the real principles of Marxism which it could not assimilate.

Surrealist Themes: Post-War Continuity

Surrealism was being dismissed as irrelevant or counterrevolutionary on all sides, and one of the most common criticisms leveled at it was its lack of ideological consistency. But a careful study of its politics does reveal an underlying continuity. True to their internationalist convictions, the Surrealists supported the Garry Davis "citizen of the world" movement that, along with a parallel world disarmament organization, the *Front humain,* attracted a great deal of attention in France.[25] Even the Existentialists favored it for a time in spite of Simone de Beauvoir's condescending remark that "Sartre was in complete agreement with the Communists that the Garry Davis affair was nothing but hot air. . . . The significant thing was that he should have been taken seriously by European 'left-wing' intellectuals."[26] Breton withdrew his support when Davis began to demand the legalization of conscientious objection in France because it was such a trivial issue compared with total disarmament, and when Davis began to encourage the support of religious groups, Breton became thoroughly disgusted with him.[27] Nevertheless, he and his friends demonstrated the persistence of their internationalism, their desire to play a political role and also of their anti-clerical and anti-religious sentiments.

One of their first post-war manifestoes, published in 1947, was *Liberté est un mot Vietnamien,* denouncing the French intervention in Indochina.[28] As always, Surrealism was anti-militarist and anti-colonialist, opposing the resurgence of imperialism in France just as it had done in 1925 at the time of the Riff war in Morocco. Another tract condemned the colonialist French government and demanded an immediate cease-fire in Algeria.[29] Most important, Breton was one of the signers of the famous *Manifesto of the 121* against the Algerian war signed by 121 of the foremost artists and intellectuals of France. It was a courageous document whose signers understood that their words could be legally construed as treason, and it declared that

> we respect and we justify the refusal to take arms against the Algerian people. . . . We respect and we justify the conduct of Frenchmen who believe it their duty to bring aid and protection to oppressed Algerians in the name of the people of France. The cause of the Algerian people, which has contrib-

uted in decisive fashion to the overthrow of the colonial system, is the cause of all free men.[30]

The Surrealists also maintained their anti-Stalinist position, while continuing to regard themselves as Marxists. They published a protest against the Soviet intervention in Hungary in 1956,[31] and in *Au Tour des livrées sanglantes,* they defended their ideological position against the Stalinists.

> For twenty years, Surrealism has been in complete opposition to Stalinism which, however, implies no abandonment of revolutionary objectives but, on the contrary, such an opposition is demanded as a moral guarantee, and in addition, Surrealism claims a *truly* dialectic conception of individual revolt: force and unlimited *negation* transformed into a positive revolutionary consciousness.[32]

Thus, they persisted in regarding Stalinism as a betrayal of revolutionary principles. Breton, who always maintained that you could not be friends with a man whose politics you disagreed with, went so far as to break off a lifelong friendship with Picasso because he had joined the Communist Party.[33]

In several postwar essays, Breton again denounced the theory and practice of socialist realism, calling it, among other things, a means of "moral extermination."[34] While many critics have pointed out that there were inherent philosophical contradictions between Surrealism and Marxism that made a break inevitable, it was actually their refusal to accept the doctrine of socialist realism which turned out to be the key factor in the severing of relations. Sartre, who was close to the Party for years after the war, also attacked them for this refusal and condemned them for lacking a working-class public.

> The Surrealists have no readers in the proletariat. . . . Their public is elsewhere, among the cultivated bourgeoisie. The C. P. [Communist Party] knows this and uses them simply to stir up trouble in ruling class circles. Thus, their revolutionary doctrines remain purely theoretical, . . . and find no echo among the workers; they remain the parasites of the class they insult; their revolt remains on the margin of the revolution.[35]

This criticism was often made by leftists.[36] Yet, if the bourgeoisie did co-opt Surrealism, it could be argued that it was, at

least partly, the fault of the Party that had determined in advance
that its art had no appeal for the masses and therefore made no
attempt to present it to them. Even during the period of relatively
good relations between the Surrealists and the Communists, an art
critic in *L'Humanité* could praise Dali's paintings and the Surrealist
film, *L'Age d'or,* while remarking, in what can only be described as
a patronizing manner that, of course, this kind of art was not for
the proletariat. It is at least conceivable that the masses could be
educated to appreciate Surrealism and other non-representational
kinds of art, but no such attempt was ever made. On the contrary,
the Party did all it could to foster socialist realism as the only truly
revolutionary art, while condemning Surrealism as bourgeois and
counter-revolutionary.

The Communists, understandably, complained of the Surrealists' penchant for Freud, their liking for erotic themes in art,
their persistent admiration for Trotsky, their outspoken condemnation of the literary qualities of *L'Humanité,* and their general
inability or refusal to accept discipline. But none of these factors
proved to be the decisive one. It was ultimately the quarrel over
socialist realism that provoked their expulsion and made them try
to join forces with Trotsky. Matthew Josephson has pointed out
that this refusal to acquiesce in the dictates of a policy they could
not approve of was actually a *moral* stand and this is precisely how
they themselves saw it.[37]

The underlying conflict, apparent from the beginning, finally
erupted into open antagonism over the *affaire Aragon.* At issue
were two fundamentally different attitudes toward art and the role
of the artist in society. The Communist International developed
the concept of proletarian literature and later of socialist realism in
the belief that art must immediately serve the cause of revolution.
The Surrealists, without actually disagreeing with this assertion,
were primarily concerned with upholding the absolute freedom of
the artist which, they insisted, is a necessary precondition for
artistic creation. Art can serve the revolution in many ways, even if
it lacks an overtly revolutionary content, they believed. They also
maintained that to subject art to an outside discipline, even a
Marxist discipline, would destroy the atmosphere that art must
have to flourish, therefore, they denounced socialist realism in the
name of freedom of art and of the artist. They were the first to see
that its principles were antipathetical to true creativity, and indeed,
the doctrine became something of an embarrassment, even in

orthodox Communist circles. The "thaw," which began after the death of Stalin, ushered in a more liberal era for which many left-wing intellectuals were profoundly grateful. Ironically, it was Ehrenburg, formerly so hostile to Surrealism, who was the first to take advantage of the new dispensation by publishing *The Thaw*, a novel that attacked the rigidity of socialist realism. From then on, he continued to plead for a "Soviet humanism," by which he meant greater artistic freedom than the regime had yet permitted. But it was Breton who was the first to insist that a revolutionary message cannot be conveyed through a conservative form and style.

As Alquié said in *The Philosophy of Surrealism*, Breton whole-heartedly believed that revolutionary techniques in art do serve the revolution in spirit, and he asked

> Why does it have to be then that the bourgeoisie, which Breton detests, often receives favorably artistic innovation, while the officials of Communism appreciate only paintings in all points similar to those of the academic artists at the end of the last century? . . . Is there no connection between the will to social revolution and the will to cultural revolution? . . . This so simple and so essential a question, it is surprising to note, has in our time practically been posed only by André Breton.[38]

Alquié also thought that the greatest contribution of Surrealism was to have linked together the spiritual emancipation of the individual with the social liberation of man, seeing both as necessary to the revolution.

After the war, the Surrealists were concerned with reaffirming the validity of their ideology and with proclaiming their positions on current political issues. In the 1960s the group admired the Cuban Marxist experiment.[39] Castroism seemed to them to symbolize the possible emegence of a "third force," neither Russia nor the West, that the Surrealists had called for in the late 1930s, but mounting evidence of political repression eventually disillusioned them. Even the strain of anarchy in Surrealist thought continued to be expressed in a collaboration with the anarchist organ, *Le Libertaire*,[40] yet, as Breton explained, this was not to be construed as a return to the early negativist phase of the movement. His intention was to hail the black flag of anarchism in the name of liberty.

The only remedy . . . is to go back to the principles . . . of anarchism—not to the caricature that is made of it, nor the terror—but to . . . socialism, no longer conceived of as the simple resolution of political and social problems, but as the expression of the exploited masses in their desire to create a classless society where all human values and aspirations can be realized.[41]

The intimate connection between Surrealism and social revolution has not always been made, but there were student groups and youth movements in the 1960s and 1970s that understood its essential message. Among the many slogans scrawled on the walls of the Sorbonne during the May 1968 student revolt in France were ones that said, "Vive la révolution surréaliste!" which suggests that at least some students were very knowledgeable about Surrealist ideology. They shared the same view of the French Communist Party and they too accused the Party of betraying its revolutionary origins, becoming class collaborationist, and part of the "establishment." "These demonstrations in the Latin Quarter . . . were Surrealism in action, revolution in all its purity," according to the journalist, André Billy,[42] and it is certainly true that the May revolt cannot be understood without a grasp of Surrealist ideology.[43] Among its leaders on the strike committee of the "liberated" Sorbonne, were some former *Lettrists* who had founded a group called the *Situationist international* in 1957 and their program had been borrowed almost entirely from Surrealism. It was anti-capitalist, anti-bureaucratic, anti-consumerist and in favor of complete freedom, spontaneity and *autogestion,* or worker control of factories. Their mottoes, "The revolutionary movement can tolerate neither prophets nor guides,"[44] and "All power to the imagination," could just as easily have been said by the Surrealists. The Situationists opposed the Communist Party from the start precisely because of the unhappy experience of the Surrealists who had tried to maintain their independence while in the Party but had been expelled over the issue of artistic freedom. Afterwards, as the Situationists saw it, Surrealist art was co-opted by the bourgeoisie which loves the *avant-garde* as long as it is safely tamed and shorn of its revolutionary potential. In order to avoid either being swallowed up by a purely political movement or being co-opted by the capitalists, the Situationists simply disbanded after 1968, deliberately destroying their organization. But their influence, especially in film and in the theoretical work of their leader, Guy Debord, who wrote the Situationist text, *La Societé du spectacle,* continues to grow.[45]

There was also a group of young people in Chicago in the late 1960s who made a connection between Surrealism and the old I. W. W. *The Rebel Worker,* in which translations of Surrealist writings appeared, was their journal, and they also published an anthology of Surrealist political texts in which the editor, Franklin Rosemont, explained how Surrealism was relevant to his movement.

> Surrealism is at the same time an arsenal, a drug, a way of *seeing* [and] a kind of total guerilla warfare. . . . Little understood on these shores, so systematically lied about by academicians and journalists, it is nevertheless making its seditious presence felt. The Surrealist miracle, without any eclecticism, unites strands of Marxism, anarchism, utopianism, psychoanalysis, hermetic philosophy, "poetry of the damned," Zen, psychedelic drugs, mythology, nonsense literature, anthropology, madness, play, cinema, relativity theory and popular culture. . . . Long live Surrealism at the service of the revolution![46]

In addition, *Radical America,* journal of the Students for a Democratic Society, put out a special issue called *Surrealism in the service of the Revolution,* with translations of Surrealist texts and placed the movement firmly in the Marxist tradition of revolution.

> We are told . . . that Surrealism is only an artistic and literary movement; or that it is exclusively French; or that it somehow "disappeared" as a movement during the second World War. Critics . . . have formed a veritable holy alliance to exorcise the Surrealist spectre. . . . But Surrealism knows well the reasons why it must be attacked. The bourgeois protagonists of "art-for-art's sake" (including its recent incarnations under the names Pop, Op, Minimal Art, etc.) despise the Surrealist movement because of its solidarity with the cause of proletarian revolution, and its adherence to the principles of Marxism-Leninism. . . . Sartre and Camus, while climbing the ladder of literary and philosophical success, also found it auspicious to fulminate against the Surrealist insurrection: their invertebrate polemics against André Breton are classics of incomprehension and calumniation. Stalinists . . . pretend to see in Surrealism only decadence, "idealism," and even

mysticism, doubtless because the Surrealists have never succumbed to the bureaucratic superficiality of so-called "socialist" realism. The liberal humanist Herbert Muller absurdly reduces Surrealism to a "glorification of the irrational, the unconscious," and accordingly manages to read into it similarities with—of all things—fascism.

The Statement concluded with the hope that these misunderstandings of the fundamental nature of Surrealism will be dispelled and it will assume its rightful role as the "inspiration for the theory and practice of total revolution."[47] As is clear from both these comments, there are left-wing organizations that cherish Surrealism precisely because it has been attacked and misunderstood by both Left and Right. They admire it for refusing to be untrue to itself by following the precepts of socialist realism, and they want to rescue it from conservative critics who profess to admire its art while stripping it of its revolutionary ideology. Indeed, Surrealist art without Surrealist ideology is the form without the substance, as those artists believed who demonstrated in New York at the Museum of Modern Art retrospective exhibit of 1968. They objected to the "sanitized" apolitical version of Surrealism that the Museum had presented.

The movement has achieved a truly original and creative synthesis of Marxist and Freudian ideas, a synthesis which appears to have passed almost unnoticed, since it is rarely commented upon. It has tried to link together two revolutions: that of the mind, by liberating the unconscious, and the social and economic revolution of the masses. The Surrealists always maintained that one of the most important ways to undermine capitalism is to destroy the supremacy of bourgeois rationalism and this is precisely what they aimed for in their art. Their most original contribution lay in the way they put Freudian theory to a revolutionary, rather than a therapeutic, use. Their goal was not the treatment of neurosis, but the release of the creative powers of the unconscious from the prison of logical thought. To orthodox Marxists, Freudian theory is, of course, unacceptable. But it could be argued that the Surrealists, in their collective and anonymous art forms, succeeded in creating an anti-elitist art that acquired a new social meaning. Their belief that talent is irrelevant, and that everyone has creative potential in his unconscious, could be a perfect vehicle for a truly revolutionary art. In fact, there were even a few Communist intellectuals who agreed and who tried to defend them on

these grounds. That the official art of a Party dedicated to revolution should be merely an adaptation of a nineteenth century bourgeois aesthetic is an irony that has become increasingly apparent.
Breton and his group were the most consistent opponents of this
narrow view of art, criticizing it from within while they were
members of the Party, and continuing their dissent after they were
forced out.

Their first loyalty was always to the idea of liberty, in every
sense of the word. Many critics have erroneously thought that
Surrealism was an inconsistent, protean movement responsive
only to the whims of the moment, with no coherent underlying
principle. Dreams, séances, eroticism, anarchism, Marxism, were
all, according to this view, taken up only as intellectual toys, and
the movement stands accused of an irresponsible nihilism. But, in
fact, Surrealism was remarkably consistent in its love of liberty.
Seen in this light, its adherence to the Communist Party, its
subsequent anti-Stalinism, its admiration for Trotsky, for Freud,
for de Sade, for the Spanish anarchists, for the Garry Davis movement, and for automatic writing, acquires coherence. Its apparent
contradictions are resolved, unified by its dedication to liberty,
both for the artist and for the masses. Liberty to the Surrealists
meant the absence of all constraints upon human beings. Hence,
their demands to "open the prisons," "disband the army," "free the
mental patients," and their insistence on sexual freedom which
seemed so frivolous and shocking to hostile Communist officials.
It is true that they had their own definition of revolution, but they
recognized the need for political and economic freedom and they
detested the capitalist system because it is based on exploitation
and for this reason, they felt it necessary to ally themselves with
the Party of revolution. Even after they were expelled by the
Communists, they remained Marxists although, again in the name
of liberty, they became vehemently anti-Stalin. Even now, those
who still call themselves Surrealists consider themselves anti-Soviet Marxist revolutionaries. Unlike so many disillusioned intellectuals, they did not drift to the Right after turning against the
Communist Party, but preferred to risk failure and to suffer isolation, by remaining in opposition to both the capitalist West and the
Soviet East.

But liberty for the individual was just as important to them as
mass revolution and this was the underlying cause for all their
conflicts with the Party. They held that the task for which they

were best suited was the freeing of men's minds from bourgeois morality and from Christian religious beliefs which were nothing more than insidious forms of subjection imposed by the dominant class. These were simply another kind of prison from which men had to be freed. Most of all, to Breton and his followers, liberty was needed for art because creative genius could not live unless allowed free expression. This was the reason for the savage denunciation of such former friends as Aragon who, from the Surrealists' point of view, betrayed the cause of artistic freedom by voluntary servitude to a political ideology. This was the reason for Breton's condemnation of censorship, and especially of socialist realism, as totally incompatible with art. This was also why they stressed the importance of poetry and dreams as instruments of liberty and of revolution, much to the consternation of Communist bureaucrats. Finally, this is the explanation of their later adherence to the cause of anarchism, after the narrow, bureaucratic nature of orthodox Communism became obvious to them. When, in the 1950s, they collaborated with the anarchist journal, *Le Libertaire,* it was not a new departure for them; on the contrary, it was perfectly consistent with Surrealist philosophy from the very beginning, it was a collaboration made in the name of liberty.

Notes

CHAPTER **1**

Introduction: Dada and the Great War

1. Ilya Ehrenburg, *Memoirs: 1921–1941* (New York: Grosset and Dunlap, 1966), 12.

2. Jean Arp, *On My Way: Poetry and Essays 1912–1947,* ed. by Robert Motherwell (New York: Wittenborn, Schultz, 1948), 37.

3. Hugo Ball, "Lorsque je fondis le Cabaret Voltaire," *Cabaret Voltaire,* I (May 1916). n.p.

4. Richard Huelsenbeck, *En Avant Dada: Eine Geschichte des Dadaismus;* (Hanover: Paul Steegemann Verlag, 1920), 27.

5. Arp, *On My Way,* 39.

6. Tristan Tzara, *An Introduction to Dada* (n.p., 1951) n.p.

7. Hans Richter, *Dada: Art and Anti-Art* (New York: McGraw-Hill, 1966), 35.

8. Huelsenbeck, *Eine Geschichte des Dadaismus,* 25.

9. Richter, *Art and Anti-Art,* 41.

10. Max Ernst, *Beyond Painting and Other Writings by the Artist and His Friends* (New York: Wittenborn, Schultz, 1948), 13.

11. Richter, *Art and Anti-Art,* 41.

12. Tzara, "Zurich Chronicle 1915–1919," Robert Motherwell, *The Dada Painters and Poets: An Anthology* (New York: Wittenborn, Schultz, 1951), 236–237.

13. Richter, *Art and Anti-Art,* 66.

14. *Ibid.,* 34.

15. The Futurists' glorification of war is apparent in their many manifestoes. See Joshua C. Taylor, *Futurism* (New York: Doubleday, 1961), *passim*.

16. Huelsenbeck, *Eine Geschichte des Dadaismus*, 27.

17. Tzara, "Dégoût dadaiste," *Sept manifestes DADA: Lampisteries* (Paris: Jean-Jacques Pauvert, 1963), 33–35.

18. Tzara, "Pour faire un poème dadaiste," *ibid.*, 64.

19. Louis Aragon, "Manifeste du mouvement dada," *Littérature,* XIII (May 1920), 2.

20. Richter, *Art and Anti-Art,* 16. On the subject of Lenin, one of the Zurich group, Marcu, remembered an encounter with him which is interesting for the complete divergence of views that it shows. Lenin asked, "Do you know the real meaning of this war? One slaveholder, Germany, who owns one hundred slaves is fighting another slaveholder, England, who owns two hundred slaves for a fairer distribution of the slaves." Marcu responded, "How can you expect to foster hatred of this war if you are not in principle against all wars? I thought that as a Bolshevik you were a really radical thinker and refused to make any compromise with the idea of war. . . . I see that we young people can only count on ourselves. . . ." Lenin replied, "I don't know how radical you are or how radical I am. One can never be radical enough; that is, one must always try to be as radical as reality itself." Quoted in Motherwell, *Dada Painters and Poets,* xviii.

21. Richter, "DADA XYZ," Motherwell, *op. cit.,* 285.

22. André Breton, "Patinage dada," *Littérature,* XIII (May 1920), 9.

23. Georges Hugnet, "The Dada Spirit in Painting," Motherwell, *op. cit.,* 131.

24. *Ibid.,* 157.

25. Quoted in Richter, *Art and Anti-Art,* 111–112.

26. Huelsenbeck, "En Avant dada," Motherwell, *op. cit.,* 41–42.

27. Johannes Baader, et al., "Dadaisten gegen Weimar," in Richter, *Art and Anti-Art,* 126.

28. Tzara, "Memoirs of Dadaism," in Edmund Wilson, *Axel's Castle: A Study in the Imaginative Literature of 1870–1930* (New York: Scribner's, 1954), 309–311.

29. Hugnet, "The Dada Spirit in Painting," Motherwell, *op. cit.,* 152.

30. Richter, *Art and Anti-Art,* 109–112.

31. Huelsenbeck, "Dada Lives," *Fall,* No. 25 (1936), 2.

32. Huelsenbeck, "En Avant dada," Motherwell, *op. cit.,* 44.

33. Huelsenbeck, *Dada Manifesto 1949* (New York: Wittenborn, Schultz, 1951. n.p.

34. Adolf Hitler, *Mein Kampf* (Cambridge: Houghton Mifflin, 1943), 258.

35. Huelsenbeck, "En Avant dada," Motherwell, *op. cit.,* 44.

36. Man Ray, *Self Portrait* (Boston: Little Brown, 1963), 390.

37. Breton, *Les Pas perdus* (Paris: Gallimard, 1924), 181–182, 206.

38. Georges Ribemont-Dessaignes, "History of Dada," Motherwell, *op. cit.*, 109.

39. Ribemont-Dessaignes, "L'heure est aux héroes," *391* XI (February 1920). n.p.

40. Matthew Josephson, *Life Among the Surrealists* (New York: Holt, Rinehart, 1962), 119.

41. André Gide, *Les Nourritures terrestres* (Paris: Mercure de France, 1897), 90.

42. Ribemont-Dessaignes, "History of Dada," Motherwell, *op. cit.*, 114.

43. Maurice Nadeau, *The History of Surrealism* (New York: Macmillan, 1965), 45–46.

44. Samuel Putnam, quoted in Motherwell, *Dada Painters and Poets*, xxxiv.

45. Breton, ed., *Les Lettres de guerre de Jacques Vaché* (Paris: Grou-Radenez, 1949), 7.

46. *Ibid.*, 25.

47. *Ibid.*, 9.

48. Breton, *Les Pas perdus*, 9.

49. *Ibid.*, 24.

50. Tzara, "Memoirs of Dadaism," 308.

51. Malcolm Cowley, *Exile's Return* (New York: Viking, 1951), 139.

52. "L'Affaire Barrès," *Littérature*, XX (August 1921), 3.

53. Tzara, "A Letter on Hugnet's 'Dada Spirit in Painting,'" Motherwell, *op. cit.*, 303.

54. Benjamin Péret, "A Travers mes yeux," *Littérature*, XVII (October 1922), 13.

55. Breton, *Les Pas perdus*, 131–132.

56. Georges Lemaître, *From Cubism to Surrealism in French Literature* (Cambridge: Harvard University Press, 1947), 176.

CHAPTER 2

The Negation of Negation

1. Jacques Rigaut, *Littérature*, V (December 1920), 5–7.

2. J. H. Matthews, *An Introduction to Surrealism* (University Park, PA: Pennsylvania State University Press, 1965), 40.

3. André Breton, "Interview du Professeur Freud," *Les Pas perdus* (Paris: Gallimard, 1924), 118.

4. Quoted in Nicolas Calas, "Surrealist Intentions," *Trans/formation: Arts Communication, Environment: A World Review* I, No. 1 (1950), 51–52.

5. Breton, *Manifestes du surréalisme* (Paris: Jean-Jacques Pauvert, 1962), 36–37.

6. Maurice Nadeau, *The History of Surrealism* (New York: Macmillan, 1965), 80.

7. *Ibid.*, 82.

8. Louis Aragon, *Traité de style* (Paris: Gallimard, 1928), 22.

9. Breton, "Entrée des médiums," *Littérature,* nouvelle série, VI (November 1922), 3.

10. Nadeau, *History of Surrealism,* 83.

11. Georges Ribemont-Dessaignes, *Déjà jadis, ou du mouvement Dada à l'espace abstrait* (Paris: Julliard, 1958), 116.

12. Marie-Rose Carré, "René Crevel: Surrealism and the Individual," *Yale French Studies,* No. 21 (May 1964), 79.

13. Ferdinand Alquié, *The Philosophy of Surrealism,* trans. by Bernard Waldrop (Ann Arbor: University of Michigan Press, 1965), 20.

14. *La Révolution surréaliste,* I (December 1924), 1.

15. Breton, *Manifestes du surréalisme,* 27.

16. Anna Balakian, *André Breton: Magus of Surrealism* (New York: Oxford University Press, 1971), 31.

17. William S. Rubin, *Dada, Surrealism and Their Heritage* (New York: Museum of Modern Art, 1968), 64.

18. André Breton, Paul Eluard, and René Char, *Ralentir travaux* (Paris: Editions surréalistes, 1930). There were, of course, counterparts to these literary techniques in painting which were practiced by the Surrealist artists.

19. Breton, *Manifestes du surréalisme,* 25.

20. *Ibid.*, 17–18.

21. *Ibid.*, 40.

22. *Ibid.*, 44–45.

23. *Ibid.*, 57.

24. Julien Levy, *Surrealism* (New York: Black Sun Press, 1936), 3.

25. Breton's mother was so angry when he quit medical school that she said she would have preferred to hear that he had died on the battlefield. (Balakian, *André Breton,* 46). Aragon's family also virtually disowned him when he deliberately failed his exams.

26. Nadeau, *History of Surrealism,* 96.

27. *Ibid.*, 233–237.

28. *Ibid.*, 114–115.

29. *Ibid.*, 238–239.

30. *La Révolution surréaliste,* II (January 1925), 32.

31. Aragon, "Germaine Berton," *La Révolution surréaliste,* I (December 1924), 12.

32. Kriegel refers to the "Dadaists and Surrealists returning from the bloodiest of wars" becoming anarchists as a result of the impact of World War I. Annie Kriegel, *Les Communistes français: Essai d'ethnographie*

politique (Paris: Editions du Seuil, 1968), 122. Joll has made the same point, placing Surrealism squarely in the context of the anarchist tradition. James Joll, *The Anarchists* (Boston: Little, Brown, 1964), 280.

33. *La Révolution surréaliste*, n.p., n.d.

34. "Ouvrez les prisons, licenciez l'armée: Il n'y a pas de crimes de droit commun." *La Révolution surréaliste*, II (January 1925), 18.

35. Aragon, *et al.*, "Declaration of 27 January 1925," *Surrealism and Revolution*, n.p., n.d., 5.

36. Nadeau, *History of Surrealism*, 104.

37. Antonin Artaud, "Lettre aux recteurs des universités européenes," *La Révolution surréaliste*, III (April 1925), 11.

38. Artaud, "Adresse au Pape, *ibid.*, 16.

39. Jean Koppen, "Comment accomoder le prêtre," *La Révolution surréaliste*, XII (December 1929), 31.

40. Artaud, "Adresse au Dalaï-Lama," *La Révolution surréaliste*, III (April 1925), 17.

41. Artaud, "Lettre aux médecins-chefs des asiles de fous," *ibid.*, 29.

42. Eluard, "La Suppression de l'esclavage," *La Révolution surréaliste*, III (April 1925), 19.

43. Robert Desnos, "Description d'une révolte prochaine," *ibid.*, 25–26.

44. Desnos, "Pamphlet contre Jérusalem," *ibid.*, 8–9.

45. Pierre Naville, *La Révolution et les intellectuels: Que peuvent faire les surréalistes?* (Paris: n.p., 1926), 15.

46. Breton, "Léon Trotsky: Lenine," *La Révolution surréaliste*, V (October 1925), 29.

47. André Masson, "Lettre d'André Masson," *ibid.*, 30.

48. David Gascoyne, *A Short Survey of Surrealism* (London: Cobden-Sanderson, 1935), 70–72.

49. "La Révolution d'abord et toujours," *La Révolution surréaliste*, V (October 1925), 31–32.

50. Marcel Fourrier, "De *Clarté* à *La Guerre civile*," *Clarté*, No. 79 (December 1925–January 1926), 10.

51. Breton, *What Is Surrealism?*, 51–52.

52. Kriegel, *Les Communistes français*, 121.

CHAPTER 3

Surrealists and the Clarté Movement

1. Nicole Racine, "The *Clarté* Movement in France 1919–1921," *The Journal of Contemporary History*, Vol. 2, No. 2 (1967), 207.

2. The Communists only got 7.9% of the vote in the 1924 elections,

in spite of a program that was "more reformist than revolutionary—ranging from the seizure of the great private fortunes to the suppression of a standing army." Jacques Fauvet, *Historie du parti communiste français: De la Guerre à la guerre 1919–1939* (Paris: Librairie Arthème Fayard, 1964), 70.

3. Pierre Naville, *La Révolution et les intellectuels: Que peuvent faire les surréalistes?* (Paris: n.p, 1926), 20.

4. Marcel Fourrier, "De *Clarté* à *La Guerre civile,*" *Clarté,* No. 79 (December 1925–January 1926), 10.

5. Jean Bernier, "Un Cadavre," *Clarté,* No. 68 (November 15, 1924), 485.

6. Victor Crastre, *Le Drame du surréalisme* (Paris: Editions du Temps 1924), 32.

7. Crastre, *André Breton* (Paris: Editions arcanes, 1952), 122.

8. Crastre, *Le Drame du surréalisme,* 16.

9. André Breton, *Entretiens 1913–1952 avec André Parinaud* (Paris: Gallimard, 1952), 91–92.

10. *Ibid.,* 118.

11. Breton, "What Is Surrealism?" in *Paths to the Present: Aspects of European Thought from Romanticism to Existentialism,* ed. Eugene Weber (New York: Dodd, Mead, 1962), 258–259.

12. Maurice Nadeau, *The History of Surrealism* (New York: Macmillan, 1965), 118.

13. Crastre, *Le Drame du surréalisme,* 44–45.

14. Crastre, "Le Suicide est-il une solution?" *Clarté,* No. 72 (March 1, 1925), 3.

15. Crastre, "Explosion surréaliste," *Clarté,* No. 74 (May 1925), 200–201.

16. Crastre, "Scandale," *Clarté,* No. 75 (June 1925), 37.

17. Crastre, *Le Drame du surréalisme,* 73.

18. "Appel aux travailleurs intellectuels: Oui ou non, condamnez-vous la guerre?" *Clarté,* No. 76 (July 15, 1925), 284.

19. *Ibid.,* 296.

20. *Ibid.,* 285.

21. Georges Altmann, *et al.,* "La Révolution d'abord et toujours," *Clarté,* No. 77 (October 15, 1925), 301.

22. Naville, *La Révolution et les intellectuels,* 20–21.

23. Naville, "Les Tendances confusionistes du group 'L'Esprit,'" *Clarté* No. 3, nouvelle série (August–September 1926), 24.

24. Bernier, "Ou nous en sommes," *Clarté,* No. 78 (November 30, 1925), 2.

25. *L'Humanité,* November 8, 1925, 2 [italics in original].

26. Bernier, "Ou nous en sommes," 3.

27. As Breton said later, "We are fairly well acquainted with the *Holy Family,* the *Philosophical Works,* the *Poverty of Philosophy,* the *Anti-*

Dühring of Engels, and the *Materialism and Empirocriticism* of Lenin, to cite only the most basic works." Breton, *Entretiens,* 124.

28. Bernier, "Ou nous en sommes," 5–6.

29. Louis Aragon, "Le Prolétariat de l'esprit," *ibid.,* 9.

30. Aragon, "Le Prix de l'esprit," *Clarté,* nouvelle série no. 4 (October–December 1926), 122–123.

31. Robert Desnos, "Le Sens révolutionnaire du surréalisme," *ibid.,* 10.

32. Crastre, "Europe," *La Révolution surréaliste,* VI (March 1926), 28.

33. Fourrier, "L'Opportunisme impuisant," *La Révolution surréaliste,* VII (June 1926), 29.

34. Crastre, *Le Drame du surréalisme,* 87–88.

35. *Clarté,* No. 79 (December 1925).

36. Fourrier, "De *Clarté* à *La Guerre civile,*" *ibid.,* 9–10.

37. Breton, "La Force d'attendre," *ibid.,* 12–13.

38. Nadeau, *History of Surrealism,* 123.

39. Breton, *Entretiens,* 122.

40. Crastre, *Le Drame du surréalisme,* 89–90.

41. Annie Kriegel, *Les Internationales ouvrières 1864–1943* (Paris: Presses universitaires de France, 1964), 89.

42. Crastre, *Le Drame du surréalisme,* 90.

43. Fourrier, "Lettre aux lecteurs de *Clarté,*" *Clarté,* nouvelle série, I (June 15, 1926), 27.

44. Naville, "L'Activité de *Clarté, Clarté,* nouvelle série, XI (July 15, 1927), 20.

45. *Ibid.,* 21.

46. David Caute, *Communism and the French Intellectuals 1914–1960* (New York: Macmillan, 1964), 92.

CHAPTER 4

The Surrealists Join the Communist Party

1. Quoted in Pierre Naville, *La Révolution et les intellectuels: Que peuvent faire les surréalistes?* (Paris: n.p., 1926), 7.

2. *Ibid.,* 25.

3. *Ibid.,* 17.

4. *Ibid.,* 23.

5. *Ibid.,* 26.

6. *Ibid.,* 30.

7. *Ibid.,* 27.

8. André Breton, "What Is Surrealism?" in *Paths to the Present: Aspects of European Thought from Romanticism to Existentialism,* ed. Eugen Weber (New York: Dodd, Mead, 1962), 268.

9. Breton, "Legitimate Defense," in Maurice Nadeau, *The History of Surrealism* (New York: Macmillan, 1965), 243–248.

10. David Caute, *Communism and the French Intellectuals 1914–1960* (New York: Macmillan, 1964), 77.

11. Breton, *Legitimate Defense,* 249–255.

12. Breton, *Entretiens 1913–1952 avec André Parinaud* (Paris: Gallimard, 1952), 133.

13. Edouard Kasyade, *Prétexte à la fondation d'un organe de révolte suivi d'une "Lettre à André Breton"* (Paris, n.p., 1927), 8.

14. *Ibid.,* 23–24.

15. *Ibid.,* 31.

16. Louis Aragon and André Breton, *A Suivre: Petite contribution au dossier de certains intellectuels à tendances révolutionnaires* (Paris, n.p., 1929), 27.

17. Breton, *Entretiens,* 120–121.

18. Paul Eluard, *et al., Au Grand jour* (Paris: Les Editions surréalistes, 1927), 7.

19. Victor Crastre, "Changer l'homme," *Almanach surréaliste du demisiècle numéro spécial de La Nef* (Paris: Editions du Sagittaire, 1950), 26–27.

20. Eluard, *et al., Au Grand jour,* 10–11.

21. Paul Nougé, "A l'Occasion d'un manifeste," *Histoire de ne pas rire* (Brussels: Editions de la revue les levres nues, 1956), 30.

22. Eluard, *et al., Au grand jour,* 14–17.

23. *Ibid.,* 22–27.

24. Antonin Artaud, "A la Grande nuit ou le bluff surréaliste," *Oeuvres complètes* (Paris: Gallimard, 1956), I, 283–286.

25. *Ibid.,* 290.

26. Ruby Cohn, "Surrealism and Today's French Theatre," *Yale French Studies,* No. 31 (May 1964), 160.

27. Pierre Naville, "Mieux et moins bien," *La Révolution surréaliste,* IX–X, 54–57.

28. *Ibid.,* 60.

29. Breton, *Entretiens,* 126–127.

30. André Thirion, *Revolutionaries Without Revolution,* trans. by Joachim Neugroschel (New York: Macmillan, 1975), 116.

31. Maxime Alexandre, *et al.,* "Permettez!" in Nadeau, *The History of Surrealism,* 258–259.

32. Eluard, "D.A.F. de Sade, écrivain fantastique et révolutionnaire," *La Révolution surréaliste,* VIII (December 1926), 8–9.

33. Alexandre, *et al.,* "Hands Off Love!" *La Révolution surréaliste,* IX–X (October 1927), 2. The title is in English in the original.

34. Anna Balakian, *André Breton: Magus of Surrealism* (New York: Oxford University Press, 1971), 175.

35. Quoted in Whitney Chadwick, *Women Artists and the Surrealist Movement* (Boston: Little, Brown, 1985), 12.

36. Hayden Herrera, *Frida: A Biography of Frida Kahlo* (New York: Harper and Row, 1983), 252.

37. Robert Short, *Dada & Surrealism* (London: John Calmann & Cooper, 1980), 165.

38. Mary Ann Caws, "Ladies Shot and Painted: Female Embodiment in Surrealist Art," in *The Female Body in Western Culture: Contemporary Perspectives,* edited by Susan Rubin Suleiman (Cambridge: Harvard University Press, 1986), 267. There are a number of recent articles exploring the question of a separate feminine Surrealist aesthetic created by the women painters and writers. See, for example, Gloria Orenstein, "Women of Surrealism," *Feminist Art Journal,* 2 (Spring 1973), and her "La Vision surréaliste de Kay Sage et la nouvelle conscience féministe," *Mélusine* 3, (1982); Janet Kaplan, "Remedios Varo: Voyages and Visions," *Woman's Art Journal,* 1, No. 2 (Fall 1980/Winter 1981); Josephine Withers, "The Famous Fur-Lined Teacup and the Anonymous Meret Oppenheim," *Arts* 52, No. 3 (November 1977); and Nancy B. Mandlove, "Humor in the Service of the Revolution: Leonora Carrington's Feminist Perspective on Surrealism," *Perspectives on Contemporary Literature,* Volume 7 (1981), in which she argues that in her novels, Carrington creates a fusion of Surrealist and feminist ideals.

39. "Recherches sur la sexualité part d'objectivité, déterminations individuelles, degré de conscience," *La Révolution surréaliste,* XI (March 1928), 33–34.

40. *Ibid.,* 39.

41. J. Frois-Wittman, "Mobiles inconscients du suicide," *La Révolution surréaliste,* XII (December 1929), 41.

42. Horace M. Kallen, "Surrealism as Program and as Achievement," *Art and Beauty: Use and Freedom in Western Civilization from the Greeks to the Present Day,* II (New York: Duell, Sloane and Pierce, 1942), 826.

43. Breton, *Entretiens,* 133–134.

44. Georges Hugnet, ed., *Petite anthologie poétique du surréalisme* (Paris: Editions Jeanne-Bucher, 1934), 35.

45. Jacques Fauvet, *Histoire du parti communiste français* (Paris: Librairie Arthème Fayard, 1964), 98.

CHAPTER 5

At the Service of the Revolution

1. Louis Aragon and André Breton, *A Suivre: Petite contribution au dossier de certains intellectuels à tendances révolutionnaries* (Paris: n.p., 1929), 7–8.

2. *Ibid.*, 24–26.

3. George Ribemont-Dessaignes, *Déjà jadis ou du mouvement dada à l'espace abstrait* (Paris: René Juilliard, 1958), 141.

4. Aragon and Breton, *A Suivre*, 29–31.

5. André Thirion, *Revolutionaries without Revolution*, trans. by Joachim Neugroschel (New York: Macmillan, 1975), 164–170.

6. Arturo Schwarz, *André Breton, Leone Trotskij Storia di un'amicizia tra arte e rivoluzione* (Roma: Edizioni Savelli, 1974), 143 *et passim*.

7. "Le Monde au temps des surréalistes," *Varietés numéro hors séries: Le Surréalisme en 1929* (June 1929), 26–27.

8. Thirion, "A Bas le travail," *ibid.*, 43–46.

9. Breton, *Manifestes du surréalisme* (Paris: Jean-Jacques Pauvert, 1962), 153–157.

10. *Ibid.*, 40.

11. *Ibid.*, 160.

12. *Ibid.*, 188–191.

13. *Ibid.*, 173–174.

14. Maxime Alexandre, *Mémoires d'un surréaliste* (Paris: La Jeune Parque, 1968), 153–154.

15. Breton, *Manifestes du surréalisme*, 171–174.

16. *Ibid.*, 211.

17. Raymond Queneau, *et al.* (n.p., [1930]), 1–4.

18. Robert Desnos, "Troisième manifeste du surréalisme," in Maurice Nadeau, *Histoire du surréalisme: documents surréalistes* (Paris: Editions du Seuil, 1948), II, 157.

19. Marcel Jean and Arpad Mezei, *The History of Surrealist Painting* (New York: Grove, 1960), 207.

20. *Le Surréalisme au service de la révolution*, I (July 1930), hereafter referred to in footnotes as *LSASDLR*.

21. Alexandre, *et al.*, "Déclaration," *LSASDLR*, 41.

22. Max Ernst, "Danger de pollution," *LSASDLR*, III (December 1931), 22–24.

23. Georges Sadoul, "Le bon Pasteur," *LSASDLR*, IV (December 1931), 23–26.

24. Aragon, "Guerre à la mode," *LSASDLR*, II (October 1930), 14–16.

25. René Char, "Les Porcs en liberté," *LSASDLR*, II (October 1930), 20.

26. René Crevel, "Bobards et fariboles," *LSASDLR*, II (October 1930), 17.

27. Benjamin Péret, "La Vie de l'assassin Foch," *LSASDLR*, II (October 1930), 24.

28. Albert Valentin, "Le Haut du pavé," *LSASDLR*, II (October 1930), 21.

29. Pierre Unik, "La France des cinq parties du monde," *LSASDLR,* III (December 1931), 28.

30. Paul Eluard and Benjamin Péret, "Revue de la presse," *LSASDLR,* V (May 1933), 23.

31. *LSASDLR,* VI (May 1933), 41.

32. Char, "Hommage à D.A.F. de Sade à Paul Eluard," *LSASDLR,* II (October 1930), 6.

33. Jean Frois-Wittman, "Les Mots de l'esprit et l'inconscient," *LSASDLR,* II (October 1930), 26–29.

34. Oscar Davitcho *et al.,* "Belgrade 23 décembre, 1930," *LSASDLR,* III (December 1931), 32.

35. Crevel, "Les Surréalistes yougoslaves sont au bagne," *LSASDLR,* VI (May 1933), 36–39.

36. Some of the original group, Ristitch and Dussan Matic, later contributed to a volume on Breton, published after his death, *André Breton 1896–1966 et le mouvement surréaliste* (Paris: La Nouvelle revue française, 1967).

37. Aragon, "Découverte du nouveau monde," *LSASDLR,* I (July 1930), 28–30.

38. Thirion, "Réponse à un recours en grâce," *LSASDLR,* II (October 1930), 32–36.

39. Jacques Rigaut, *Papiers posthumes* (Paris: Au sans pareil, 1934), 82.

40. Breton, "La Barque de l'amour s'est brisée contre la vie courante," *LSASDLR,* I (July 1930), 21–22.

41. *L'Humanité,* June 2, 1930, 3.

42. Sadoul, "Mémoire," *LSASDLR,* I (July 1930), 34–35.

43. Clément Vautel, "Editorial," *Le Journal,* June 4, 1930, 7.

44. Alexandre, *et al., L'Age d'or* (Paris: Corti, 1931), 3.

45. Y. Cloud, *A Note on the Affair of the Surrealist Film, "L'Age d'or"* (n.p., n.d.), 1–2.

46. *Figaro,* December 7, 1930, 3.

47. *Ami du peuple,* December 7, 1930, 5.

48. Alexandre, *et al., L'Affaire de l'age d'or* (n.p., n.d.), 6.

49. *L'Humanité,* December 7, 1930, 4.

50. *L'Humanité,* December 13, 1930, 4.

51. Breton, *et al., Ne Visitez pas l'exposition coloniale* (n.p., [1931]), 1.

52. Yves Tanguy, *et al., Premier bilan de l'exposition coloniale* (n.p., [1931]), 1.

53. Péret, *et al., Au Feu!* (n.p., [1931]), 1.

CHAPTER 6

L'Affaire Aragon and Proletarian Literature

1. Louis Aragon, *Pour un réalisme socialiste* (Paris: Denöel et Steele, 1935), 15.

2. Jan Topass, *La Pensée en révolte: Essai sur le surréalisme* (Bruxelles: René Henriquez, 1935), 105.

3. *L'Humanité,* January 6, 1931, 4.

4. Unpublished letter from André Thirion to the Party Bureau, January 9, 1931. This letter is in a collection of unpublished documents, many of which relate to the *Affaire Aragon,* that Paul Eluard had compiled for the years 1930–1934. It will be referred to hereafter as *Eluard's Notebook.*

5. André Thirion, *Revolutionaries Without Revolution,* trans. by Joachim Neugroschel (New York: Macmillan, 1975), 263–264.

6. René Char et al., *Paillasse! (Fin de "L'Affaire Aragon")* (Paris: Gallimard, 1932), 3.

7. *LSASDLR,* II (October 1930), 42–43.

8. "Reports, Resolutions and Debates: Second International Congress of Revolutionary Writers," *Literature of the World Revolution,* Special Number (November 1931), 4.

9. *Ibid.,* 88.

10. *Rabcors* was an abbreviation of a Russian word meaning "worker-correspondents," and it was simply one of the many words that entered the vocabulary of French Communists during this period. Annie Kriegel, *Les Communistes français: Essai d'ethnographie politique* (Paris: Editions du Seuil, 1968), 220.

11. *Literature of the World Revolution,* 6.

12. *Ibid.,* 87.

13. Roger Garaudy, *L'Itinéraire d'Aragon* (Paris: Gallimard, 1961), 215.

14. *Literature of the World Revolution,* 19.

15. *Ibid.,* 89.

16. *Ibid.,* 103.

17. *Ibid.,* 109.

18. *Ibid.,* 180.

19. *Ibid.,* 245.

20. Caute has formulated "five principles of utility" to explain the ways in which the Communist Party made use of intellectuals. In the case of Barbusse, the first principle, "pure prestige, or eminence, reflecting favorably on the Party," would be a sufficient explanation of why his many deviations did not result in his expulsion. David Caute, *Communism and the French Intellectuals 1914–1960* (New York: Macmillan, 1954), 35.

21. *Literature of the World Revolution,* 103.

22. *Ibid.*, 213.

23. *Ibid.*, 182.

24. *Ibid.*, 211.

25. *Ibid.*, 181.

26. *Ibid.*, 227.

27. Char, *et al.*, *Paillasse*, 4.

28. *Literature of the World Revolution*, 227.

29. Thirion, *Revolutionaries Without Revolution*, 268–269. Daix confirms that the French Communist Party worked against the Surrealists at Kharkov. "It was clear the Party was not willing to allow two suspect Surrealists to represent the French Party in the international organizations created at Kharkov." Pierre Daix, *Aragon une vie à changer* (Paris: Seuil, 1975), 255.

30. Daix, *Une vie à changer*, 251.

31. Char, *et al.*, *Paillasse*, 6–7.

32. See my "Elsa Triolet: The Politics of a Committed Writer," *Women's Studies International Forum*, Vol. 9, No. 4, 1986, for a fuller treatment of the role played by Triolet in the *Affaire Aragon* and her conception of socialist realism. Gershman argues that "Aragon left Surrealism less for Communism than for Elsa," although the reasons are actually more psychologically—and politically—complex than he suggests. Herbert S. Gershman, *The Surrealist Revolution in France* (Ann Arbor: University of Michigan Press, 1969), 100. Daix and Thirion, who knew her, also stress Triolet's importance in the *Affaire*: Daix, *Une vie à changer*, 253; Thirion, *Révolutionnaires sans révolution*, 169–170.

33. Louis Aragon, Georges Sadoul, "Aux Intellectuels révolutionnaires," in Maurice Nadeau, *Histoire du surréalisme: Documents surréalistes*, Vol. II (Paris: Editions du Seuil, 1948), 226–227.

34. Char, *et al.*, *Paillasse*, 9.

35. Aragon, "Le Surréalisme et le devenir révolutionnaire," *LSASDLR*, III (December 1931), 2, 8.

36. Maxime Alexandre, "Un Professeur révoqué," *LSASDLR*, III (December 1931), 11.

37. Clifford Browder, *André Breton: Arbiter of Surrealism* (Geneva: Librairie Droz, 1967), 32.

38. *Literature of the World Revolution*, III (1931), 1.

39. Garaudy, *L'Itinéraire d'Aragon*, 228.

40. André Breton, *Misère de la poésie: "L'Affaire Aragon" devant l'opinion publique* (Paris: Editions du Seuil, 1932), 25–27.

41. By the second charge, Aragon was being held responsible, not only for his own work, but also, as one of the editors of *Literature of the World Revolution*, for the contribution of another poet, *The Cavalry of Boudionny* by V. Vichnevsky. David Gascoyne, *A Short Survey of Surrealism* (London: Cobden-Sanderson, 1935), 112.

42. Alexandre, *et al.*, "L'Affaire Aragon," in Nadeau, 205–207.

43. Breton, *Misère*, 25–27.

44. René Magritte, *et al.*, *La Poésie transfigurée* (Bruxelles, January 20, 1932) and E. L. T. Mesens, *et al.*, *Protestations* (Bruxelles, March 22, 1932) in *Eluard's Notebook*.

45. Breton, *Misère*, 29–30.

46. "L'Inculpation d'Aragon," *L'Humanité*, February 9, 1932, 2.

47. This is a reference to Paul Ruegg, a secretary of the International Trade Unions, who was condemned to death for espionage by the Kuomintang. The Surrealists were among those who signed a petition demanding his release. *L'Humanité*, December 23, 1931, 3.

48. Unpublished letter from Briand, Secretary of Cell 638, to *L'Humanité*, [March (?) 1932], *Eluard's Notebook*.

49. Unpublished letter from André Berthon to Aragon, February 11, 1932, *Eluard's Notebook*.

50. Unpublished form letter from Aragon, [March (?) 1932], *Eluard's Notebook*.

51. Caute, *Communism and the French Intellectuals*, 93–94.

52. "Les Arts," *L'Humanité*, January 14, 1932, 4.

53. *L'Humanité*, January 28, 1932, 4.

54. Salvador Dali, "Rêverie," *LSASDLR*, IV (December 1931), 31–36.

55. Alexandre, *Mémoires d'un surréaliste* (Paris: La Jeune Parque, 1968), 209–210. According to Eluard, Aragon did try to persuade the Surrealists to break with Dali because the Party demanded it. "He dared to ask us, he, author of three books illegally printed, to eliminate Dali, on the pretext that ill-disposed minds wanted to call the collaboration of Dali in our publications pornographic." Eluard, "Certificat," in Nadeau, 228.

56. Breton, *Entretiens*, 167.

57. Breton, *Misère*, 9.

58. *Ibid.*, 12–17.

59. *Ibid.*, 30.

60. *Ibid.*, 18.

61. Daix, *Aragon une vie à changer*, 264.

62. *L'Humanité*, March 10, 1932, 2.

63. Char, *et al.*, *Paillasse*, 9.

64. Eluard, *Certificat*, 229.

65. Alexandre, *Mémoires d'un surréaliste*, 211–212.

66. Maxime Alexandre and Pierre Unik, *Autour d'un poème* (April 1932), 3–4.

67. *Eluard's Notebook*.

68. Tristan Tzara, *Protestation* (December 22, 1932), *Eluard's Notebook*.

69. Tzara, *et al.*, *Minutes*, December 22, 1932, *Eluard's Notebook*.

70. Aragon, "Complainte des chômeurs," *La Lutte anti-réligieuse et prolétarienne* (April 1932), *Eluard's Notebook*.

71. Garaudy, *L'Itinéraire d'Aragon*, 8.

72. Aragon, "Pour qui écrivez-vous?" *Commune* (December 1933), 329.

73. Aragon, *Réalisme socialiste*, 53.

74. *Ibid.*, 79.

75. Garaudy, *L'Itinéraire d'Aragon*, 223.

76. Breton, "Surrealism Yesterday, Today and Tomorrow," *This Quarter: Surrealist Number* (September 1932), 40.

77. Breton, "A Propos du concours de littérature prolétarienne organisé par *L'Humanité*," *LSASDLR*, V (May 1933), 16–18.

78. Breton, *Misère*, 19.

79. Robert S. Short, "The Politics of Surrealism 1920–1936," *Journal of Contemporary History*, I, No. 2 (1966), 17.

80. Gascoyne, *Short Survey of Surrealism*, 119–120.

CHAPTER **7**

Final Rupture and the Doctrine of Socialist Realism

1. Adson, et al., "Protestez!" n.d., n.p., *Eluard's Notebook*.

2. Printed invitation dated March 21, 1933, *Eluard's Notebook*.

3. Louis Aragon, et al., "*L'A.E.A.R.* s'incline devant les victimes et fait appel aux correspondants ouvriers," Maurice Nadeau, *Histoire du surréalisme: Documents surréalistes,* Vol. II (Paris: Editions du Seuil, 1948), 368.

4. André Breton, "M. Renault est très affecté," Nadeau, 369.

5. Philippe Robrieux, *Histoire intérieure du parti communiste 1920–1945,* Vol. I (Paris: Librairie Arthème Fayard, 1980), 455.

6. Breton, *et al., La Mobilisation contre la guerre n'est pas la paix: Les Raisons de notre adhésion au congrès international contre la guerre,* n.p. [1933], n.p.

7. Breton, *Entretiens 1913–1952 avec André Parinaud* (Paris: Gallimard, 1952), 169.

8. Because of lack of funds, the Surrealists stopped publishing *Le Surréalisme au service de la révolution* after the fifth and sixth issues appeared as a double number in May 1933. Until 1938, they collaborated on *Minotaure,* an art review edited by Skira. *Minotaure* was non-political in content, but they also contributed to a leftist Belgian review, *Documents,* until 1935, when it became the organ of the Marxist *Association révolutionnaire culturelle.* There was also the *Bulletin international du surréalisme* of 1935, devoted to Surrealist movements abroad. In addition, various periodicals had special issues on Surrealism from time to time such as the

March 1938 *Cahiers G.L.M.*, but there was no Surrealist review again until after World War II

9. Ferdinand Alquié, "A André Breton," *LSASDLR,* V (May 1933), 43.

10. Years later, Alquié expressed his gratitude for this refusal but added, "I happen to be moved, even more than by interhuman loyalty, by fidelity to impersonal truth, truth that we should in fact prefer to our friends and to ourselves." Alquié, *The Philosophy of Surrealism* (Ann Arbor: University of Michigan Press, 1964), 164.

11. Paul Nizan, "Revues des revues," *Commune,* I (July 1933), 85–87. Timing, however, was of crucial importance as Nizan discovered when, in 1939, he was vilified by the Party because he insisted on fighting the Germans even though the Nazi-Soviet Pact had just been concluded. He was killed in 1940, but much later was exonerated, his reputation was restored, and he is now described as having been a "premature anti-fascist."

12. Guy Mangeot, *Histoire du surréalisme* (Brussels: René Henriquez, 1934), 98.

13. "Les Livres," *L'Humanité,* February 27, 1933, 4.

14. Ilya Ehrenburg, "The Surrealists," *Partisan Review,* II, No. 9 (October–November 1935), 11–13.

15. Ehrenburg, *Post-War Years: 1945–54* (New York: World Publishing, 1967), 287.

16. Copies of three telegrams from Paul Eluard, René Crevel and André Breton, dated February 28, 1933, *Eluard's Notebook.*

17. Maurice Nadeau, *Histoire du surréalisme* (Paris: Editions du Seuil, 1964), 159.

18. Tristan Tzara, *Le Surréalisme et l'après-guerre* (Paris: Editions Nagel, 1948), 31.

19. The manuscript of Eluard's speech is undated but it was clearly given after the Surrealists were expelled from the *A.E.A.R.* since he said "I cannot speak this evening as a member of the *A.E.A.R.*" Also, he mentioned "le front unique," a term of Party policy current in 1934. *Eluard's Notebook.*

20. Alain, *et al.,* "Appel à la lutte," *Documents 34: Numéro spécial: Intervention surréaliste,* I, nouvelle série (June 1934), 5–6.

21. Breton, *Entretiens,* 174.

22. Jean Audard, *et al.,* "Enquête sur l'unité d'action," *Documents 34,* 6–7.

23. David Caute, *Communism and the French Intellectuals 1914–1960* (New York: Macmillan, 1964), 113–114.

24. Breton, "Discours au congrès des écrivains," *Position politique du surréalisme* (Paris: Editions du Sagittaire, 1935), 91.

25. Breton, *et al.,* "La Planète sans visa," *Documents 34,* 9–10. The list of those who signed this pamphlet in defense of Trotsky is rather

small but it does include a number of new recruits. Besides Breton, the names were Roger Caillois, Char, Crevel, Eluard, Maurice Heine, Maurice Henry, Hugnet, Valentine Hugo, Marcel Jean, Jean Levy, Fernand Marc, Jehan and Marie-Louise Mayoux, J. M. Monnerot, Henri Pastoureau, Péret, Guy Rosey, Tanguy, Robert Valançay, and Pierre Yoyotte. In addition there were "a rather large number of foreign comrades" whose names, presumably because of possible legal consequences, were not given.

26. Maxim Gorky, "Soviet Literature," in *Problems of Soviet Literature: Reports and Speeches at the First Soviet Writers' Congress,* ed., H. G. Scott (New York: International Publishers, 1935), 132–133.

27. A. A. Zhdanov, "Soviet Literature—The Richest in Ideas, the Most Advanced Literature," in *Problems of Soviet Literature,* 20–22.

28. Gorky, "Soviet Literature," in *Problems of Soviet Literature,* 67.

29. Zhdanov, "Soviet Literature," in *Problems of Soviet Literature,* 21.

30. Nikolai Bukharin, "Poetry, Poetics and the Problems of Poetry in the U.S.S.R." in *Problems of Soviet Literature,* 250–252.

31. Gorky, "Soviet Literature," in *Problems of Soviet Literature,* 157.

32. *Ibid.,* 142. It is said that Gorky, who played a courageous role in protecting artists and writers, was coerced into giving this speech, the implications of which, as he very well understood, were a virtual denial of artistic freedom.

33. Jürgen Rühle, *Literature and Revolution: A Critical Study of the Writer and Communism in the Twentieth Century* (New York: Praeger, 1969), 136–138.

34. Breton, "La Grande actualité poétique," *Minotaure,* VI (December 1934), 62.

35. E. L. T. Mesens, "Editorial," *Documents 34,* II nouvelle série trimestrielle (November 1934), 3.

36. Ehrenburg, *Memoirs: 1921–1941* (New York: World Publishing, 1964), 62.

37. René Magritte, *et al.,* "L'Action immédiate," *Documents 34 Numéro spécial: Intervention surréaliste,* I nouvelle série (June 1934), 1–3, and Pierre Yoyotte, "Réflexions conduisant à préciser la signification antifasciste du surréalisme," *ibid.,* 90.

38. Breton, *What is Surrealism?* trans. by David Gascoyne (London: Faber and Faber, 1934), 47–48.

39. *Ibid.,* 90.

40. *Ibid.,* 69.

41. Claude Spaak, "Libération de l'esprit," *Documents 34,* II nouvelle série trimestrielle (November 1934), 30–33.

42. Louise Périer, "Livres," *Commune,* XI (December 1934), 359–360.

43. Roger Shattuck, "Writers for the Defense of Culture," *Partisan Review,* Volume LI, Number 3, (1984), 404, *et passim.*

44. Elmer Peterson, *Tristan Tzara: Dada and Surrational Theorist* (New Brunswick, New Jersey: Rutgers University Press, 1971), 123–135. The Congress had set up an *International Writers Association for the Defense of Culture* which held its next meeting, with Tzara as delegate, in Madrid, in the middle of the Spanish Civil War.

45. Breton, *et al.*, "Du Temps que les surréalistes avaient raison," in *Position politique du surréalisme,* 101–102.

46. Marie-Rose Carré, "René Crevel: Surrealism and the Individual," *Yale French Studies, XXXI* (May 1964), 85–86.

47. Breton, "Discours au congrès des écrivains," 84–89.

48. *Ibid.,* 96–98.

49. Ehrenburg, *Memoirs,* 307.

50. *L'Humanité,* June 21, 1935, 3.

51. *Commune,* XXIII (July 1935), 1202.

52. Pierre Vermelen, "La Défense de la culture," in *Documents 35. Revue mensuelle de l'association révolutionnaire culturelle,* III (May 1935), 24–27; and Jean Lavachery, "Pour les Réalités contre les entités," *Documents 35,* 21.

53. Breton, *Entretiens,* 176.

54. Breton, et al., "Du Temps que les surréalistes avaient raison," 107–112. Those who signed this formal declaration of defiance of the Communist Party were Breton, Dali, Oscar Domingez, Eluard, Ernst, Fourrier, Heine, Henry, Hugnet, Sylvain Itkine, Jean, Dora Maar, Magritte, Léo Malet, M.-L. Mayoux, J. Mayoux, E. L. T. Mesens, Nougé, Oppenheim, Henri Pariscot, Péret, Man Ray, Maurice Singer, André Souris, Tanguy, and Valançay. It is interesting that at this time Camus took a position similar to that of the Surrealists. He joined the Communist Party in 1934, but soon left it because, like them, he disapproved of the Franco-Soviet Pact, and also of the weakening of the anticolonialist line which was a necessary tactic in the creation of the Popular Front. Caute, *Communism and the French Intellectuals,* 207–209.

55. Jules Monnerot, *La Poésie moderne et le sacré* (Paris: Gallimard, 1945), 76.

56. George Lichtheim, *Marxism in Modern France* (New York: Columbia University Press, 1966), 86.

57. P. O. Lapie, "L'Insurrection surréaliste," *Cahiers du sud* (January 1935), 102.

58. Claude Cahun, *Les Paris sont ouverts* (Paris: José Corti, 1934), 23.

59. *Ibid.,* 9.

60. *Ibid.,* 26–31.

61. V. Nezval, "Correspondance à André Breton," *LSASDLR* V (May 1933), 31.

62. Editorial, *Bulletin international du surréalisme,* I (April 1935), 3–4.

63. Magritte, *et al.*, "Le Couteau dans la plaie," *Bulletin international du surréalisme,* III (August 1935), 2.

64. Herbert Read, "On the Social Aspects of Surrealism," *Bulletin international du surréalisme,* IV (September 1936), 9–12.

65. Breton, *Position politique du surréalisme,* 14.

66. Georges Bataille, *et al.,* "Contre-Attaque," *Position politique du surréalisme,* 168–174.

67. Nadeau, *Histoire du surréalisme,* 447–451.

68. Robert Short, "Contre-Attaque" in *Le Surréalisme: Entretiens dirigés par Ferdinand Alquié,* (Paris: Mouton, 1968), 160–165.

69. Hugh Sykes Davies, "Surrealism in this Time and Place," in Read, *Surrealism,* 166.

70. Georges Hugnet, "1870–1936," in Read, *Surrealism,* 246.

CHAPTER 8
Trotsky and the Surrealists

1. Claude Courtot, *Introduction à la lecture de Benjamin Péret* (Paris: La Terrain vague, 1965), 22.

2. André Breton, *L'Amour fou* (Paris: Gallimard, 1937), 87.

3. Adolphe Acker, *et al.,* "Il n'y a pas de liberté pour les ennemis de la liberté (Robespierre)," in Maurice Nadeau, *Histoire du surréalisme suivie de documents surréalistes* (Paris: Editions du Seuil, 1964), 456–457.

4. Hugh Thomas, *The Spanish Civil War* (New York: Harper, 1961), 67.

5. Acker, *et al.,* "Neutralité? Non-sens, crime et trahison!" in Nadeau, 458–459.

6. Courtot, *Introduction à Benjamin Péret,* 28–32.

7. Eric Losfeld, ed., *Tracts surréalistes et déclarations collectives 1922–1939,* Tome I (Paris: Le terrain vague, 1970), 512.

8. Courtot, *Introduction à Benjamin Péret,* 34–36.

9. Nadeau, *Histoire du surréalisme,* 460.

10. Breton, *Entretiens 1913–1952 avec André Parinaud* (Paris: Gallimard, 1952), 179.

11. Nadeau, *Histoire du surréalisme,* 462–466.

12. Breton, "Visite à Léon Trotsky," *La Clé des champs* (Paris: Jean-Jacques Pauvert, 1967), 55.

13. Breton, *Entretiens,* 183.

14. *Ibid.,* 187.

15. Breton, *Clé des champs,* 55–56.

16. Letter from Breton to Leon Trotsky, August 9, 1938, quoted in Isaac Deutscher, *The Prophet Outcast Trotsky: 1929–1940* (London: Oxford University Press, 1963), 431–432.

17. Letter from Trotsky to Breton, August 31, 1938, *ibid.,* 432.

18. This admiration was expressed in the form of a loose collaboration with the Fourth International, at least to the extent of signing an

occasional manifesto. In 1956, Breton signed a Trotskyist protest against the general suppression of revolutionary and nationalist movements. The pamphlet denounced Russian aggression in Hungary, French aggression in Algeria, and the Anglo-French military expedition in Egypt. H. Baratier, *et al., Appel pour la libération du mouvement ouvrier* [1956].

19. Deutcher, *The Prophet Outcast,* 432.

20. Trotsky, *Culture and Socialism and a Manifesto: Art and Revolution* (London: New Park Publications, 1963), 11–12.

21. Trotsky, "Art and Politics," *Partisan Review,* V, No. 3 (August–September 1938), 4.

22. *Ibid.,* 7–10.

23. Breton, *Clé des champs,* 63.

24. Deutcher, *The Prophet Outcast,* 432. Schwarz, too, concludes that Trotsky co-authored the manifesto and he interviewed Jacqueline Lamda, Breton's wife at the time, on the collaboration between Trotsky and Breton. Arturo Schwarz, *André Breton, Leone Trotskij* (Rome: Guilio Savelli, 1974).

25. Quoted in Trotsky, *Culture and Socialism,* 35–36.

26. Breton, *Clé des champs,* 63.

27. Trotsky, *Culture and Socialism,* 37–39.

28. *Ibid.,* 39.

29. Trotsky, "Leon Trotsky to André Breton," *Partisan Review,* VI, No. 2 (Winter 1939), 126–127.

30. Sandro Burgi, *Jeu et sincerité dans l'art* (Neuchâtel: A La Baconnièrre, 1943), 86.

31. [René] Etiemble, "The Tibetan Dog," *Yale French Studies,* No. 31 (May 1964), 130.

32. Clifford Browder, *André Breton: Arbiter of Surrealism* (Geneva: Librairie Droz, 1967), 38.

33. Breton, *Entretiens,* 191.

34. Louis Chaigne, *Les Lettres contemporaines* (Paris: editions mondiales, 1964), 323.

35. Sean Niall, "Paris Letter," *Partisan Review,* VI, No. 1 (Fall 1938), 105.

36. Breton, "Lettre ouverte à Paul Eluard," *La Clé des champs,* 284–286.

37. John Richardson, "School for Scandal Forty Years On," *Sunday Times* (London), December 14, 1965, 31.

38. Frank Caspers, "Surrealism in Overalls," *Scribner's Magazine,* 104, No. 2 (August 1938), 19.

39. Breton, *Entretiens,* 181.

40. Breton, *Situation du surréalisme entre les deux guerres* (Paris: Editions de la rue Fontaine, 1945).

41. Salvador Dali, *Diary of a Genius* (New York: Doubleday, 1945), 15–16.

42. Nadeau, *Histoire du surréalisme,* 177.

43. Breton, "Freud at Vienna," *London Bulletin,* No. 2 (May 1938), 2.

44. Le Groupe surréaliste, "Ni de votre guerre, ni de votre paix," in Nadeau, 476–477.

45. Herbert S. Gershman, *The Surrealist Revolution in France* (Ann Arbor: University of Michigan Press, 1969), 232.

46. *Clé: Bulletin mensuel de la F.I.A.R.I.,* I (January 1939), 1.

47. Breton, "Et Vous?" *Clé: Bulletin mensuel de la F.I.A.R.I.,* I (January 1939), 407.

48. Niall, "Paris Letter," 102–104.

49. Nadeau, *Histoire du surréalisme,* 478. I am indebted to Claus and Carol Mueller for obtaining microfilms of *Clé* from the Bibliothèque nationale in Paris.

50. Yves Allégret, *et al.,* "Protestation contre la zénophobie," *Clé* I (January 1939), 1.

51. Henri Pastoureau, "Editorial," *Cle,* 6.

52. Jean Giono, "Précisions (Fragments)," *Clé,* I (January 1939), 2.

53. *F.I.A.R.I.,* "M. Daladier et la grève des fonctionnaires," *Clé,* I (January 1939), 6.

54. Maurice Heine, "Les Fruits de l'automne," *Clé,* I (January 1939), 3.

55. N. C., [Nicolas Calas], "Revue des revues," *Clé,* I (January 1939), 8.

56. "Lettre à nos amis de Londres," *Clé,* I (January 1939), 8.

57. Heine, "Les Fruits de l'automne," in *ibid.,* 1.

58. *F.I.A.R.I.,* "Persécutions démocratiques," *Clé,* I (January 1939), 6.

59. Benjamin Péret, "Un Ennemi declaré," *Clé,* II (February 1939), 2.

60. Victor Serge, "Disparitions en URSS," *Clé,* II (February 1939), 8.

61. Philippe Saint-Placide, "Frankreich erwache!," *Clé,* II (February 1939), 10.

62. *F.I.A.R.I.,* "N'imitez pas Hitler," *Clé,* II (February 1939), 9.

63. Diego Rivera, *Clé,* II (February 1939), 9.

64. Michel Collinet, "L'Homme à la recherche de lui-meme," *Clé,* II (February 1939), 6.

65. Herbert Read, "L'Artiste dans le monde moderne," *Clé,* II (February 1939), 7.

66. Michel Carrouges, "Kropotkine: L'Entre'aide," *Clé,* II (February 1939), 4.

67. Nadeau, *Histoire du surréalisme,* 479–483.

68. Breton, *Entretiens,* 218.

CHAPTER 9

The Revolutionary Legacy

1. Clifford Browder, *André Breton: Arbiter of Surrealism* (Geneva: Librairie Droz, 1967), 39.

2. Herbert Gershman, *The Surrealist Revolution in France* (Ann Arbor: University of Michigan Press, 1969), 155.

3. Claude Courtot, *Introduction à la lecture de Benjamin Péret* (Paris: Terrain vague, 1965), 201.

4. Gershman, *The Surrealist Revolution,* 155.

5. Nöel Arnaud, ed., *Avenir du surréalisme* (Paris: Quatre vingt et un, 1944).

6. Eric Losfeld, ed., *tracts surréalistes et déclarations collectives, Tome II 1940–1969* (Paris: Terrain vague, 1982), xvii.

7. André Breton, *Situation du surréalisme entre les deux guerres* (Paris: Editions de la revue Fontaine, 1945).

8. Jean-Louis Bédouin, *Vingt ans de surréalisme 1939–1959* (Paris: Editions Denöel, 1961), 73.

9. Much of the information on Breton in Haiti was given to me by Professor René Bélance of Williams College who, at that time, was a young Haitian journalist who interviewed Breton and took part in the events of January, 1946.

10. Colbert Bonhomme, *Révolution et contre-révolution en Haiti de 1946 à 1957* (Port-au-Prince: Imprimerie de l'état, 1957), 25.

11. John Fagg, *Cuba, Haiti and the Dominican Republic* (Englewood Cliffs, N.J.: Prentice-Hall, 1965), 154.

12. Breton, *Entretiens 1913–1952 avec André Parimaud* (Paris: Gallimard, 1952), 243–244.

13. Personal letter to the author from René Bélance, February 16, 1969.

14. Tristan Tzara, *La Surréalisme et l'après-guerre* (Paris: Nagel, 1948), 73–74.

15. *Ibid.,* 33–35.

16. *Ibid.,* 73–74.

17. Roger Vailland, *Le Surréalisme contre la révolution* (Paris: Editions sociales, 1948), 47–48, 57.

18. Bédouin, *Storia del Surrealismo 1945 ai nostri Giorni,* trans. Livio Maitan and Tristan Sauvage (Milan: Schwartz, 1960), 256–257.

19. Bédouin, *Vingt ans de surréalisme,* 87.

20. Isidore Isou, *Réflexions sur André Breton* (Paris: Editions lettristes, 1948), 20.

21. Albert Camus, *The Rebel,* trans. Anthony Bower (New York: Alfred A. Knopf, 1956), 96.

22. Jean-Paul Sartre, *What is Literature?* trans. Bernard Frechtman (New York: Harper and Row, 1965), 190–191.

23. *Ibid.*, 129.

24. *Ibid.*, 175.

25. Bédouin, *Vingt ans du surréalisme*, 130–131.

26. Simone de Beauvoir, *Force of Circumstance* (New York: Putnam, 1965), 171.

27. Bédouin, *Vingt ans du surréalisme*, 154–155.

28. Adolphe Acker *et al.*, "Libertà è una Parola Vietnamita," in Bédouin, *Storia del Surrealismo*, II, 253–255.

29. Anne Bédouin, *et al.*, "Au Tour des livrées sanglantes," in Bédouin, *Vingt ans de surréalisme*, 320–322.

30. *The New York Post*, September 14, 1960, 46.

31. Bédouin, *et al.*, "Hongrie, soleil levant," in Bédouin, *Vingt ans de surréalisme*, 323–324.

32. Bédouin, *et al.*, "Au Tour des livrées sanglantes," *ibid.*, 319.

33. Herbert Lottman, *The Left Bank: Writers, Artists, and Politics from the Popular Front to the Cold War* (Boston: Houghton Mifflin, 1982), 261.

34. Breton, "Du Réalisme socialiste comme moyen d'extermination morale," *La Clé des champs* (Paris: Editions du Sagittaire, 1953), 335–339, and "Pourquoi nous cache-t-on la peinture russe contemporaine?", *ibid.*, 316–324.

35. Sartre, *What is Literature?*, 178–179.

36. A typical example of this was the comment of the Marxist critic, Edgell Rickword, on the Surrealist art exhibit in London in 1936: "It is no accident that the Surrealist Exhibition last year was thronged by excessively well-to-do people. The violence of the fantasy satisfied their sense of the necessity of criticizing social reality, while effectively short-circuiting any impulse to action." Quoted in Martin Turnell, "The Social Background of Contemporary Poetry," *Arena*, I, No. 3 (October–December 1937), 227.

37. Personal interview with Matthew Josephson, May 8, 1969.

38. Ferdinand Alquié, *The Philosophy of Surrealism* (Ann Arbor: University of Michigan Press, 1965), 65–66.

39. "Ce qui est important," *L'Archibras: Le Surréalisme,* II (October 1967), 78. *L'Archibras* was the major postwar Surrealist review and was similar in many respects to *Le Surréalisme au service de la révolution* of the pre-war era. In the same issue, an interview with Herbert Marcuse appeared applauding his views of revolutionary poetry as "the true language of politics." Michel Pierson, "Herbert Marcuse," *L'Archibras*, II (October 1967), 17–20.

40. J. Pierre, ed., *Surréalisme et anarchie: Les "billets surréalistes" du Libertaire 12 octobre 1951–8 janvier 1953* (Paris: Plasma, 1983), *passim*.

41. Breton, "La Claire tour," *La Clé des champs*, 327.

42. Quoted in *Tracts surréalistes, Tome II, vii*.

43. Bernard F. Brown, *Protest in Paris: Anatomy of a Revolt* (Morristown, New Jersey: General Learning Press, 1964), 103 *et passim*. Brown

states that "every aspect of Situationist theory (and, by extension, of the ideology of the May revolt that so impressed the public) can be found in the older Surrealist movement. . . . Situationism is Surrealism resurgent," 103. Alfred Willener, in *The Action Image of Society: On Cultural Politicization* (New York: Pantheon Books, 1970), also stresses the students' debt to Surrealism in the character of their revolt.

44. Quoted in Willener, *The Action Image,* 146.

45 Myriam D. Mayan, "From Avant-Garde Aesthetics to the Occupation of the Sorbonne: The Career of the Situationist International, 1957–1968" (Paper delivered at the Fourteenth Annual Conference of the Western Society for French History (Baltimore, Maryland, 21 November 1986), 14–15. I am indebted to Dr. Mayan for her analysis of the Situationists.

46. Franklin Rosemont, *Preface: Surrealist Ambush,"* Surrealism and Revolution (Chicago: n.p., 1966), 4.

47. Rosemont, "Introduction," *Radical America: Special Issue: Surrealism in the Service of the Revolution* (January 1970), 1–3.

Bibliography

Primary Sources: Books

Alexandre, Maxime. _Mémoires d'un surréaliste_. Paris: La Jeune parque, 1968.

Alquié, Ferdinand, ed. _Entretiens sur le surréalisme sous la direction de Ferdinand Alquié_. Paris: Mouton, 1968.

————. _The Philosophy of Surrealism_. Translated by Bernard Waldrop. Ann Arbor: University of Michigan Press, 1965.

André Breton 1896–1966 et le mouvement surréaliste. Hommages—Témoignages. L'Oeuvre—le Mouvement surréaliste. Paris: La Nouvelle revue française, 1967.

Aragon, Louis. _Littératures sovietiques_. Paris: Denoël, 1955.

————. _Pour un réalisme socialiste_. Paris: Denoël et Steele, 1935.

————. _Traité du style_. Paris: Gallimard, 1928.

Aragon, Louis and Breton, André. _A Suivre: petite contribution au dossier de certains intellectuels à tendances révolutionnaires_. Paris: n.p., 1929.

Arnaud, Nöel, ed. _Avenir du surréalisme_. Paris: Quatre Vingt et un, 1944.

Arp, Jean. _On My Way: Poetry and Essays 1912–1947_. Edited by Robert Motherwell. New York: Wittenborn, Schultz, 1948.

Arpad, Mezei. _Le Surréalisme en 1947_. Paris: Editions Pierre à Feu, 1947.

Artaud, Antonin. _Oeuvres complètes_. Paris: Gallimard, 1956.

Baron, Jacques. _L'Ani du surréalisme suivi de l'an dernier_. Paris: Denoël, 1969.

de Beauvoir, Simone. _Force of Circumstance_. Translated by Richard Howard. New York: Putnam, 1965.

Bédouin, Jean-Louis. *André Breton*. Paris: Editions Pierre Seghers, 1950.

———. *La Poésie surréaliste*. Paris: Editions Seghers, 1964.

———. *Storia de Surrealismo 1945 ai nostri Giorni*. Translated by Livio Maitan and Tristan Sauvage. Milan: Schwartz, 1960.

———. *Vingt ans de surréalisme 1939–1959*. Paris: Editions de Noël, 1961.

Breton, André. *L'Amour fou*. Paris: Gallimard, 1937.

———. *Arcane 17: Enté d'Ajours*. Paris: Editions du Sagittaire, 1947.

———. *La Clé des champs*. 2d ed. Paris: Jean-Jacques Pauvert, 1967.

———. *Entretiens 1913–1952 avec André Parinaud*. Paris: Gallimard, 1952.

———. *Introduction au discours sur le peu de realité*. Paris: Gallimard, 1927.

———. *Légitime défense*. Paris: Editions surréalistes, 1926.

———. *Manifestes du surréalisme*. Paris: Jean-Jacques Pauvert, 1962.

———. *Misère de la poésie: "L'Affaire Aragon" devant l'opinion publique*. Paris: Editions du Seuil, 1932.

———. *Nadja*. Translated by Richard Howard. New York: Grove Press, 1960.

———. *Ode à Charles Fourier commentée par Jean Gaulnier*. Paris: Librairie C. Klincksieck, 1961.

———. *Les Pas perdus*. Paris: Gallimard, 1924.

———. Point du jour. Paris: Gallimard, 1934.

———. *Position politique du surréalisme*. Paris: Editions du Sagittaire, 1935.

———. *Qu'est-ce que le surréalisme?* Brussels: René Henriquez, 1934.

———. *Situation du surréalisme entre les deux guerres*. Paris: Editions de la rue Fontaine, 1945.

———. *Les Vases communicants*. Paris: Gallimard, 1955.

———. *What is Surrealism?* Translated by David Gascoyne. London: Faber and Faber, 1936.

Breton, André and Eluard, Paul. *L'Immaculée conception*. Paris: Editions surréalistes, 1930.

Breton, André; Eluard, Paul; and Char, René. *Ralentir travaux*. Paris: Editions surréalistes, 1930.

Breton, André, and Soupault, Philippe. *Les Champs magnétiques*. Paris: Au sans pareil, 1920.

Brunius, Jacques B., and Mesens, E.L.T. *Idolatry and Confusion*. London: n.p., 1944.

Burgi, Sandro. *Jeu et sincerité dans l'art*. Neuchâtel: A la Baconnière, 1943.

Cahun, Claude. *Les Paris sont ouverts*. Paris: José Corti, 1934.

Calas, Nicolas. *Confound the Wise*. New York: Arrow Editions, 1942.

Camus, Albert. *The Rebel*. Translated by Anthony Bower. New York: Alfred A. Knopf, 1956.

Carrouges, Michel. *André Breton et les données fondamentales du surréalisme*. Paris: Gallimard, 1950.

Cloud, Y. *A Note on the Affair of the Surrealist film, "L'Age d'Or."* n.p., n.d.

Crastre, Victor. *André Breton*. Paris: Editions arcanes, 1952.

———. *Le Drame du surréalisme*. Paris: Editions du temps, 1963.

Dali, Salvador. *La Conquête de l'irrationnel*. Paris: Editions, Surréalistes, 1935.

———. *Diary of a Genius*. New York: Doubleday, 1945.

Ehrenburg, Ilya. *Memoirs 1921–1941*. New York: Grosset and Dunlap, 1966.

———. *People and Life: 1891–1921*. New York: Alfred A. Knopf, 1962.

———. *Post-War Years: 1945–1954*. New York: World Publishing, 1967.

———. *The Thaw*. Translated by Manya Harari. Chicago: H. Regnery, 1955.

Eigeldinger, Marc, ed., *André Breton: Essais et témoignages*. Neuchâtel: A la Baconnière, 1950.

Eluard, Paul. *Poèmes politiques*. Preface by Louis Aragon. Paris: Gallimard, 1948.

Ernst, Max. *Beyond Painting and Other Writings by the Artist and His Friends*. New York: Wittenborn, Schultz, 1948.

Freud, Sigmund. *The Interpretation of Dreams*. Translated by A. A. Brill. London: George Allen, 1913.

Garaudy, Roger. *L'Itinéraire d'Aragon*. Paris: Gallimard, 1961.

Gascoyne, David. *A Short Survey of Surrealism*. London: Cobden-Sanderson, 1935.

Gide, André. *Les Caves du vatican*. Paris: Editions de la nouvelle revue française, 1914.

Hercourt, Jean. *La Leçon du surréalisme suivie de Jules Supervielle*. Fribourg: Editions du verbe, 1947.

Huelsenbeck, Richard. *En Avant Dada: Eine Geschichte Des Dadaïsmus*. Hanover: Paul Steegeman Verlag, 1920.

Hugnet, Georges. *L'Aventure dada* (1916–1922). Introduction by Tristan Tzara. Paris: Seghers, 1971.

Hugnet, Georges, ed. *Petite anthologie poétique du surréalisme*. Paris: Editions Jeanne-Bucher, 1934.

Isou, Isidore. *Réflexions sur André Breton*. Paris: Editions lettristes, 1948.

Josephson, Matthew. *Life among the Surrealists*. New York: Holt, Rinehart, 1962.

Kasyade, Edouard. *Prétexte à la fondation d'un organe de révolte suivie d'une "Lettre à André Breton."* Paris: n.p., 1927.

Lautréamont, Comte de [Isidore Ducasse.] *Les Chants de Maldoror*. Paris: José Corti, 1953.

Lemaître, Georges. *From Cubism to Surrealism in French Literature*. Cambridge, MA: Harvard University Press, 1947.

Losfeld, Eric, ed. *Tracts surréalistes et déclarations collectives Tome 1, 1922–1939*. Paris: Le Terrain vague, 1980.

———. *Tracts surréalistes et déclarations collectives Tome 2, 1940–1969*. Paris: Le Terrain vague, 1982.

Mangeot, Guy. *Histoire du surréalisme*. Brussels: René Henriquez, 1934.

Monnerot, Jules. *La Poésie moderne et le sacré*. Paris: Gallimard, 1945.

Motherwell, Robert, ed. *The Dada Painters and Poets: An Anthology:* New York: Wittenborn, Schultz, 1951.

Nadeau, Maurice, *Histoire du surréalisme, documents surréalistes*. 2 Volumes. Paris: Editions du Seuil, 1948.

———. *Histoire du surréalisme suivie de documents surréalistes*. 2nd edition. Paris: Editions du Seuil, 1964.

———. *The History of Surrealism*. Translated by Roger Shattuck. New York: Macmillan, 1965.

Naville, Pierre. *La Révolution et les intellectuels: Que peuvent faire les surréalistes?* Paris: n.p., 1926.

———. *Le Temps du suréel*. Paris: Editions Galilée, 1977.

Nougé, Paul. *Histoire de ne pas rire*. Brussels: Editions de la revue les lèvres nues, 1956.

Orwell, George. *Homage to Catalonia*. Boston: Beacon, 1952.

Pierre, J., ed. *Surréalisme et anarchie: les "billets surréalistes" du Libertaire 12 octobre 1951–8 janvier 1953*. Paris: Plasma, 1983.

Read, Herbert, ed. *Surrealism*. London: Faber and Faber, 1936.

Reports, Resolutions and Debates: Second International Congress of Revolutionary Writers. Literature of the World Revolution. Moscow: International Union of Revolutionary Writers, 1931.

Ribemont-Dessaignes, Georges. *Déjà jadis ou du mouvement dada à l'espace abstrait*. Paris: René Juilliard, 1958.

Richter, Hans. *Dada: Art and Anti-Art*. New York: McGraw Hill [1966].

Rigaut, Jacques. *Papiers posthumes*. Paris: Au sans pareil, 1934.

Rosey, Guy. *André Breton*. Paris: Editions surréalistes, 1934.

Sartre, Jean-Paul. *What Is Literature?* Translated by Bernard Frechtman. New York: Harper and Row, 1965.

Scott, H. G., ed. *Problems of Soviet Literature: Reports and Speeches at the First Soviet Writers' Congress* New York: International Publishers, 1935.

Thirion, André. *Revolutionaries without Revolution*. Translated by Joachim Neugroschel. New York: Macmillan, 1975.

Topass, Jan. *La Pensée en révolte: Essai sur le surréalisme*. Brussels: René Henriquez, 1935.

Trotsky, Leon. *Culture and Socialism and a Manifesto: Art and Revolution*. London: New Park, 1963.

Tzara, Tristan. *An Introduction to Dada*. New York: n.p., 1951.

———. *Morceaux choisis*. Preface by Jean Cassou. Paris: Bordas, 1957.

———. *Oeuvres complètes*. Henri Behar, ed. Paris: Flammarion, 1975.

———. *Sept manifestes dada: Lampisteries*. Paris: Jean-Jacques Pauvert, 1963.

———. *Le Surréalisme at l'après-guerre*. Paris: Editions Nagel, 1948.

Vaché, Jacques. *Les Lettres de guerre de Jacques Vaché*. Edited by André Breton. Paris: Grou–Radenez, 1949.

Vailland, Roger. *Le Surréalisme contre la révolution*. Paris: Editions sociales, 1948.

Articles and Essays

"L'Affaire Barrès." *Littérature*, XX (August 1921).

Alexandre, Maxime. "Un Professeur revoqué." *Le Surréalisme au service de la révolution*, III (December 1931), 11–12.

Alquié, Ferdinand. "A André Breton." *Le Surréalisme au service de la révolution*, V (May 1933), 41–44.

Aragon, Louis. "Complainte des chômeurs." *La Lutte anti-réligieuse et prolétarienne* (April 1932), 29.

———. "Découverte du nouveau monde." *Le Surréalisme au service de la révolution*, I (July 1930), 28–30.

———. "Germaine Berton." *La Révolution surréaliste*, I (December 1924), 12.

———. "Guerre à la mode." *Le Surréalisme au service de la révolution*, II (October 1930), 14–16.

———. "Pour qui écrivez-vous?" *Commune* (December 1933), 326–332.

———. "Le Prix de l'esprit." *Clarté*, nouvelle série, No. 4 (October–December 1926), 121–125.

———. "Le Prolétariat de l'esprit." *Clarté*, No. 78 (November 30, 1925), 79–84.

———. "Le Surréalisme et le devenir révolutionnaire." *Le Surréalisme au service de la révolution*, III (December 1931), 2–6.

———. "Une Vague de rêves." *Commerce*, II (Autumn 1924), 89–122.

Aragon, Louis and Breton, André. "Le Cinquantenaire de l'hystérie." *La Révolution surréaliste*, XI (March 1928), 18–23.

Artaud, Antonin. "Lettre aux médicins-chefs des asyles de fous." *La Révolution surréaliste*, III (April 1925), 29–34.

———. "Lettre à personne." *Les Cahiers du sud*, XXXI (July 1926), 3–9.

Ball, Hugo. "Lorsque je fondis le Cabaret Voltaire." *Cabaret Voltaire*, I (May 1916).

Bernier, Jean. "Un Cadavre." *Clarté*, No. 68 (November 15, 1924), 4–11.

———. "Ou nous en sommes." *Clarté*, No. 78 (November 30, 1925), 2–10.

Blin, Georges. "Procès du surréalisme." *La Revue hébdomadaire*. Année 47 Tome 6 (June 11, 1938), 212–225.

de Boully, Monny. "L'Art des fous." *La Révolution surréaliste*, IV (July 1925), 18–19.

Breton, André. "La Barque de l'amour s'est brisée contre la vie courante." *Le Surréalisme au service de la révolution,* I (July 1930), 16–22.

———. "Entrée des médiums." *Littérature nouvelle série,* VI (November 1922), 2–20.

———. "Et vous?" *Clé: Bulletin mensuel de la F.I.A.R.I.,* I (January 1939), 4–7.

———. "La Force d'attendre." *Clarté,* No. 79 (December 1925), 10–15.

———. "La Grande actualité poétique." *Minotaure,* VI (December 1934), 60–62.

———. "Léon Trotsky: Lenine." *La Révolution surréaliste,* V (October 1925), 25–29.

———. "Patinage dada." *Littérature,* XIII (May 1920), 6–20.

———. "A propos du concours de littérature prolétarienne organisée par *L'Humanité.*" *Le Surréalisme au service de la révolution,* V (May 1933), 10–18.

———. "Surrealism Yesterday, Today and Tomorrow." *This Quarter: Surrealist Number* (September 1932), 40–46.

N. C. [Nicolas Calas]. "Revue des revues." *Clé: Bulletin mensuel de la F.I.A.R.I.,* I (January 1939), 8–9.

Calas, Nicolas. "Surrealist Intentions." *Trans/formation: Arts, Communication, Environment: A World Review,* I (1950), 49–56.

Carrouges, Michel. "Kropotkine: L'Entre'aide." *Clé: Bulletin mensuel de la F.I.A.R.I.,* II (February 1939), 3–4.

"Ce Qui est importante." *L'Archibras: Le Surréalisme,* II (October 1967), 78.

Char, René. "Hommage à D.A.F de Sade à Paul Eluard." *Le Surréalisme au service de la révolution,* II (October 1930), 6.

———. "Les Porcs en liberté." *Le Surréalisme au service de la révolution,* II (October 1930), 20.

Charlot, Jean. "Surrealism: The Reason for Unreason." *American Scholar* (April 1938), 230–242.

Collinet, Michel. "L'Homme à la recherche de lui-même." *Clé: Bulletin de la F.I.A.R.I.,* II (February 1939), 5–6.

Crastre, Victor. "Changer l'homme." *Almanach surréaliste du demisiécle. Numéro spécial de La Nef.* Paris: Editions du Sagittaire, 1950.

———. "Europe." *La Révolution surréaliste,* VI (March 1926).

———. "Explosion surréaliste." *Clarté,* No. 74 (May 1925), 200–203.

———. "Scandale." *Clarté,* No. 75 (June 1925), 96–108.

———. "Le Suicide est-il une solution?" *Clarté,* No. 72 (March 1925), 3–6.

———. "Sur le suicide de Jacques Rigaut." *La Nouvelle revue française* (August 1, 1930), 251–255.

Crevel, René. "Bobards et fariboles." *Le Surréalisme au service de la révolution,* II (October 1930), 17.

———. "Les Surréalistes yougoslaves sont au bagne." *Le Surréalisme au service de la révolution,* VI (May 1933), 36–39.

Dali, Salvador. "Rêverie." *Le Surréalisme au service de la révolution,* IV (December 1931), 31–36.

Desnos, Robert. "Description d'une révolte prochaine." *La Révolution surréaliste,* III (April 1925), 24–28.

———. "Pamphlet contre Jérusalem." *La Révolution surréaliste,* III (April 1925), 8–9.

———. "Le Sens révolutionnaire du surréalisme." *Clarté,* No. 78 (November 30, 1925), 10–13.

Doriot, Jacques, and Sémard, Pierre. "Télégramme historique du parti communiste à Abd-el-Krim." *Commune,* IV (December 1933), 379.

Drieu La Rochelle, Pierre. "La Véritable erreur des surréalistes." *La Nouvelle revue française,* No. 143 (August 1925), 166–171.

"Editorial." *Bulletin international du surréalisme,* I (April 1935), 3–4.

"Editorial." *Bulletin international du surréalisme,* III (August 1935), 3–4.

"Editorial." *Commune,* XXIII (July 1935), 1201–1206.

Ehrenburg, Ilya. "The Surrealists." Partisan Review, II, No. 9 (October–November 1935), 9–20.

Eluard, Paul. "D.A.F. de Sade, écrivain fantastique et révolutionnaire." *La Révolution surréaliste,* VIII (December 1926), 7–10.

———. "La Suppression de l'esclavage." *La Révolution surréaliste,* III (April 1925), 19–23.

Eluard, Paul and Péret, Benjamin. "Revue de la presse." *Le Surréalisme au service de la révolution,* V (May 1933), 23–25.

"Enquête sur le suicide." *La Révolution surréaliste,* I (December 1924), 2–11.

Ernst, Max. "Danger de pollution." *Le Surréalisme au service de la révolution,* III (December 1930), 22–24.

Etiemble. [René]. "The Tibetan Dog." *Yale French Studies,* XXXI (May 1964), 127–134.

Fourrier, Marcel. "De Clarté à la guerre civile." *Clarté,* No. 79 (December 1925–January 1926), 3–10.

———. "Lettre aux lecteurs de Clarté." *Clarté,* I, nouvelle série (June 15, 1926), 19–28.

———. "L'Opportunisme impuisant." *La Révolution surréaliste,* VII (June 1926), 28–30.

Frois-Wittman, Jean. "Mobiles inconscients du suicide." *La Révolution surréaliste,* XII (December 1929), 3–10.

———. "Les Mots de l'esprit et l'inconscient." *Le Surréalisme au service de la révolution,* II (October 1930), 26–29.

Gide, André. "Literature and Society." Partisan Review, II, No. 9 (October–November 1935), 1–2.

Giono, Jean. "Précisions (Fragments)." *Clé: Bulletin mensuel de la F.I.A.R.I.,* I (January 1939), 1–2.

Glicksberg, Charles I. "The Aesthetics of Surrealism." *T'ien Hsia Monthly* (Shanghai), IX (1939), 364–374.

Heine, Maurice. "Les Fruits de l'automne." *Clé: Bulletin mensuel de la F.I.A.R.I.,* I (January 1939), 2–3.

Huelsenbeck, Richard, "Dada Lives." *Fall,* XXV (1936), 2–10.

Huelsenbeck, Raoul [Richard]. "En Avant." *Littérature nouvelle série,* IV (September 1922), 19–22.

Koppen, Jean. "Comment accommoder le prêtre." *La Révolution sur-réaliste,* XII (December 1929), 29–33.

Lapie, P. O. "L'Insurrection surréaliste." *Cahiers du sud (January 1935),* 100–108.

Lavachery, Jean. "Pour les realités contre les entités." *Documents 35: Revue mensuelle de l'Association révolutionnaire culturelle,* III (May 1935), 14–21.

"Lettre à nos amis de Londres." *Clé: Bulletin mensuel de la F.I.A.R.I.,* I (January 1939), 8.

Masson, André. "Lettre d'André Masson." *La Révolution surréaliste,* V (October 1925), 30–31.

Mesens, E.L.T. "Editorial." *Documents 34,* II nouvelle série trimestrielle (November 1934), 3–7.

Miller, Henry. "An Open Letter to the Surrealists Everywhere." *Selected Prose: I.* London: MacGibbon and Kee, 1965.

"Le Monde au temps des surréalistes." *Varietés. numéro hors séries: Le Surréalisme en 1929* (June 1929), 26–27.

Naville, Pierre. "L'Activité de Clarté, XI, nouvelle série (July 15, 1927).

———. "Mieux et moins bien." *La Révolution surréaliste,* IX–X (October 1927).

———. "Les Tendances confusionistes du group 'L'Esprit.' " *Clarté,* III, nouvelle série (August–September 1926), 24–31.

Nezval, V. "Correspondance à André Breton." *Le Surréalisme au service de la révolution,* V (May 1933), 31.

Niall, Sean. "Paris Letter." *Partisan Review,* VI, no. I (Fall 1938), 101–106.

Nizan, Paul. "Revues des revues." *Commune,* I (July 1933), 82–89.

Pailthorpe, Grace W. "The Scientific Aspect of Surrealism." *London Bul-letin,* VII (December 1938–January 1939), 10–16.

Pastoureau, Henri. "Editorial." *Clé: Bulletin mensuel de la F.I.A.R.I.,* I (January 1939), 3–4.

Péret, Benjamin. "A travers mes yeux." *Littérature,* nouvelle série, XVII (October 1922).

———. "The Dishonor of Poets." *Radical America,* IV, No. 6 (August 1970), 15–21.

———. "Un Ennemi declaré." *Clé: Bulletin mensuel de la F.I.A.R.I.,* II (February 1939), 2–3.

————. "La Vie de l'assassin Foch." *Le Surréalisme au service de la révolution*, II (October 1930), 24–26.

Périer, Louise. "Livres." *Commune*, XI (December 1934), 355–361.

Pierson, Michel. "Herbert Marcuse." *L'Archibras: Le Surréalisme*, II (October 1967), 17–20.

Read, Herbert. "L'Artiste dans le monde moderne." *Clé: Bulletin mensuel de la F.I.A.R.I.*, II (February 1939), 6–8.

————. "On the Social Aspects of Surrealism." *Bulletin international du surréalisme*, IV (September 1936), 7–15.

"Recherches sur la sexualité, Part d'objectivité, déterminations individuelles, degré de conscience." *La Révolution surréaliste*, XI (March 1928), 28–36.

Rivière, Jacques. "Reconnaissance à dada." *La Nouvelle revue française*, no. 83 (August 1920), 216–237.

Rosemont, Frank. "Introduction to 1970." *Radical America: Special Issue: Surrealism in the Service of the Revolution* (January 1970), 1–4.

————. "Preface: Surrealist Ambush." *Surrealism and Revolution*. Chicago: n.p., 1966.

Sadoul, Georges. "Le Bon pasteur." *Le Surréalisme au service de la révolution*, IV (December 1931), 23–26.

————. "Manifestations révolutionnaires à la Sorbonne." *Le Surréalisme au service de la révolution*, III (December 1931), 35–40.

————. "Mémoire." *Le Surréalisme au service de la révolution*, I (July 1930), 34–40.

Saint-Placide, Philippe. "Frankreich erwache!" *Clé: Bulletin mensuel de la F.I.A.R.I.*, II (February 1939), 10–12.

"Secours rouge internationale." *Le surréalisme au service de la révolution*, VI (May 1933).

Serge, Victor. "Disparitions en U.R.S.S." *Clé: Bulletin mensuel de la F.I.A.R.I.*, II (February 1939), 8–10.

Spaak, Claude. "Libération de l'esprit." *Documents 34*, II, nouvelle série trimestrielle (November 1934), 24–34.

Strachey, John. "Marxism and the Heritage of Culture." *Partisan Review*, II, No. 9 (October–November 1935), 28–33.

Thirion, André. "A Bas le travail." *Varietés. numéro hors séries: Le Surréalisme en 1929* (June 1929), 41–47.

————. "En lisant Hegel." *Le Surréalisme au service de la révolution*, III (December 1930), 1–3.

————. "Réponse à un recours en grâce." *Le Surréalisme au service de la révolution*, II (October 1930), 33–36.

Trotsky, Leon. "Art and Politics." *Partisan Review*, V, No. 3 (August–September 1938), 2–7.

————. "Leon Trotsky to André Breton." *Partisan Review*, VI, No. 2 (Winter 1939), 123–129.

Tzara, Tristan. "Memoirs of Dadaism." Edmund Wilson. *Axel's Castle:*

A Study in the Imaginative Literature of 1870–1930. New York: Scribner's, 1954.

Unik, Pierre. "La France des cinq parties du monde." *Le surréalisme au service de la révolution,* III (December 1931), 28.

――――. "Un Panier de crabes." *Le Surréalisme au service de la révolution,* IV (December 1931), 29–30.

"Un Insulteur de Majakowsky reçoit une visite désagréable." *Le Surréalisme au service de la révolution,* I (July 1930), 21–22.

Valentin, Albert. "Le Haut du pavé." *Le Surréalisme au service de la révolution,* II (October 1930), 21.

Vermelen, Pierre. "La Défense de la culture." *Documents 35: Revue mensuelle de l'Association révolutionnaire culturelle,* III (May 1935), 22–28.

Yoyotte, Pierre. "Réflexions conduisant à préciser la signification antifasciste du surréalisme." *Documents 34: numéro spécial: Intervention surréaliste,* I, nouvelle série (June 1934), 90–95.

Protest Manifestoes, Tracts and Pamphlets

Dégout dadaiste. Zurich, 1918. Signed by Tristan Tzara. Published in *Sept manifestes DADA: Lampisteries.* Violent denunciation of Western bourgeois culture.

Dadaïsten Gegen Weimar. Berlin, 1920. Signed by Johannes Baader and seven others. Published in Hans Richter, *Dada: Art and Anti-Art.* German Dadaists ridicule the Weimar Republic.

L'Heure est aux héroes. Paris, 1920. Signed by Georges Ribemont-Dessaignes. Published in *391,* XI, February 1920. Ironic denunciation of the war. The heroes are imbeciles.

Manifeste du mouvement dada. Paris, 1920. Signed by Louis Aragon. Published in *Littérature,* XIII (May 1920). A nihilist protest.

Un Cadavre. Paris, 1924. Signed by Philippe Soupault, Paul Eluard, André Breton, Louis Aragon. Protests eulogies of famous writer, Anatole France.

La Révolution surréaliste. Paris, [1924], n.p. Announcement of publication of a new revolutionary journal.

Adresse au Dalaï Lama. Paris, 1925. Signed by Antonin Artaud. Published in *La Révolution surréaliste,* III (April 1925). In praise of Eastern mysticism.

Adresse au Pape. Paris, 1925. Signed by Antonin Artaud. Published in *La Révolution surréaliste,* III (April 1925). Vehement anticlerical diatribe.

Appel aux travailleurs intellectuels: Oui ou non, condamnez-vous la guerre? Paris, July 1925. Signed by editors of *Clarté.* Published in *Clarté,* No. 76 (July 15, 1925). Protest against resurgence of French imperialism in the Riff war in Morocco.

Déclaration du 27 janvier 1925. Paris, 1925. Signed by Aragon, Breton and twenty-four others. Published in *Surrealism and Revolution,* edited by Frank Rosemont. Announcement that Surrealism must be revolutionary in the material sense.

Lettre aux écoles du Buddha. Paris, 1925. Signed by Antonin Artaud. *La Révolution surréaliste,* III (April 1925). Against materialism of the West.

Lettre aux recteurs des universités européennes. Paris, 1925. Signed by Antonin Artaud. Published in *La Révolution surréaliste,* III (April 1925).

Ouvrez les prisons, licenciez l'armée: Il n'y a pas de crimes de droit commun. 1925. Published in *La Révolution surréaliste,* II (January 1925). Protest against conscription.

La Révolution d'abord et toujours! Paris, October 1925. Signed by Louis Aragon, Victor Crastre, and fifty others. Published in *La Révolution surréaliste,* V (October 1925) and *Clarté,* No. 77 (October 15, 1925). Call for immediate disarmament and revolution in protest against the French War with the Riff.

A l'Occasion d'un manifeste. Brussels, 1926. Signed by Paul Nougé. Published in Paul Nougé, *Histoire de ne pas rire.* Brussels: Editions de la revue les lévres nues, 1956. Belgian Surrealists announce they will sign no more political protests.

A La Grande nuit ou le bluff surréaliste. Paris, June 1927. Signed by Antonin Artaud. Published in Antonin Artaud, *Oeuvres complètes.* Paris: Gallimard, 1956. Denouncing Surrealists for joining the Communist Party.

Au Grand jour. Paris, 1927. Signed by Paul Eluard, Louis Aragon, André Breton, Pierre Unik and Benjamin Péret. (*Au Grand jour.* Paris: Les Editions surréalistes, 1927). Statement of the five Surrealists who joined the Communist Party.

Hands Off Love. Paris, 1927. Signed by Maxime Alexandre and thirty others. Published in *La Révolution surréaliste,* IX–X (October 1927). A defense of Charlie Chaplin on trial for sex offenses.

Permettez! Paris, October 1927. Signed by Maxime Alexandre and twenty-eight others. Reprinted in Nadeau, *The History of Surrealism,* 3rd edition. Against attempts to "rehabilitate" Rimbaud's reputation.

Un Cadavre. Paris, [1929]. Signed by Raymond Queneau and eleven others. n.p. Insults André Breton in reply to his attacks on them in the *Second Manifesto of Surrealism,* 1929.

Belgrade 23 Décembre 1930. Belgrade, 1930. Signed by Oscar Davitcho and ten others. Published in *Le Surréalisme au service de la révolution,* III (December 1931). Statement of support from the Yugoslav surrealists.

Question. Réponse. Paris, July 1930. Published in *Le Surréalisme au service de la révolution,* I, July, 1930. Statement of adherence to the Third International by the French Surrealists.

Troisième manifeste de surréalisme. Paris, 1930. Signed by Robert Desnos. Published in Nadeau, *Histoire du surréalisme,* first edition. Personal attack on Breton.

L'Affaire de l'age d'or. Paris [1931]. Signed by Maxime Alexandre and fifteen others (n.p.). Protests censorship of Dali and Buñuel film, *L'Age d'or.*

L'Age d'or. Paris, 1931. Signed by Maxime Alexandre and twelve others. (*L'Age d'or.* Paris: Corti, 1931). Protest against growth of fascism and anti-Semitism in France.

Au Feu! Paris, [1931]. Signed by Benjamin Péret and twenty-one others. (n.p.) In praise of church-burnings in Spain.

Ne Visitez pas l'exposition coloniale. Paris, [1931]. Signed by André Breton and eleven others. (n.p.) Urges boycott of Colonial Exposition.

Premier bilan de l'exposition coloniale. Paris, July 1931. Signed by Yves Tanguy and eleven others. Published in Nadeau, 3rd edition. Tract denouncing European imperialism.

Autour d'un poème. Paris, April 15, 1932. Signed by Maxime Alexandre and Pierre Unik. (n.p.) Attempt to reconcile the Surrealists and the Communist Party after "L'Affaire Aragon."

Certificat Paris, [1932]. Signed by Paul Eluard. Published in Nadeau, *Histoire du surréalisme,* 1st edition. Declaration of Eluard's contempt for Aragon's stand in "L'Affaire Aragon."

L'Affaire Aragon. Paris, 1932. Signed by Maxime Alexandre and eleven others. Protest Aragon's arrest for publishing "Front rouge."

Manifeste de l'A.E.A.R. Paris, 1932. Signed by Louis Aragaon *et al.* Denounces Surrealism as counterrevolutionary.

Paillasse! (Fin de "l'Affaire Aragon"). Paris, March 1932. Signed by René Char and nine others. [*Paillasse! (Fin de "l'Affaire Aragon").* Paris: Editions surréalistes, 1932.] Protest against Aragon's "defection" to the Communist Party and socialist realism.

La Poésie transfigurée. Brussels, January 30, 1932. Signed by René Magritte and twenty others (Eluard's Notebook). Belgian Surrealists protest Aragon's arrest for his seditious poem, "Front rouge."

Protestation. Brussels, March 22, 1932. Signed by E. L. T. Mesens and fifty-four others (Eluard's Notebook). Belgian artists protest Aragon's arrest for his seditious poem, "Front rouge."

Protestation. Paris, December 22, 1932. Signed by Tristan Tzara. Promise to abide by the "rules" of not publishing in conservative journals (Eluard's Notebook).

L'A.E.A.R. s'incline devant les victimes et fait appel aux correspondants ouvriers. Paris, 1933. Signed by Louis Aragon *et al.* Published in Nadeau, *Histoire du surréalisme,* 3rd edition. *A.E.A.R.* tract denouncing Renault factory after accident in which workers were killed.

La Mobilisation contre la guerre n'est pas la paix: Les Raisons de notre adhésion au Congrès International contre la guerre. Paris, 1933. Signed by André Breton and nine others. Published in Nadeau, *Histoire du surréalisme,* 1st edition. Criticism of Communist Party's Amsterdam-Pleyel tactic.

M. Renault est très affecté. Paris, 1933. Signed by André Breton. Published in Nadeau, *Histoire du surréalisme,* 1st edition. Protest against industrial accident that killed factory workers.

Protestez! Paris, [1933]. Signed by Adson *et al.* (Eluard's Notebook). *A.E.A.R.* anti-fascist protest that the Surrealists signed.

Appel à la lutte. Paris, February 1934. Signed by Alain and thirty-four others. Published in *Documents 34: Numéro spécial: Intervention surréaliste,* I (June 1934). Call for general strike to protest fascist demonstration of February 6, 1934.

L'Action immédiate. Brussels, 1934. Signed by René Magritte and twenty-two others. Published in *Documents 34: Numéro spécial: Intervention Surréaliste* (June 1934). Belgian Surrealists demand anti-clerical demonstrations against fascism.

Enquête sur l'unité d'action. Paris, April 1934. Signed by Jean Audard and ninety-four others. Published in *Documents 34: Numéro spécial: Intervention surréaliste,* I, June 1934. Surrealist questionnaire asking for united anti-fascist action.

La Planète sans visa. Paris, 1934. Signed by André Breton and twenty others and "a number of foreign comrades." Published in *Documents 34: Numéro spécial: Intervention surréaliste,* I (June 1934). Surrealists denounce French government for refusing Trotsky asylum.

Contre-Attaque! Paris, 1935. Signed by Georges Bataille and thirteen others. Published in *Position politique du surréalisme.* Paris: Editions du Sagittaire, 1935. Predicts failure of *Popular Front.* Demands return to true revolutionary tactics under new organization, *Contre-Attaque.*

Le Couteau dans la plaie. Brussels, 1935. Signed by René Magritte *et al.* Published in *Bulletin international du surréalisme* III (August 1935). Belgian Surrealists' manifesto opposing the Franco-Soviet Pact of 1935.

Du Temps que les surréalistes avaient raison. Paris, 1935. Signed by André Breton and twenty-five others. Published in *Position politique du surréalisme.* Paris, Editions du Sagittaire, 1935. Announcement of break with Communist Party because of its collaborationist policies.

Il n'y a pas de liberté pour les ennemis de la liberté (Robespierre). Paris, 1936. Signed by Adolphe Acker and fourteen others and "foreign comrades." Published in Nadeau, *Histoire du surréalisme,* 2nd edition. Demands arrest of Gil Robles in exile in France.

Neutralité? Nons-sens, crime et trahison! Paris, August, 1936. Signed by Adolphe Acker and eleven others. Published in Nadeau, *Histoire du surréalisme,* 2nd edition. Demands that the French Popular Front government aid the Spanish loyalists.

La Verité sur le procès de Moscou. Paris, 1936. Signed by Adolphe Acker and eleven others. Published in Nadeau, *Histoire du surréalisme,* 3rd edition. Denounces purge trials in Moscow and Russian intervention in Spain against the *C.N.T.,* the *F.A.I.,* and the *P.O.U.M.*

Déclaration d'André Breton à propos des seconds procès de Moscou. Paris, January 1937. Signed by André Breton. Published in Nadeau, *Histoire du surréalisme,* 2nd edition. Against purge of old Bolsheviks—Kamenev, Zinoviev and Radek. Praises Trotsky, and Spanish revolutionaries.

Freud at Vienna. Paris, 1938. Signed by André Breton. Published in *London Bulletin,* II (May 1938). Demand for Freud's immediate release from Nazi custody.

Ni de votre guerre, ni de votre paix. Paris, September 1938. Signed "Le group surréaliste." Published in Nadeau, *Histoire du surréalisme,* 2nd edition. Manifesto denouncing Munich talks and inevitable imperialist war.

Towards a Free Revolutionary Art. Mexico, 1938. Signed by André Breton and Diego Rivera. Published in Leon Trotsky, *Culture and Socialism and a Manifesto: Art and Revolution,* 1963. Actually written by Trotsky and Breton. Protests socialist realism. Calls for creation of a Federation of Independent Revolutionary Artists.

A Bas les lettres de cachet! A Bas la terreur grise! Paris, 1939. Signed by the *F.I.A.R.I.* Published in Nadeau, *Histoire du surréalisme,* 3rd edition. Against arrest without charge in France of three Leftists.

M. Daladier et la grève des fonctionnaires. Paris, January, 1939. Signed by the *F.I.A.R.I.* Published in *Clé: Bulletin mensuel de la F.I.A.R.I.,* I (January 1939). Tract denouncing Daladier for ordering strikers back to work.

N'Imitez pas Hitler. Paris, February 1939. Signed by the *F.I.A.R.I.* Published in *Clé: Bulletin mensuel de la F.I.A.R.I.,* II (February 1939). Protests Mexican government's ban of O'Gorman frescoes.

Persécutions démocratiques. Paris, 1939. Signed by the *F.I.A.R.I.* Published in *Clé: Bulletin mensuel de la F.I.A.R.I.,* I (January 1939). Denunciation of decree laws against foreign Spanish civil war veterans residing in France.

Protestation contre la xénophobie. Paris, January 1939. Signed by Yves Allégret and nineteen others. Published in *Clé: Bulletin mensuel de la F.I.A.R.I.,* I (January 1939). Against "stateless persons" decree.

Liberté est un mot vietnamien. Paris, 1947. Signed by Adolphe Acker and others. Published in Bédouin, *Storia del Surrealismo 1945 ai nostri Giorni.* Against French intervention in Indochina.

Dada Manifesto. New York, 1949. Signed by Richard Huelsenbeck. (*Dada Manifesto.* New York: Wittenborn, Schultz, 1951). Against betrayers of true spirit of Dada, especially Tristan Tzara.

Appel pour la libération du mouvement ouvrier. [1956] by H. Baratier *et al.* (n.p.) Trotskyist manifesto denouncing Algerian war, Russian intervention in Hungary, and Anglo-French military expedition into Egypt, which Breton signed.

Au Tour des livrées sanglantes. Paris, 1956. Signed by Anne Bédouin *et al.* Published in Bédouin, *Vingt ans de surréalisme 1939–1959.* Demanded immediate cease fire in Algeria.

Hongrie, soleil levant. Paris, 1956. Signed by Anne Bédouin *et al.* Published in Bédouin, *Vingt ans de surréalisme 1939–1959.* Denunciation of Russian intervention in Hungary.

Manifeste des 121. Paris, 1960. Signed by 121 of most famous French artists and writers, including André Breton. Published in the *New York Post,* September 14, 1960. Supports Algerian fighters for independence.

Secondary Sources: Books, Articles, and Essays

Balakian, Anna. *André Breton: Magus of Surrealism.* New York: Oxford University Press, 1971.

———. *Literary Origins of Surrealism.* New York: King's Crown, 1947.

———. *Surrealism: The Road to the Absolute.* New York: Noonday, 1959.

Barr, Alfred H., Jr., ed. *Fantastic Art, Dada, Surrealism.* 2nd edition. New York: Museum of Modern Art, 1937.

Baudouin, Dominique, ed. *Cahiers de l'Association internationale pour l'étude de dada et du surréalisme.* Paris: Editions lettres modernes, 1970.

Bernard, J.-P. *Le Parti communiste français et la question littéraire 1921–1939.* Grenoble: Presses universitaires de Grenoble, 1972.

Bonhomme, Colbert. *Révolution et contre-révolution en Haiti de 1946 à 1957.* Port-au-Prince: Imprimerie de l'etat, 1957.

Bonnet, Marguerite. *André Breton: Naissance de l'aventure surréaliste.* Paris: Librairie José Corti, 1975.

Borkenau, Franz. *The Communist International.* London: Faber and Faber Ltd., 1938.

Browder, Clifford. *André Breton, Arbiter of Surrealism.* Geneva: Librairie Droz, 1967.

Brown, Bernard E. *Protest in Paris: Anatomy of a Revolt.* Morristown, N.J.: General Learning Press, 1974.

Carmody, Francis J. "Eluard's Rupture with Surrealism." *Publications of the Modern Language Association,* LXXVI, No. 4 (September 1961), 436–446.

Carré, Marie-Rose. "René Crevel: Surrealism and the Individual." *Yale French Studies,* XXI (May 1964), 74–88.

Caspers, Frank. "Surrealism in Overalls." *Scribners Magazine,* August, 1938, 17–21.

Caute, David. *Communism and the French Intellectuals 1914–1960.* New York: Macmillan, 1964.

Caws, Mary Ann. "Ladies Shot and Painted: Female Embodiment in Surrealist Art." Susan Rubin Suleiman, ed., *The Female Body in Western Culture: Contemporary Perspectives.* Cambridge: Harvard University Press, 1986.

Chadwick, Whitney. *Women Artists and the Surrealist Movement.* Boston: Little, Brown, 1985.

Cohn, Ruby. "Surrealism and Today's French Theatre." *Yale French Studies,* XXXI (May 1964), 159–166.

Courtot, Claude. *Introduction à la lecture de Benjamin Péret.* Paris: La Terrain vague, 1965.

Cowles, Fleur. *The Case of Salvador Dali.* Boston: Little, Brown, 1959.

Cowley, Malcolm. *Exile's Return.* New York: Viking, 1951.

Daix, Pierre. *Aragon une vie à changer.* Paris: Seuil, 1975.

Deutscher, Isaac. *The Prophet Outcast: Trotsky 1929–1940.* London: Oxford University Press, 1963.

Droz, Jules Humbert. *L'Oeil de Moscou à Paris.* Paris: René Julliard, 1964.

Durozoi, Gérard, and Lecherbonnier, Bernard. *Le Surréalisme: Théories, thèmes, techniques.* Paris: Librairie Larousse, 1972.

Egbert, Donald Drew. *Social Radicalism and the Arts: Western Europe.* New York: Alfred A. Knopf, 1970.

Fauvet, Jacques. *Histoire du parti communiste français: De la guerre à la guerre 1917–1939.* Volume I. Paris: Librairie Arthème Fayard, 1964.

Figuères, Leo, ed., *Le Parti communiste français la culture et les intellectuels.* Paris: Librairie José Corti, 1975.

Fowlie, Wallace. *Age of Surréalism.* Bloomington: Indiana University Press, 1962.

Gauthier, Xavière. *Surréalisme et sexualité.* Paris: Gallimard, 1971.

Gershman, Herbert S. "Futurism and the Origins of Surrealism." *Italica,* XXXIX, No. 2 (June 1962), 114–123.

———. *The Surrealist Revolution in France.* Ann Arbor: University of Michigan Press, 1969.

Harap, Louis. *Social Roots of the Arts.* New York: International Publishers, 1949.

Haupt, Georges and Marie, Jean-Jacques. *Les Bolcheviks par eux-mêmes.* Paris: François Maspero, 1969.

Herrera, Hayden. *Frida: A Biography of Frida Kahlo.* New York: Harper and Row, 1983.

Histoire du parti communiste français. Paris: Editions sociales, 1964.

Janover, Louis. *Surréalisme art et politique.* Paris: Editions galilée, 1980.

Jederman, ed., *La "Bolchévisation" du P.C.F. (1923–1928).* Paris: François Maspero, 1971.

Joll, James. *The Anarchists.* Boston: Little, Brown, 1964.

Kallen, Horace M. "Surrealism as Program and as Achievement." *Art and Beauty, Use and Freedom in Western Civilization from the Greeks to the Present Day.* Volume II. New York: Duell, Sloane and Pierce, 1942.

Kaplan, Janet. "Remedios Varo: Voyages and Visions," *Woman's Art Journal* 1, No. 2 (Fall 1980/Winter 1981), 13–18.

Kelly, Michael. *Modern French Marxism.* Baltimore: Johns Hopkins University Press, 1982.

Kriegel, Annie. *Les Communistes français: Essai d'ethnographie politique.* Paris: Editions de Seuil, 1968.

———. *Les Internationales ouvrières 1864–1943.* Paris: Presses universitaires de France, 1964.

Lecherbonnier, Bernard. *Les Critiques de notre temps et Aragon.* Paris: Garnier frères, 1976.

Levy, Julien. *Surrealism.* New York: Black Sun, 1936.

Lewis, Helena. "Elsa Triolet: The Politics of a Committed Writer." *Women's Studies International Forum,* Vol. 9, No. 4 (1986), 385–394.

Lichtheim, George. *Marxism in Modern France.* New York: Columbia University Press, 1966.

Lottman, Herbert. *The Left Bank Writers, Artists, and Politics from the Popular Front to the Cold War.* Boston: Houghton Mifflin Company, 1982.

Mandlove, Nancy. "Humor in the Service of the Revolution: Leonora Carrington's Feminist Perspective on Surrealism." *Perspectives on Contemporary Literature,* Volume 7 (1981), 117–122.

Matthews, J. H. *André Breton.* New York: Columbia University Press, 1967.

———. *An Introduction to Surrealism.* University Park, PA: Pennsylvania State University Press, 1965.

Mauriac, Claude. *André Breton.* Paris: Editions de Flore, 1949.

Orenstein, Gloria. "Women of Surrealism," *Feminist Art Journal,* 2 (Spring 1973), 7–9.

Passeron, René. *Phaidon encyclopedia of Surrealism.* Oxford: Phaidon, 1978.

Peterson, Elmer. *Tristan Tzara: Dada and Surrational Theorist.* New Brunswick, NJ: Rutgers University Press, 1971.

Picon, Gaeton. *Surrealists and Surrealism 1919–1939* (Geneva: Skira, 1977).

Racine, Nicole. "The *Clarté* Movement in France, 1919–1921," *The Journal of Contemporary History,* Vol. 2, No. 2 (1967), 206–213.

Racine, Nicole, and Bodine, Louis. *Le Parti communiste français pendant l'entre-deux-guerres.* Paris: Armand Colin, 1972.

Redfern, W. D. *Paul Nizan: Committed Literature in a Conspiratorial World.* Princeton, NJ: Princeton University Press, 1972.

Richardson, John. "School for Scandal Forty Years On." *Sunday Times* (London), December 14, 1965.

Robrieux, Philippe. *Histoire intérieure du parti communiste 1920–1945.* Paris: Librairie Arthème Fayard, 1980.

Roy, Claude. *Aragon.* Paris: Seghers, 1945.

Rubin, William S. *Dada, Surrealism and Their Heritage.* New York: Museum of Modern Art, 1968.

Rühle, Jürgen. *Literature and Revolution: A Critical Study of the Writer and Communism in the Twentieth Century.* New York: Praeger, 1969.

Sanouillet, Michel. *Dada à Paris.* Paris: Jean-Jacques Pauvert, 1965.

Schmeller, Alfred. *Surrealism.* New York: Crown, n.d.

Shapiro, Theda. *Painters and Politics: The European Avant-Garde and Society, 1900–1925.* New York: Elsevier, 1976.

Shattuck, Roger. "Writers for the Defense of Culture," *Partisan Review,* Vol. 1, No. 3 (1984), 393–416.

Short, Robert. *Dada and Surrealism.* London: John Calmann and Cooper, 1980.

————. "The Politics of Surrealism 1920–1936." *Journal of Contemporary History,* I, No. 2, (1966), 3–25.

Taylor, Joshua C. *Futurism.* New York: Doubleday, 1961.

Thomas, Hugh. *The Spanish Civil War.* New York: Harper, 1961.

Trilling, Lionel. "Freud and Literature." *Criticism: The Foundations of Modern Literary Judgment.* Edited by Mark Schorer, Josephine Miles, Gordon McKenzie. New York: Harcourt, Brace, 1948.

Turnell, Martin. "Surrealism: The Social Background of Contemporary Poetry." *Arena,* I, No. 3 (October–December 1937), 212–228.

Verkauf, Willy; Janco, Marcel; Bollinger, Hans. *Dada: Monographie einer Bewegung.* St. Gallen, Switzerland: Verlag Arthur Niggli A.G., 1965.

Waldberg, Patrick, ed. *Surrealism.* Translated by Stuart Gilbert. New York: McGraw-Hill, 1978.

Weber, Eugen, ed. *Paths to the Present: Aspects of European Thought from Romanticism to Existentialism.* New York: Dodd, Mead, 1962.

Willener, Alfred. *The Action Image of Society: On Cultural Politicization.* Translated by A. M. Sheridan Smith. New York: Pantheon, 1970.

Withers, Josephine. "The Famous Fur-Lined Teacup and the Anonymous Meret Oppenheim," *Arts* 52, No. 3 (November 1977), 88–93.

Index

219